SHADOWRUN:
SHADOWS DOWN UNDER

JEAN RABE

SHADOWRUN: SHADOWS DOWN UNDER
Cover art by Laura Diaz Cubas
Design by Matt Heerdt

Published by Catalyst Game Labs,
an imprint of InMediaRes Productions, LLC
PMB 202 • 303 91st Ave NE • E502 • Lake Stevens, WA 98258

DEDICATION
For Uncle Wes
And Most Marvelous Mitzi

PROLOGUE

The storm came before sunset on a Christmas Eve long ago.

Birthed over the Outback from a single, nacreous cloud at the top of the sky, all milky blue and opalescent gray, shimmering, beautiful, shiny, a hint of rosy pink, it invited the original people—the Aborigines—to stand beneath its pulsing strands in wonder and appreciation.

And later in terror.

And then in understanding.

And finally in appreciation again.

First the cloud darkened, roiling as if it seethed with a righteous anger. A mean wind grew with it, escalating to such a gale force that even the original people had to seek refuge. Fingers of lightning arced down to spear those who had harmed the once-fair Earth. Thunder made the ground leap and dance.

The devastation was awesome, wiping away small towns, slaughtering dozens and injuring hundreds. It wreaked havoc on the astral plane, too.

When the tempest eased, all but the original people relaxed and considered it a freak of nature and magic; a mana storm. They went back to their lives, started rebuilding their small towns, and then gaped in disbelief when the terrible cloud returned weeks later and expanded, and the rain came at them sideways, driven by winds the land had not seen in a long, long memory.

Then came another storm.

And another.

And the time between downpours became shorter, and the winds that came after each one were fiercer.

Thousands died.

It was as if the Awakening had declared war on Australia. Clouds churned across the island continent, and the magic that hammered down drove all but the original people into the sprawls, which were mostly unaffected. The Aborigines had found safe places and a more appropriate name for the weather: *madjitil boroong*, or magic rain. It had chased the white men back to the cities, where they belonged.

The continent-wide deluge eventually, mercifully, subsided—though scattered mana storms appeared from time to time, they stayed only briefly, perhaps to remind everyone to leave the Outback to its original occupants.

Only one big cloud persisted.

A mother-of-pearl beauty, all milky blue and opalescent gray, shimmering, shiny, with just a hint of rosy pink at the edges. Frightening on some days when it darkened like a great charcoal smudge. Wholly terrifying when it turned the world blackest-black and wicked magic coursed down from it.

That cloud had settled over Sydney and stretched out into the bay.

That isolated storm had remained there.

For more than sixty years.

ONE
ELLA'S LAMENT

The room was long and narrow, the walls shot through with sections of corrugated metal, giving it the feel of a big, antique boxcar that had been canted so one end was higher than the other, descending to the stage down front. Fog clung to the ceiling—or rather what looked like fog, the dense sort that rolls into the harbor and up the pilings of the ruined bridge. The fog was tobacco smoke; the nightclub, unlike many establishments in the city, had no restrictions on that particular vice.

"Welcome one and all on this rare, stormless night!" the announcer boomed through hidden speakers. *"Our extravaganza opens with a damsel fair who creates her own thunder, the one–the only–Miss Ella Gance!"*

The crowd erupted with applause and catcalls as the house lights dimmed. An alto saxophone wailed; the first of many notes lost amid the cheers. Then the crowd quieted, and the sax's seductive melody rose, joined by a muted trombone. The curtains parted, and a single, bright spotlight bathed her.

Ella's coral lips edged up into a suggestive smile, and her perfectly manicured hands smoothed the red silk dress hugging her hips. The slender torch singer swayed gently on her rhinestone-studded heels and crooned.

"Love is where you find it, find it.
And if you find it, keep it, keep it.
Keep it close to your heart, where it's yours alone.
'Cause if someone else finds it, they'll steal it, steal it."

Ella's voice, tempered by expensive vocal range enhancers, trilled as she stepped to the edge of the stage and reached a finger up to brush a single strand of shiny, raven hair off her face. Her liquid brown eyes scanned the crowd as she finished the chorus and waited for the English horn's nasal notes to slice through the strains of the rest of the woodwinds. It was real music, played by actual musicians; finely dressed elves and humans on fourteen instruments comprised the small orchestra. The dwarf who played the cello was absent tonight. Some people came just to hear the ensemble, a rarity in the neighborhood . . . real music getting to be a rarity in the entire city.

She blew a kiss to an elderly ork sitting to the left of the stage, staring at her in rapt fascination, and rolled her shoulders.

Cadigal's Corner was packed tonight, and Ella knew it was because of her. She was perhaps the most popular singer in Kings Cross, and she drew them in every night—all kinds.

Purists captivated by the neighborhood's outmoded atmosphere that was still mostly stylish, yet slightly going to seed.

Businessmen passing through Sydney who came out of curiosity, or because they could still appreciate a good act.

Craggy-faced laborers from the surrounding blocks who drooled when she gave them a sexy pout.

A few women were wedged here and there between the men; Ella believed they secretly envied her. A pair of choobs she recognized; sometimes they caused trouble, but the pair looked subdued tonight; an obvious Azzie in the middle of the second row; a stage manager from a joint downtown. Several tourists were here too, mostly Americans and Japanese, and mostly young— they stood out like that proverbial sore thumb. She could effortlessly tell the locals from the foreigners, the regulars from those who were here for the first time. The latter were always marked by the expressions on their faces. They hadn't known what to expect from the old-fashioned Australian tawdry house.

Ella vowed to give them a show they wouldn't soon forget.

"Lover, won't you find me, find me?
I'm lonely, won't you keep me, keep me?
Keep me close to your heart, I'll be yours alone.
'Til another catches my eye and steals me, steals me."

In the front row, a pudgy elf with obvious cybereyes lit up a cig. She ran her index finger down her throat to her chest and stared at him. Ella grinned as his hand shook, and she drew her finger lower. The cig fell from his doughy fingers and struck his pantsleg. He awkwardly patted it out and looked up, but the singer had already moved on to a new target.

She leaned forward, batting her thick lashes and teasing the top of a young dwarf's carefully-trimmed mohawk. He stood next to the footlights, mutely gaping at her. *A newcomer,* she thought, *one who dresses well and smells faintly of White Cristal cologne.* His breath carried a hint of graypuppy, and made her yearn for a slip. *He'll have something to tell the boys in the office tomorrow—if he doesn't think this is all a hallucination.* She coyly winked at him, then pivoted smoothly and returned to the center of the stage.

"Hot passion, let it find you, find you.
Let it burn inside you, 'side you.
Your heart sings a melody, sings you'll be mine alone.
'Til another comes along and steals you, steals you.
'Til another comes and steals you away..."

Ella shut her eyes and hummed the last few notes, the alto sax wailing a sad, haunting riff as her voice faded. The spotlight shrank, allowing the shadows of the stage to reach up and envelope her. The crowd responded wildly, clapping, hooting, whistling, and shouting as the curtain closed. Ella hiked her dress up to her knees and strode off.

"Beautiful, beautiful, beautiful, beautiful Ella dear!" gushed Cadi Hamfyst, the hulking, one-tusked troll who owned Cadigal's Corner. He gently patted her shoulder as she glided past. "Beautiful, beautiful, beautiful Ella my sweet. I love that song."

Ella pressed against the wall as a trio of song-and-dance girls tap-tap-tapped past, dressed in silver and blue tights, feathered skirts low around their hips. They were a new act, come up from Canberra, and Ella thought Cadi should have watched their vids closer before signing them. All elven, the tall one in the middle had overdone it with her breast implants, and looked so top heavy that she might fall forward at the slightest shuffle-ball-change. The shortest had fiberoptic hair that was never the same color twice. The third was simply unremarkable, too plain for the live stage. Amateurs.

After they'd passed. Ella headed down a twisting corridor filled with clothes racks and lined with dressing rooms. She was the only entertainer at Cadigal's that commanded her own room—

MISS ELLA GANCE painted above the door. She'd told Cadi to put a star above it, but that hadn't happened yet. Maybe she'd get a star elsewhere someday—if she ever made it into one of Brisbane's top nightclubs. She was always "away with the pixies," thinking about getting out from under this near-constant mana storm, to a place where fate and a random bolt of magic couldn't turn someone walking down the sidewalk into a wombat.

But that would never happen, would it? She'd pay her dues in the Cross—amid its antiquated strip shows, sex parlors, tawdry houses, and pubs—until she died. The few-square-block area was Sydney's armpit, civilized folk claimed, the neighborhood still clinging to the past and its outdated constructions, right down to the original bricks that made up the streets and sidewalks and the metal keys that opened many of the doors.

Despite the area's backwater vibe, Ella and her friends considered Kings Cross the heart of the city. It pulsed with a rhythm found nowhere else, and everyone of every background and sexual persuasion was welcomed with open arms. The purist Aborigines. The fanatically moral RighteousRight. The wide-eyed tourists. The jaded locals. The zealots of every stripe—from those who embraced the time of Sydney's founding as halcyon days to the ones who held dear more recent years. Even the cyber-addicts, ever searching for new enhancements and attachments, ever drunk on the technology spewing from Sydney's research centers...even they came here. The Cross attracted them all like a magnet, enfolded them in its shadowy arms, and hugged them to its big, stormy bosom.

The Cross had welcomed her more than thirty years ago, in an earlier incarnation of herself. And though she wanted to be a star in Brisbane, where the nuyen flowed faster, the weather was kinder, and the audience more sophisticated—thought about picking up stakes and going to Brisbane every day—she knew she'd miss this place terribly if she did. Going somewhere else would just kill her. So she could fragging well dream about leaving, but she knew she was staying.

Ella reached her room and nudged the door open. Twenty-five minutes before her next number. Plenty of time. She grabbed her sequined purse and darted to the back door, looking over her shoulder to make sure Cadi wasn't around. The troll discouraged the girls from leaving the building between acts—fearful, she imagined, that they'd get it in their pretty heads to keep going.

Satisfied no one was watching, she slipped out the security door and felt the alley's sweltering night air wash over her.

She squatted and groped for the brick, her insurance against getting locked out. There was no handle on the alley side. It was dark behind Cadigal's Corner; the streetlight a half-block away was broken—again. Had the neighborhood accepted the hydroposts the rest of the city used, there wouldn't be such problems. But just enough light spilled out from the opened security door and twinkled down from the stars in the rare gap in the cloud so Ella could see a little. At last her hand closed on an empty Toohey's bottle. It would work. She stuffed the neck into the jamb and the door caught against it.

Padding across the alley, she sat on a crate and fumbled in her purse, retrieving a small compact that held her slips. The lighted mirror showed her face, tiny wrinkles at the edges of her eyes. She shuddered. *Need to get them gone, another treatment...and before the week's out.* Her fingers had also been feeling a little stiff in the morning. Another treatment would fix that, too, and shouldn't be that all expensive. And right now a slip would make her forget the tiny wrinkles.

Just one slip, she admonished, as she placed it under her tongue and felt a rush akin to swallowing a few shots of expensive whiskey. She edged her fingers beneath the gold choker and rubbed her Adam's apple. The balmy night, coupled with the slip of graypuppy, made her sweat. *No, glow,* she corrected.

The heat felt good; she never complained about hot weather.

She let the delicious sensation roll through her, imagining herself by a waterfall eternally cascading over some tropical sunbaked cliff. Then the experience ended all too soon, and she nearly reached for another slip.

"Don't," she whispered. "Too easy." Way the hell too easy to pop one after another and be swept away by the rapture, to lose all track of herself, and miss her next number. She'd done it before.

Ella wasn't sure how much time had passed. She'd put the chrono in her purse, but without the streetlight she wouldn't be able to read it. *Better get back inside to be safe.*

She stood, brushed off her bottom, and started for the door, but stopped when she heard a trash bin fall over behind the Chinese restaurant two doors down. *Cats,* she thought with a smile. Cadi often kidded that the restaurant served Siamese cats with ribs attached. But then another bin tipped over, and

Ella heard something shuffling in the debris. Something much bigger than a cat.

From the shadows, the stranger watched the singer. He sniffed the air, sorting out the smells of beef and lamb and soyjerky, of rotten vegetables and redfish. He was hungry, and his stomach rumbled with the thought of the discarded food. But he also smelled the singer, and the singer was what he'd come here for.

He was pleased; this one was walking slowly in the sparkly high heels, unable to move too quickly over the brick alleyway. The one he'd killed nearly four weeks ago had been a more challenging target, faster in flats, athletic, an elf, almost got away. He was glad this singer wasn't an elf; in another life he'd loved her. That voice. Good thing she was human, wasn't an elf. Hated elves. Most elves were nimble and quick.

He preferred easier targets, and humans fit that bill; took less time to deal with.

The stranger stuck out his tongue, licked his bulbous lips, and started toward his prey.

This one should be easy enough.

This one wasn't an elf.

The regulars knew the girls came out back between acts to grab a smoke or some fresh air. They often waited here to buy some of the girls' services—the ones who were joygirls on the side—or sell them slips, though they didn't usually do either amid the refuse. But it was a good spot to set up arrangements.

Ella peered into the shadows and saw a man, very dark and well over six feet tall.

"Sorry, mate," she said. "Break's over. No time for fun."

The man walked closer, and Ella guessed he was likely a bum or a pug—Lord knew the Cross had enough of them. *Scrounging in the alley for food, no doubt.*

"Try the trash behind Wesley's Diner. The tucker's much better there—Australian-style." When she said 'Australian,' it came out 'Strine' like the Loyalists desperately hanging onto the land's original accent pronounced it. "Grilled redfish. Smell it? Yum."

Ella stepped toward the back of Cadigal's, but the man slid around her even faster. One more large step, and he blocked her from the door. Maybe he was a troll; he was certainly wide enough, and taller than Cadi, maybe taller than seven feet. Ella watched the figure stoop, remove the Toohey's bottle. The door closed, and the light disappeared.

Ella bolted, but she couldn't match the large man's speed. Several long strides and the stranger came even with her, and then shot past, stepping to the center of the alley as he flicked open a long-bladed knife that *thrummed* softly. He slashed the air with it, the *thrum* growing louder and the knife's edge glowing pale red-orange.

A heater. Like some of the bangers carried. Ella felt faint, and nearly toppled off her high heels.

"Please, m-m-mate. Let's not have any trouble here." She started backing up, and the stranger followed. "I'm not even a woman. So if women're what you're interested in, you can look elsewhere." Ella reached down the front of her dress and pulled out a piece of sweat-soaked foam. "See? I'm a false sheila. I'm an impersonator. N-not a joygirl, either."

He took another step forward, and Ella took another one back. The singer was sweating profusely now—from the heat that she'd never minded, from fear, from thinking about how she might get out of this without a scratch on her perfect and oh-so-expensive body with its high-end vocal range enhancers.

"No!" Ella sputtered as her heel caught in a crack between the bricks. She tugged her foot free of the shoe, and then kicked off the other one. Out of the corner of her eye, she saw the stranger lean in, the superheated blade edge glowing in the darkness.

She whirled and ran down the long alley, leaving Cadigal's Corner and the Chinese restaurant behind. She felt her beautiful sequined purse slip from her sweat-slick fingers, heard her bare feet slapping against the bricks, and then heard a louder sound catching up to her from behind—the stranger's pounding feet.

Her heart hammered madly as she took in great gulps of the humid air. Her lungs burned, and her temples throbbed like her head was going to explode. But she willed herself to run even faster. If she could just break out of the alley on the other side, she'd be near the park. There'd be people around the restored El Alamein Fountain, there always were. They'd help her.

Ella grabbed her aching side, then felt herself flying forward, her feet tangled in her long dress. The ground rushed up, and she slammed hard into the bricks.

The stranger bent down and his muscled arm shot out, fingers closing on a slender ankle. Ella flailed, grabbing at the cracks between the bricks and trying to pull herself toward the end of the alley—closer to the park and to the people gathered there, who were always by the fountain late at night, drinking and laughing and wading in the water.

She felt her battered knees, her sore ribs, which were probably cracked because she'd never bothered with bone lacing, had never thought she'd need it. But she also felt like she was making progress. Clawing at the street with all her strength, Ella dragged the man with her, until at last she saw faint light filtering into the end of the alley. The streetlight from the park.

"Help!" she screamed as the stranger tightened his grip. *So strong. Impossibly strong.* Pain shot up her left leg as the bones in her ankle broke, then she felt the stranger's hands on her other leg, squeezing until those bones splintered, too.

Tears spilled from Ella's eyes, and her chest heaved as she was harshly rolled over. Pain stabbed up from her shattered legs, and she stared in mute terror as the stranger placed a heavy foot on her silk-covered stomach.

Ella whimpered, tears slid down her perfectly sculpted face. She felt the heated knife pierce her skin, heard her blood begin to sizzle, and in that instant, she caught a glimpse of an empty Brisbane stage, and knew she'd never see the real thing.

TWO
HANGOVER CURE

"January." The word rolled off Nininiru Tossinn's tongue like a curse. *Probably snowin' in Chicago right now.*

She pictured big, wet flakes lazily floating down to join the wind-carved drifts. The air cold enough to see her breath. Ice skimmers at the edge of Lake Michigan, and hot chocolate and after-Christmas sales that filled the sidewalks with bundled-up bargain-hunters.

Ruefully shaking off the image, Ninn headed down Roslyn Street toward a growing crowd illuminated by flashing nightclub signs and elevated police spotlights.

"I hate summer," she muttered. This one had been brutal, with record temperatures. It was just past midnight, two days after New Year's Eve, and still too annoyingly warm, despite the late hour. Ninn felt drops of sweat trickling down her face, and tugged up the edge of her shirt to wipe them off.

As she drew closer, she spotted an Aborigine at the edge of the crowd. Thin, old, out of place among the sea of white bodies; he futilely stood on his bare tiptoes to see over the shoulders of those in front of him. *Out of place in the Cross*, she thought. *Hell, I'm outta place here, too. I should go back to Chicago.*

Nearby were four men in soiled green coveralls, with satchels over their shoulders and dirt caked on their shoes. Likely opal miners who'd hopped off the late tram and stopped on their way home to get a look at what everybody else was gaping at. Impossible for them to see through the crowd that Ninn estimated at seven or eight bodies deep, a good-sized assembly for the middle of the week and time of day.

Teenagers—bangers, no doubt, judging by their ragged leather, plastic, and denim clothes, vivid purple and blue hair, and glowing tats—darted in and out of the fringes of the crowd, taunting people who snapped at them. *They're up to somethin', definitely, the bangers,* Ninn decided. *But none of my business.* And she had no nuyen in her pockets for them to steal.

There were entertainers, too, scattered in the crowd. She noted a second-rate dwarf magician from the Bayswater Hole. Seen him once. Not good enough to go back for a repeat viewing. A pair of dancers, maybe from the magician's act, tittered within arms' reach of the man; the taps of their polished black shoes clicking on the bricks. A member of the RighteousRight stood a tad farther back, the ink tat on his bulging bicep announcing his affiliation and prejudice.

They should be in bed. All of them. Where I should be, she thought. *Too fraggin' hot out tonight. Too much to drink an hour ago. Fraggin' voices in my head won't shut up.*

Ninn recalled how cool the drinks had been that slid down her throat and found that sweet, sweet place in her soul that only addicts possessed. Ruefully dismissing the fine sensation, she shouldered her way into the mass, noting a few more RighteousRight members as she went. The odor of going too long without a shower clung like a second skin to many of the gawkers. Bright clothes meant for dance clubs competed with guttercrawlers' mismatched shirts and ragged pants. High heels, sandals, yawns, wagging tongues, cyber attachments, less obvious augmentations. Ninn took it all in, recorded the faces and scattered conversations that added to her throbbing, alcohol-fueled headache. Might need the pictures later, she knew from experience. Often criminals hung around to watch the aftermath of their handiwork.

"Wotter ya doin', keebler? I was 'ere first!" An ork opal miner objected to Ninn cutting through the crowd. "An ill-bred whacka you are."

Locals, most of them, she decided, as they rudely jostled her back and made assorted crude comments. She winced while passing a particularly fetid old drunk, and squinted when she caught the flash of the glittery dresses of joygirls working the middle of the pack. One squeezed toward her, smiling. Very young. Expensive-looking. Probably new to the Cross—Ninn hadn't seen her around before. Her vinyl dress made inviting crinkling sounds. Ninn tuned in on the noise, cut out the chatter of the crowd, and amplified the crinkling with her audio receptor. It reminded her of snow crunching underfoot, and made her pine for Chicago even more.

I should go back. Home, she thought. *Someday. When I get enough money. Get out from under the fragging mana storm, back to where I belong. At least the cloud's quiet at the moment.*

"G'day, sweetie." The joygirl's feigned Aussie accent was poor, but her voice was pleasant enough. A human, she barely came up to Ninn's shoulder. Fluttering her long lashes, wetting her lips, she smiled temptingly. Her heart-shaped face filled Ninn's vision. "Lonely? Need some company, sweetie?" she purred. "I can be very good company."

Need your company? That could be interesting, definitely.

"The best company." She blew Ninn a kiss.

"No," Ninn said with a sigh. *If I'd needed company, I would have brought Mordred.*

"Show you the city?" the joygirl persisted. "The Cross? Anything you like?"

Thinks I'm a tourist. Ninn's skin was tanned from the many days she'd spent on Sydney's nude beach. Work had been slow lately—her own fault; and she'd rationalized that this month-long hot spell was more endurable with her tush on the sand next to the ocean. Her blond hair hung in a braid from the nape of her neck to just below her shoulder blades.

The joygirl reached out a crimson-nailed hand and wrapped the end of the braid around her thumb as the crowd wedged them together. She looked up into Ninn's bright green eyes and gave a sexy pout.

"I can show you all of Sydney, sweetie—and a lot more. Show you things you've only dreamed about...never thought to dream about. Show you things better than this." She waved a thin hand; in a small gap between the bodies at the front of the crowd, Ninn spotted the tip of a police hat. Being a tall elf had its advantages. "Show you the real Cross, the pleasure of being with a human woman. I know a place we could go."

Definitely thinks I'm a tourist.

"It's a very nice place. Quiet."

"Well, that'd take nuyen, wouldn't it? And time. Neither of which I have at the moment." Ninn grinned.

"I treat tourists very special," she whispered.

I'm not a tourist.

But she had to admit she looked like one. Her khaki jeans were frayed at the bottom, showing off her sandaled feet. Her tank top was patterned with beige kangaroos hopping in unison in perfectly-spaced stripes all the way around. In a semi-circle above her left breast the words "I Visited Circular Quay" were embroidered in shiny ocher thread. Tourist attire. It had been the only relatively clean shirt within reach when she'd rolled off the couch.

"Some other day," Ninn said almost sadly. "Broke. Seriously, no nuyen for you. Not kiddin', busted flat." She turned out her pockets to prove her point.

The joygirl frowned and backed away, squirming between the bodies, her heart-shaped face receding into the crowd, the crinkling of her dress fading as she sought out another mark. Ninn worked her way to the front rank of gawkers, mystically held back by an *AISE Investigation–Do Not Cross* banner stretched between two buildings that blocked off the alley.

AISE, or "Ace," as most Aussies called them, stood for Australian Investigation and Security Enforcement, for which she'd worked all too briefly. They were the "big guns," here, so to speak, and Ninn had only seen them in this neighborhood once before, two years past, when a downtown politician got caught in some sting operation. AISE didn't bother with Kings Cross's usual rabble.

Ninn was curious why they'd show up now—this time of day, this rundown alley. She waved her palm, showing her private investigator ID chip to a muscular officer on the other side. He had a few cyber enhancements that weren't easy to spot; maybe AISE covered the cost of those expensive, near-invisible attachments. During her short stint she'd not checked if that was on the benefit list. The AISE barely acknowledged her, just nodded as Ninn ducked under the banner.

Well behind the flimsy barricade, a trio of AISE's finest hovered over the victim, all harshly illuminated by the spots that contributed to the heat. Ninn glided toward them, tuning in on their conversation using her attention coprocessor, a frontal cortex limbic system implant that allowed her to shift her focus and be aware of several things going on at the same time. It had cost her more than a little bit, though she was given a discount because she was a repeat customer of the Sydney BioNet Center, a cyber-junkie paying for her electronic fix. She'd told herself that the implant, like the others she'd purchased and happily went under the knife to have installed over the past few years, was helpful in her line of work. But the electronics hadn't netted her any big contracts yet, and the only thing it was doing at the moment was amplifying her hangover.

This job wouldn't pull in any significant nuyen either; Cadi Hamfyst was tight with his funds, she knew from experience. The jobs she'd done for him before—spying on competitors, trailing his second ex-wife—hadn't yielded much. Maybe he'd try to pay her in booze like the last time. Wouldn't work today. Cold, hard nuyen was what she'd demand. She had office rent to worry about. But in the back of her mind, she again felt the cool drinks slide down her throat to drown that sweet spot, and thought booze in partial payment might not be awful.

Ninn often scolded herself for not saving nuyen and using it for a ticket home—where she suspected she could find good-paying and more legitimate work. But the scolding always came after she'd added some new piece of cyberware or bioware or upgraded what she already had...and then went out drinking to celebrate.

The implants were her main addiction, and whenever she saw some new device advertised that she came to want, she actively sought just enough work to pull in the nuyen to buy it. The tech the States had wasn't this good; they were years behind Australia. Ninn had vowed to get some contracts in the next month or so. A high-end nose filter had recently hit the Sydney market, and she was craving it. That, and she was looking to add a high frequency sound filter and spatial recognizer to her ear implant and get her eye upgraded. She desperately needed an improvement to her cyberear; it wasn't allowing her to record all the voices she heard, just picked up on the conversations in the lower ranges and within a few yards.

Though Cadi was cheap, maybe she could wrangle enough out of the old troll for the down payment on the nose job, the improved ear implant, *and* get him to throw in a case or two of his good stuff.

"Bloke was a looker," she heard one AISE investigator mutter, rousing Ninn from her musings. A detective-lieutenant, according to the AISE button on his shoulder. Kneeling, he stared into the bodybag. The man was familiar, a human with some age to him, judging by the lines at the edges of his eyes. Ninn tried to put a name to his face but came up short; must have run into him before she got the attention coprocessor that made remembering easy.

God, but her head pounded and her tongue felt dry and swollen. Why the hell hadn't she stopped after the fourth Kamikaze? "Didn't know you liked that type, Lieutenant," another AISE answered, a slight smirk on his elven face. "Thought you sided with the RighteousRight."

"I just agree with the Right sometimes, that's all. There's no law against someone making a living, but to do it like this...a man singing like a woman, and to be a *Koori*, no less."

Koori: derogatory slang for Aboriginal, Ninn learned when she called the word up from an early encephalon file.

Ninn saw the lieutenant shrug, watched the second speaker move closer. The elf—a handsome one, maybe in his late twenties, a few years younger than her, someone that under different circumstances might make good company—bent and opened the bag wider. The third cop, another human, kept his distance, almost as if whatever had killed the victim was contagious. Ninn noted his cyberarm with several tweezer-like attachments extended that helped gather evidence.

There were more AISE lumpers about, a human and a dwarf at the far end of the alley, taking statements from two people on the other side of the banner. One of the interviewees was a nattily-dressed businessman with a briefcase under his arm. The other a young woman in faded jeans, wet up to her thighs— probably from a dip in the fountain. It looked like she belonged to a 1960s clique.

Let's see the body, get it over with. I need to get back to my couch and work this head-wanger off.

Ninn glanced around the officers to get a look at the bag. She knew it was AISE policy to bag a corpse right away, to not let any extra contaminants from the officers or gawkers foul the evidence. Cops in Chicago—depending on the neighborhood— sometimes waited for hours to bag victims and have them carted to the morgue.

A dark-skinned woman inside the bag. Man, Ninn corrected when she noted the Adam's apple. *Beautiful. Very beautiful. Maybe twenty, twenty-five tops, no older. Took good care of herself. Himself. Pity. Think I heard her sing once.* A quick consult with her encephalon confirmed that: Miss Ella Gance. She'd heard the woman sing on two different visits to Cadigal's.

Rough place to die, this rundown alley, she thought, *a sad way to end the voyage.* A John Milton quote from *Paradise Lost* slipped through her mind: "Never can true reconcilement grow where wounds of deadly hate have pierced so deep..." How could someone have hated Ella Gance enough to pierce her so deep?

The AISE lieutenant studied a jagged slash that had practically decapitated the singer and snapped a thick gold neck chain. Oddly, the wound hadn't released much blood, leaving the corpse's silky dress unmarred. The AISE detective was using the latest equipment, a handheld evidence sniffer that the cops in Chicago wouldn't see for another year or more—if they were lucky.

Ninn kept up on tech, knew the sniffer could gauge the time of death by lividity and blood pooling, register skin, saliva, and hair samples, blood types—help point a finger at the murderer. The larger units could do more and faster, especially with DNA samples, do all but tell you exactly what the perpetrator wore and what he ate for breakfast that morning. But the lumpers that came into the Cross didn't tend to bring the big stuff.

The third officer stared at the singer's face—lovely even in death, save for an ugly bite mark on the left cheek. It was human-sized, deep, and had torn away a chunk of flesh, showing the muscle and bone beneath. The officer's eyes were shiny, the pupils enlarged, special implants. Not as good as Ninn's sole cybereye, but his cyberarm was seriously impressive. She noted that as his pupils expanded they flashed red, a video vulture recording the entire scene for morbid posterity. Just like Ninn intended to do.

She concentrated, and felt a wave of dizziness as her cybereye enlarged the image, getting a closer look at the bite. Ninn had been blinded in that eye during riots in Chicago and had worn a patch until she found a cybereye in Sydney that suited her. Maybe she should have had both replaced, but one was cheaper, and her real eye still worked. The cybereye was packed: flare comp, thermographic, plus a recorder. She felt the dizziness pass—an effect of having one cybereye instead of a pair—then started recording and sending the data to her encephalon, a microprocessor hardwired to her cortex that boosted her ability to manage and store information. She had enough room on her current chip to catch three-dozen hours or more. The next gen of cybereyes had just been released, and promised to triple that time. It was on her shopping list, too.

"We're just about finished 'ere, mates."

Ninn listened to the lieutenant kneeling over the corpse, cocked her head to get a close-up of the man.

Enlarge it. Good. Familiar. I should know him. I SHOULD KNOW—
He was tall, a tad over six feet like herself. His bushy brown hair
stuck out at odd angles beneath his cap; it was his nasal voice, and a
slightly bulbous red-veined drinker's nose that niggled her memory.
Definitely familiar. But memories—from her life before the
encephalon and other technological aids—were fuzzy, often
ephemeral. Too much alcohol, too many slips had eroded things,
especially what she'd deemed less important, cast into an ocean
of intangibilities and best forgotten. The lieutenant's name was
buried somewhere in there, lost. Recoverable? Maybe.

Like the other two, his uniform was crisp and pressed. They'd
all managed to get through the inspection of the scene without
getting a spot of blood on them.

"Coroner's on 'er way to slab this one. Be 'ere in a few," the
lieutenant said. "Nothin' left for us at the moment. We've swept
the alley. Review the bloody interviews tomorrow, and follow up
then if we need to."

So they've already talked to the crucial people, Ninn noted. Fast.
Efficient or careless, or a bit of both. She'd see what feeds AISE
would release to her in the next day or so, see who they talked to.

The lieutenant looked at his chrono, checked the far end of
the alley where his mates had finished talking to the businessman
and the drenched woman. "'Sides, with this bloody 'eat, she'll
start to stink real soon."

"He. *He'll* start to stink." This from the third officer, the one
with the cyberarm. He was the only one with a name displayed
on his pocket: *Mickey Dern.* He still gazed at the singer's face and
recorded the scene. Ninn thought this cop looked more sympa-
thetic. Mickey was younger than the other two, small and wiry,
and his expression revealed he was bothered by the crime. *New
to AISE work,* Ninn guessed, *at least to this kind of work.* Murder
didn't seem to bother veterans much. "I heard him sing once,
'bout a year ago. Took my wife to the show for our anniversary.
He was really something, really incredible. Reminded me of Billie Holiday."

"Billy who?" The lieutenant frowned, then shook his head.
"Never mind, Mick. Maybe somebody didn't like 'is singing. Cut
'is bloody vocal cords clean through. Maybe the Right. I spotted
a couple of 'em out front. Maybe a critic. Who knows? We got no
fingerprints. Nothing. Just a dead *Koori,* this one in an expensive
dress. Nothing."

Koori. Ninn winced and messaged at her temples, worked up some saliva.

"Not nothing. You can't say we got *nothing,* Lieutenant," the second officer, the handsome elf, said. "There's this bite on his cheek. See? The others only had their throats slit, clearly with a heater. This one was also bitten hard. See here, and here." He pointed at the injuries. "And those aren't normal teeth marks. Too deep, nicked the bone. Our murderer likely had some cyberdents. But the slash is the same even cut as the others. A heater, like I said. Can't be anything else. Perp didn't want the vic to bleed out. This has gotta be the same bloke what did the others. The bite was personal, I figure. Or maybe a loss of control. Maybe the Right, but I dunno. Doesn't Ballard strap heaters? Think he's upped his game? Think this is a serial slasher?"

Ballard. Familiar name. Ninn ran it through the encephalon, coming up with only one thread: *Jeb Ballard, two arrests for battery on Darlinghurst.* Nothing on his victims or his affiliations. She made a note to dig into that more tomorrow.

"Serial?" The lieutenant drew his lips tight. "Keep your voice down—no need to get the crowd into a panic. Some o' them behind the tape have 'tech and can 'ear us. Well, at least now we know for certain the perp's got 'tech too. Cyberdents. Eh. That certainly ain't Ballard or his cronies." He was talking softly, and Ninn had to boost the receptor to hear him clearly. Definitely needed an upgrade. "Someone with 'tech and a real bad attitude who doesn't like men masquerading as women. Not a *Koori* thing. The others weren't *Kooris.* And a Right wouldn't have 'tech, now would he?"

Mickey pulled the bodybag around the singer and closed it, covering the beautiful face. "But maybe the Right's using someone with 'tech to throw us off. Would be a tactic a mystery writer would throw in, eh? The others weren't *Kooris*, but they were... sexually confused. Could all be related. Could be a serial. Could be Right targets. Maybe, LT."

The others?

The hiss of the heat-sealed plasticene bag shot through Ninn's head, and she gritted her teeth and adjusted the noise filters down a couple steps.

The lieutenant shrugged. "Maybe. We'll relook a lot closer at the other cases, Mick. We'll 'ave a go at it tomorrow arvo. Eh. Later this arvo. Maybe there's a thread after all."

"What other cases?" Ninn interrupted, making all three officers' heads turn, focusing on her like a trio of sharks smelling a chum trail.

The lieutenant chortled. "Don't keep up on what's going on in your own neighborhood, Ninny? What the 'ell kinda private investigator are you?"

From the shadows a block away, the Slayer watched the crowd, captivated by the bright, flashing lights of the AISE vehicles. He sniffed the air and sorted out the smells of rain coming, of sweat and excitement and curiosity. His stomach growled. So hungry. He'd nearly given in to temptation and went after the discarded food behind the Chinese restaurant. People threw away so many things that were tasty and not wholly rotten. But he'd needed to deal with the singer first, and then he'd needed to leave or risk discovery. The quarry took precedence, then escape.

Always, the quarry came first. Killing would keep him alive. Escape after a killing was easy.

He listened to the crowd and picked through their conversations. Finding nothing particularly interesting, and eventually tiring of the flashing lights, he ambled away and down another alley. There was an Italian restaurant nearby, and there would be discards worth eating in the bins. He was especially fond of fetuccini with Alfredo sauce.

THREE
DREAMING TIME

The boys talked in a sing-song language that only a scattering of original people shared.

"My blood filled a cup, brother," the smaller child said. Save for the height difference, the two boys looked like mirrors of each other, skin dark like mud, noses broad, and eyes wide and unblinking. "I barely noticed the pain." The boy showed his arm with a long fresh scar. The taller child shivered.

"I painted with my blood, brother," the boy continued. "I painted lines and circles upon my arms and legs, and I painted symbols that came to me in a dream. And while my blood was still wet I pressed leaves against it, and felt myself moving ever closer to the earth. I dropped so close and then I flew and—"

"Father looked for you," the taller boy interrupted. "Days he looked. He thought you ran away to the city. He thought you left us. Yesterday he finally stopped looking. Yesterday he believed never to see you again."

The first boy shook his head. "I was walkabout, brother. I do not know how long I was gone."

"Days and days and days and days."

"The passing of time during walkabout means nothing. Gone minutes or months, it does not matter. I found the Rainbow Serpent, and he introduced me to my totem spirit, the galah. The Rainbow Serpent was wise and powerful, and he drove me down into the sky while he drank all of my blood and ate my flesh, and then returned life to me and brought me back to this world. I learned new songs and met spirits. My heart sings a melody, brother. It sings that the world will be mine. I traveled through the hills and into the belly of the land, where I rested on a bed of fire opals and listened to my heart."

The other boy laughed. "You make up stories, Barega. Father will scold you for running away. Heart sings a melody. Ha! Father will—" "Mother will love me for returning," the shorter boy countered. "Father will—"

"—understand. I will tell him of his ancestors who I talked with. I will tell him of the Great Ghost Dance I swam through. I felt the anger of the Rainbow Serpent gathered in the beautiful, horrible, most magical clouds, brother. I ran with the rain."

"You run with foolish stories. Father will call you a silly child. Father will—" The other boy stood and looked to the west, mouth falling open when he saw a *galah* circling slowly on an updraft.

"I am no longer a child, brother. I am *talmai, mekigar, wirringan—*"

"*Koradji,*" the other boy said with awe, eyes locked on the galah. "I believe you. *Koradji.*"

"Yes, and I can dream."

"I want to dream too, Barega." He dropped his gaze and grabbed his brother's shoulders. "Please. Take me walkabout! Show me the Rainbow Serpent. I will ask for a better totem than yours. Not a rosy-gray bird so small and noisy. My spirit will be a brown snake or *taipan*, or I will live near the water and choose a stone fish or a great white shark. My totem will be fearless and fearful, not a pretty parrot. My heart will also sing a melody. When I am *koradji*, my spirit and I will—"

"You are not *koradji*, brother. And you will not be. But I will dream for both of us."

Barega slipped out of dreamtime, the primordial present-past he'd been traipsing through so often of late. "I still dream for both of us." Disconnecting with his long-ago self, he concentrated upon the present, and the feel of the duracrete sidewalk beneath his bare feet. He took the city air deep into his lungs and tried to endure the scents of filth and food and things he had no names for. The sounds of the city seeped into his senses, music—which was both pleasant and unpleasant. He enjoyed the strains of a bluesy piece falling out the window of someone's second floor apartment. He had always loved good blues. So many decades he'd spent in and out of this and other cities; good blues had not changed in all that time. He detested the electronic techno-rock that throbbed out the door of an all-hours bar. Something new age that sounded like glass breaking pulsed from a nightclub.

He saw the neon lights of a dancehall; in pink and gray tubing above the entrance was the image of a flying galah. *Pella's Rosy Parrot*, the sign read. Believing his totem had led him in the correct direction, he continued east, where the duracrete gave way to bricks, stopping finally at the edge of a growing crowd.

Barega was fascinated by the races and colors assaulting his vision, and the conversations blotting out the blues and techno-rock and the shattering glass that pretended to be music. He stood on his tiptoes and peered into the darkness held back by police spotlights.

"Hey, old man," a joygirl cooed. "I can show you the real Cross, show you things you've only dreamed about."

Barega shook his head. The pretty young Asian girl knew nothing about dreaming.

FOUR
NINN'S CASE

"A private investigator, eh?" The handsome AISE elf glared at Ninn. She'd thought one of her "own kind" would have been more receptive to her presence, but he clearly didn't want her here.

"I said...where'd you come from, *mate?*" His last clipped word was anything but friendly.

She gave him an insincere smile. "Walked from my office on Darlinghurst and took a right on Roslyn." Ninn pointed to the street behind her. "Came in under your flimsy barricade."

"This is an AISE investigation," the elf stated. "You can see that." He huffed as he eased himself up, and then brushed at a spot of blood on his pant leg.

Not spotless after all. Despite the heater there was blood. The victim's? Or had she got a piece of her attacker? Ninn almost pointed it out to him.

"Don't be a yobbo. Get back behind the police line." The elf waved an arm at Ninn, revealing a cyber-relay system on the back of his hand.

Ninn shook her head. "I *am* a detective. Registered." She showed her left palm, displaying her ID chip for whatever minimal effect it might have. "Cadigal Hamfyst—Cadi, the troll over there—asked me to stop by. Hired me to see who slashed his singer. I'm fine to be here. And I'm not in your way. What other murders?"

"Don't you PIs ever take a listen to the news?" the elf looked to the lieutenant, who was busy examining the area around the singer's corpse.

Actually, I don't often hear the news, not lately. Not much reason to.

However, Ninn seemed to remember something she'd heard on the street about someone killed in the area a few weeks ago, a couple of suspicious deaths before that. She hadn't paid it any heed, though now she thought she should have. There typically weren't many murders in the Cross—not compared to the rest of Sydney. But there were plenty of other crimes and vices, most of which the neighborhood either tolerated or wholeheartedly espoused. She wished she'd brought Mordred with her; he usually paid more attention to the local scuttle, thrived on gossip, and likely could call up the details on the murders. Ninn would ask him later, but for now she'd prod AISE.

"The other murders—" Ninn pressed. "What can you tell me about them? Related, you think? And when—"

"Ninny's 'Merican, in case you're curious," the lieutenant said, identifying her accent for his fellows.

"New York?" The elf's attitude suddenly brightened.

"She's from Chicago, Draye," the lieutenant answered. "South Side, if I remember right."

"Big city girl. Chicago," Draye said. "Toddlin' Town. Big shoulders."

The lieutenant turned his attention back to the sealed bag, tagged it. "Ninny, if you're curious about the other murders, go run up some local news vids. I haven't got time to do your digging, or to get you up to speed. Don't expect AISE to help you earn a paychit. You drew one too many from us as it was." His lips pulled back into a mirthless smile.

So familiar. But I can't place him exactly. Frag it! He definitely remembers me from my time with AISE. Who the blue blazes is he? Did all the booze wash his name away?

The AISE elf stepped toward Ninn and pointed a blunt finger at the crowd. "Get back behind the bloody line, Toddlin' Town. Got a hearing problem? Don't need anyone else wandering around and contaminating—"

"It's dinky-di, officers. I want her to stay."

Ninn smelled the troll approaching, his strong aftershave lotion announcing him.

Cadigal was about the same height as Draye, short for a troll, but with thick upper arms, like pressed hanks of soybeef. He looked more like a construction worker than a businessman, particularly one who owned a tawdry house. He stood in front of a half-dozen showgirls gathered near a door propped open with a bottle, the back entrance to Cadigal's Corner. The troll patted a heavy-busted ork in a tight white dress who was crying softly, then strode toward Ninn, his ring-encrusted hand thrust out.

The AISE elf went back to the lieutenant and the bodybag, glancing toward the alley ends and calling to the other officers to watch for the coroner. Ninn kept her ear trained on the law trio and kicked in the audio inscriber so she could talk to Cadi now and later play back the AISE conversation she was missing. She turned off her visual recorder and paused while another, briefer, wave of dizziness struck. The aftereffects of too much booze still lingered. She'd captured enough images for now anyway, had the AISE officers Draye and Mickey tucked away in her noggin. Should have brought Mordred, definitely; he was good with details.

"Thanks for coming, my friend." Cadi grabbed Ninn's thin hand between his two sweaty palms and shook it vigorously. Despite his mass, there wasn't much strength in the grip. "This is terrible. Just terrible. Ella was the best. Beautiful. Beautiful. Beautiful. Beautiful. The very best. A headliner, a real crowd-pleaser. This is going to hurt business bad. I liked her a lot. I loved her." This last he said softly.

"Who found her, Cadi?"

The chunky ork in the white dress choked back a sob and waggled her thick fingers. She swaggered toward them.

"Hurdy Gertie," Cadi said by way of introduction. "Uh...Harold Naughton, actually."

"S'call me Gertie," she said. Her voice was husky and masculine, not bothering to sound like a woman at the moment. The cheeks of her round face were streaked blue and black from makeup that had run from the heat and her tears. Ninn noted that while all of the performers seemed upset by the murder, numb perhaps, Gertie was the only one actually crying. Her shoulders shook, and she shoved her fist against her mouth. "Ella," she said, her voice muffled. "Ella Gance was my best friend. We were gonna go to Brisbane someday. Talked about it just yesterday, in fact."

"You found her..." Ninn's tone gently urged her to explain.

"I already told the Aces. Fraggin' lumpers, they—"

Cadi nudged the ork.

The tears increased. "She was late, Ella was. They were calling for her from the wings. Thought she might be out here...smoking you know, maybe having a drink or a slip, most likely a slip 'cause she'd just bought some. I didn't want her to get in trouble, miss her number. So I came out to check. Didn't see her at first. S'was dark." She paused until she regained some semblance of control. "Didn't look hard enough. I really didn't think anything...*bad*...had happened. If I'd found her then, maybe...maybe medics could've saved her. Didn't look hard enough, pigs I didn't. She missed her next number, and I came out after my second, had a few minutes before I had to change. I looked again. Thought she'd, you know—been with a fan. S'wasn't like her to miss a number, but it happened every once in a while. If the nuyen was good enough. She wasn't a joygirl, never, but if the nuyen was good enough, Ella always needed nuyen, she sometimes—"

"And that's when you found her? The second time you came out here?"

She nodded. "I told you I had a few minutes. So I walked toward the park, thought I might see her by the fountain. She liked the fountain. S'was so dark. I almost tripped over her. Oh, God—"

Cadi draped an arm around the ork's shoulders. "Gertie came and got me right away. I called you a little while after I called the lumpers. Called the locals and here the Aces showed up." He laughed sadly. "Ace lumpers. Holy dooly! What the hell are they doing here? Maybe having a fifth murder down here finally woke 'em up."

Five murders, Ninn mused with an internal wince—she fragging well should have paid attention to the news.

"Five!" Gertie's demeanor changed and she snarled. "Drekkin' lumpers. They're drongoes, the lot of 'em. The Cross ain't prone to much crime, it ain't. Not *bad* crime."

Cadi cut in, "Bangers run from time to time, spray graffiti, break the antique streetlights, and sometimes harass tourists. You live around here, Ninn, you know what we got."

"Lumpers don't help with shit, 'specially Aces," Gertie hissed. "If them Aces came around once in a while, Ella'd still be breathing."

"But they're here now," Ninn whispered. Ninn knew "lumpers" was what the local police were called, and they were only noticed by their conspicuous absence in the neighborhood. And AISE, Australia's elite police, typically wasn't caught dead in the area. Apparently they were considered "lumpers" too.

The ork continued her tirade. "Another of my mates was killed nigh on four weeks ago outside a high-rise a couple of blocks away."

"That was Dezi Desire," Cadi supplied. "She was—"

"A singer at Halfway House. Sydney's lumpers had no clues," Gertie said. "Halfway's House's lead choreographer and some stagehand were found about a week later. Geeked near an all-hours pub, they were. Before all of that another impersonator from a place down the street was slashed. Don't remember who she worked for, that one, The Tattered Cat, Shattered Cat, something like that. Had cat in the title. Don't recall her name. There'd been a few other murders, too."

"Years ago and not so close to home, those murders," Cadi supplied. "Tourists getting mixed up in things they should've steered clear of. Probably before you moved here, Ninn. Hell, probably back when you were still in the States. The tourists are smarter now."

Gertie wiped at her nose. "But not the lumpers, they ain't smarter. Them Ace drongoes are dumb as parrot drek. They solve murders—not, keep the bangers in their place—not, and can't even prevent the streetlights from getting bashed to bits. Wonder why they bothered to show up for Ella?"

Ninn cocked her head, heard the click of hard soles across the bricks, fast businesslike steps, heard the lieutenant offer a greeting to the coroner, the words being recorded sounding like gnats buzzing around her ear. The coroner was in dress slacks so tight they looked painted on, her waist, breasts, everything in ideal proportion. The coroner was human, but it looked like she'd had some serious augmentations, body shaping, and bio-work done to come across nearly "perfect." Even her hair, wavy, shoulder-length, red with highlights. Covergirl face. Almost too perfect and plastic, like the way an undertaker can make the deceased look. Fitting appearance for her job, maybe.

"See anything else? Anyone else?" Ninn studied the ork.

"No."

"Did Ella owe someone nuyen?"

Gertie snorted. "Hand to mouth she lived, spending it all on Renaixement and slips and slips and more slips. Bad habit she had. Her debts were square, I think."

Everyone had at least one bad habit, Ninn thought. "Did Ella have any enemies?"

"Pigs she did!" Gertie shook her head vehemently. "No! Everyone loved her. I already told the lumpers that. And Dezi, everyone loved her, too. S'why're you asking me the same questions? I don't wanna talk about this anymore. I don't wanna—"

"What about the RighteousRight? They been giving you any trouble?"

"No." A pause. "Not really. Not anymore than usual. No."

"How about Ella's other..." Ninn paused, trying to grope for a word that wouldn't offend the entertainer. "*Him*," she started. "Who was Ella? Did *he* have any enemies?"

"Miss Ella Gance," Cadi cut in, "was Adoni Kogung. Adoni... it means 'sunset' in some Aboriginal dialect. Sadly appropriate."

The ork wailed, and Cadi continued. "Adoni came to work for me three years ago, picked her up from the Beat Red down the street. She'd been in the area a long time though, but hadn't looked quite this good until she started over there, and before that at Halfway House and the Forum, and apparently had enough nuyen to get some significant work done. God, she was beautiful."

"Yes, she was," Ninn admitted. "Go on."

"We came up with the Miss Ella Gance name right away, 'cause she was all that—elegant. Kept getting better and better and better. Was writing her own songs. Pulled 'em into my place like a siren. Beautiful. And then when she got the vocal cord work done...wow. Kept making noise about going to Brisbane. But she fit in here, you know? You've been here more than a few times Ninn, you saw her. Honestly, I was surprised I could hang on to her."

"I did see her. She was pretty incredible." Ninn remembered Ella singing "Over the Rainbow" some months back when she ducked into Cadigal's to get off the street during one of the nastier mana storm surges.

Cadi fidgeted as he watched the coroner escorting the AISE men leading a float-gurney, the bodybag atop it. They headed toward the far end of the alley, where the coroner's sleek, mirror-black vehicle, a Takaya Daimyo, had made the crowd drift back. The car looked perfectly plastic, too.

"Want to talk to the other girls, Ninn?" The troll nodded at the performers standing behind him. "A couple more're inside. Told 'em I haven't decided if I'm gonna close tomorrow...er, today. Probably should. To honor Ella. In fact, I'll have a service or—" Then Cadi's attention shifted to the AISE lieutenant, who was passing the sniffer one more time over where Ella had been found. He was the only officer remaining in the alley.

"Has AISE—" Ninn began.

"Lumpers already talked to all the girls," Cadi said as he and Ninn watched the bag floating down the alley. "I'm with Gertie. I don't need to go over it again. Not right now anyway, talked enough to the fraggin' Aces. Don't *want* to go over it again. But

I will, later. Right now I want to drink all of this nightmare away and—"

"Later, then," Ninn said as Cadi released Hurdy Gertie's shoulders. "I can get the girls' statements from Sydney Central records. Talk to them later if I need to." *Talk to them away from here, where there are no distractions.* The troll headed toward the lieutenant, leaving Ninn in front of the ork songstress.

Ninn turned up the volume on her receptor, pretended to listen to Hurdy Gertie, who was face-to-face with her now, praising Ella's performances, spittle and sweat flying. But Ninn was really listening to Cadi and the lieutenant.

"I'll need you down at Central this arvo," the lieutenant told Cadi. "Few more questions, finish my report. Won't take long. Sometime after lunch. You'll be back in plenty of time to open at night if that's what you want to do. She'll be apples."

"Everything will be all right? Pigs. And finish your report?" Cadi blustered. "There's no finishing nothing until you find Ella's killer. Takes what? Five murders to get Ace attention? And then just like that you'll finish it up tomorrow afternoon?"

"We're pretty sure it's linked to the murders of the other drag queens," the lieutenant said. "That maybe we've a serial—"

"Ella wasn't just a bloody drag queen! The others weren't drag queens!" Cadi fumed. "Ella was a talent, an impersonator. An artist. The best. You would understand that if—"

"Listen, it's an ongoing investigation. We're doing what we can." The lieutenant let a touch of sympathy drift into his voice, but Ninn wondered if it was practiced or genuine. "There's murders in other parts of Sydney, too."

"The bloody bastard's out there."

"Yes. And tell your *girls* to stay out of the alleys. Not to go anywhere alone. When you close up after a show, make sure they leave in a group. Safety in numbers, remember? Be sensible about things, and they'll be ducky."

"That's what you tell tourists? Safety in numbers? If you caught the murderer, they'd be safe. Everyone would be safe."

"See 'ere, *mate*, we're working on it. We're 'ere, ain't we?"

"Working," Cadi growled deep enough that Ninn felt the bricks tremble under her sandaled feet. His fists were balled, white at the knuckles. "If you'd been working hard, been here for the very first victim, you would've caught the bloody bastard by now. My beautiful Ella would still be alive."

The lieutenant glared. "That why you brought in the private investigator? Ninny? Because you don't think us cops work hard enough? She's only pretending to be sober. She's gonna be worthless to you, Mr. Hamfyst. You could do better."

Ninn bristled and chastised herself. She didn't have that coveted and expensive nose filter, yet she could smell the booze on herself.

"Don't think we'll work fast enough?" the lieutenant continued.

"Yeah, I don't. That's why I hired her. This is the fifth murder, and you haven't done frag-all about it. That's why I hired her. I'm spending my nuyen 'cause Ace ain't doing its bloody job."

The lieutenant chuckled.

The laugh. Ninn had never liked that laugh. And he'd called her Ninny. She spun and left Hurdy Gertie behind.

"Hope you're not paying 'er much, Mr. Hamfyst. Ninny there couldn't find a clue if it jumped up and bit 'er on the—"

"That's enough, Lieutenant Waller," Ninn cut in, at last remembering the name of the man who used to head the AISE squadroom on the morning shift—the shift before she went on duty. Jacob Waller. A man she'd tried to push out of her memory.

"Ninny 'ere was kicked out of AISE," the lieutenant continued, directing his comments to the troll. "About four, five years ago, if I remember right. She hadn't been on the force long, fresh from the States. A real prize at the beginning. But it went sour quick. Bad collar on a very big case. Sloppy, she was. Made the news. Then it came out that she'd made a bad collar back in Chicago, too, and meddled with a big fire investigation. We didn't give 'er a second chance after that all came to light. Told her to rack off. Booted 'er little elf ass."

The lieutenant turned to Ninn, a sneer twisting his thin features. "Was that why you moved 'ere to the Cross, Ninny? All that bad publicity in Sydney proper kept you from getting work anywhere else 'round 'ere? No little cop shop would take you on? You 'ad to go private?"

Ninn formed a fist and drew back, but Cadi's meaty hand shot up and caught her arm, throwing her aim off.

"Now why'd you have to go and stop 'er, Mr. Hamfyst? There're plenty of witnesses around. Tsk, tsk. Could put Ninny away for better'n a year for assaulting an AISE officer." Waller glared at Ninn. "Just give me an excuse, Ninny. Any excuse at all, and your little elf ass'll be locked up all nice and proper."

Ninn dropped back a step.

"Sure you don't want to take a shot at me, Ninny? But then where would Cadigal's precious *entertainers* be without a hard-drinking private eye poking around for them? You raise your fist to me again, and I'll be happy to file the paperwork. You might like jail. Free tucker and a free place to stay. Might thank me for that. Last I 'eard, you were living in your office. 'Course, last I 'eard of you was a couple years ago, when you got into a fight with a security cop posted by the opera."

That 'law' was harrassin' a friend of mine, he was in the wrong, and you know it. Nothin' came of the incident, charges dropped. He baited me. Just like you're baitin' me.

Ninn took a deep breath and tried to look composed, took another step back and put her hands out to her sides as a peaceful gesture.

Don't need a confrontation. Not here. Not now. Let it go. Let him go. He's looking for any excuse to arrest me. Push him to the back of my memory again. Forget his name again.

"Yeah, I'm still livin' in the office," she replied. "It's homey. Rent's reasonable. The landlord's a real peach, and doesn't even mind if I have guests."

Waller shook his head. "You're wastin' your nuyen, Mr. Hamfyst. Ninny 'ere is bad news, one bad collar after the next." He chuckled, shook a finger at Ninn, and then patted the nightclub owner on the arm. "Sorry about your girl. Really. Nobody should die like this. Just not right. Tomorrow arvo at Sydney Central, anytime after brekkies, actually." He whirled on his leather heels and headed toward the coroner's vehicle.

"You was a lumper? Ace?" Gertie strutted up to join the pair, wrinkled her nose at Ninn. "You was with them Aces?"

"A while ago," Ninn answered numbly, staring as the coroner pulled away.

"Better find someone else then, love." Gertie was talking to the troll. "Even if you claim she's a mate of yours, Cadi. Don't like the lumpers, especially a bad one. All of 'em drongoes are as dumb as parrot drek."

Ninn mentally clicked off the inscriber as the ork prattled on about the lack of interest the police had in the Cross, and how Ella's murderer would never be found.

"Would be different if a tourist had been killed!" Gertie taunted when she was sure the AISE investigators were out of earshot.

Cadi escorted the big woman toward the other performers, herded them to the back door.

Ninn stared at the spot on the alley where Ella's body had lain. The pounding in her head matched her heartbeat. She rubbed her temples harder. She heard the voices again.

"Where will you start?" Cadi had returned.

Ninn shut down her receptors and listened to Cadi with her own ears.

"Your investigation?" The troll continued. "Where will you start?"

"Sure you still want me involved? You saw it yourself. Lieutenant Waller, the guy in charge...we don't exactly get along."

Cadi shrugged. "Sod him. It doesn't bother me none, mate. Besides, I figure since the lumpers don't seem to like you, if I keep you around, they might actually try to find who killed my beautiful Ella, and Dezi before her. A race maybe. And if you do beat 'em to it, I still win." His quick smile faded. "I want my girls safe, Ninn. Safe in a hurry. Will you accept nine hundred a day?"

The known-to-be-stingy troll was deadly serious to offer that much nuyen. Ninn nodded.

Cadi thrust a voucher chit for twenty-seven hundred at her. "For starts," he said.

"Hopefully this won't take more than three days."

"If it takes less, I don't need a refund, Ninn."

Ninn pressed the chit against her credstick, tried not to visibly savor the transfer of the nuyen into her nearly empty account.

"You'll keep me posted?"

"Every day."

"Where will you start?" he repeated.

Ninn looked all around, taking in the alley, the crowd behind the barricade tape. "Right here, of course. And, I'll begin by—"

The rain came without a single warning flash of lightning. It poured out of the sky like someone had turned on an immense water faucet. There were no drops, just a solid deluge that soaked everyone in the alley in a heartbeat.

Hail spat down as the assemblage dashed for cover, rat-a-tat-tatting off the bricks and garbage bins.

"Pigs!" Gerti cursed as she swung open the rear door of Cadigal's Corner. "Pigs! Pigs I say!" Cadi was a step ahead.

The water sluiced across the bricks on its way toward the park at a lower incline. The alley had turned into a stream in the water-

and-hail onslaught, and Ninn pressed herself against the back of the tawdry house, finding the barest cover under the overhang of a fire escape. She watched the crowd the flimsy barricade had held back vanish. Then the barricade washed away.

Don't like weather in Sydney? Ninn recalled an old local comedienne quipping. *Stick around a minute or two. It will change for the worse.*

If there'd been any evidence left behind, it was gone now. There was Ella's dressing room to search, but that could wait, couldn't it? Her flat, too. Ninn inched her way along the wall, paused until the hail stopped and purple and pink threads of lightning arced overhead.

She slogged through the street, back to her office, passing a dwarf clinging to an outmoded streetlight. He'd been turned to solid stone, granite limbs wrapped tight around the post, his face forever locked in an expression of terror.

The mana storm had that effect on some people.

FIVE
CROSS HATCHINGS

The alley felt more oppressive now than it had under the AISE spotlights hours ago—not because of the summer heat, which was considerable, but because Ninn could see everything more clearly. The spots had been trained on the slain singer, not on the backs of the buildings that rose like poised talons. The noontime sun poked through a rare gap in the clouds and revealed an astonishing display of graffiti. Ninn swore the layers of paint added enough to the brickwork that it physically narrowed the alley. It gave her the creeps.

Blind Freddy is Dead, Ginger is a RATBAG, S.F.A., Mangy Bastards, Suck It Ace, Hurl the Squirrel, FrEeDoM, Poker Rocks, Belt Up Wez, Sulene for Prez.

"Australian Graffiti, 2025, Dantzel Walager and Brent Tulley."

Ignoring Mordred, she noted symbols from one go-gang or another, arguments between warring bangers displayed in fluorescent greens and oranges that somehow all of Sydney's storms had not washed away. Beneath the most recent spray-painted scrawls were remnants of previous tags, including Greek Mafia slogans, threats posed by factions within the Yakuza and Triads, and coup tallies of Vietnamese Gang recidivists who posted their prison numbers like badges of honor.

Ninn recorded everything, figuring her encephalon could pick through it and call up anything that might be related to what the area residents were now calling the Cross Slayer.

She'd waited until now to come back here, certain Cadi was away to the AISE office and the lumpers were long gone, wanting the alley to herself. Cadigal's Corner was closed tight; she couldn't get inside to take a look at Ella's dressing room. Well, she could pick the maglock, but didn't think that would be polite to her employer.

What little she'd gleaned from the AISE reports and interviews this morning—that they'd been willing to share—showed that Ella/Adoni had no arrest record, none of Cadi's girls believed she had any enemies, and apparently she'd not been mixed up in anything untoward that might have put her in the sights of the gangs or local mafia. Hurdy Gertie had, however, repeatedly mentioned that Ella was Aborigine, and that some people had retained a centuries-long prejudice against the indigenous Australians. Too, Ella Gance and all of the other victims in the past month or so had received RighteousRight holocards encouraging them to "repent for redemption."

There were no public records of any sort to be had on either Miss Ella Gance or Adoni Kogung, apparently SINless and paid under the table by Cadi. It was not uncommon for Aborigines to fly under the proverbial government radar; especially someone like a female impersonator usually paid in cash for everything and, according to her fellow performers, lived largely hand-to-mouth, spending everything on vices and enhancements. *Sounds familiar,* Ninn thought.

No bank records. No school records. Had to be some medical records out there, seeing as she'd had work done—unless it was all street doc stuff. Cadi had mentioned costly vocal enhancers, the surgery for which had kept her off the stage for two weeks. Would finding such records help find the killer?

"No," Ninn said.

"No, what?" The voice was thin.

"Finding medical records won't make a difference. This is a hate crime, Mordred. Simple, stupid hate."

"Seems to be, Keebs."

"Stop calling me that. It's offensive."

"Sorry. Sorry. Sorry."

"You don't sound sorry, Mordred." *You never sound sorry.*

"Sorry, Nininiru. Yes, it does seem to be a hate crime, a string of them."

"RighteousRight maybe." Ninn spotted a symbol behind the Chinese restaurant, a stylized ЯR in red spray paint, applied so liberally that the letters ran like blood. The elf wondered if the murderer was indeed some RighteousRight fanatic, or someone hired by them, a moralist who thought that by killing the "sexually confused" of the Cross, he'd clean up the area. And in Ella Gance's case, the killer got an impersonator *and* an Aborigine with one slash of the knife. The RighteousRight had been making its presence known lately, preaching a return to a wholesome lifestyle free of perversion and cybernetic enhancements, and acquiring more and more converts in the past few years. The fanatics believed the mana storm was God's punishment for straying from a basic, simple life. Some called them the New Amish.

"RighteousRight most likely. Best answer." Ninn thought the RighteousRight certainly would have her in its crosshairs. She wholly embraced cybernetic enhancements, bioware, anything to improve on what nature had cheaply dealt her right out of the womb...which wasn't sufficient in this teched-up world. Don't like the cards? Get yourself a whole new deck. The RighteousRight thought you should only play the hand fate provided. Some of them even opposed electricity and solar power.

ЯR. Scanning everything a second time, she noted four more ЯR tags. "Fragging KKK," she whispered. The group reminded her of old America's Ku Klux Klan. Pockets of the Klan still existed back in the States, and when she'd lived in Chicago, she'd read about a small town over the border in Wisconsin where they held a rally every summer. Burlington—that was the burg. Those *are the freaks,* she thought, not the female impersonators, or the cybered-out dwarfs and whatever and whoever else wandered these streets. Not her. Amazing that in this age prejudice could still be as thick as sludge—as thick as the graffiti on the walls.

"Step back," the thin voice said. *"You're looking too close."*

"What the hell am I looking too close at? You tell me, Mordred. What's too close?"

"You're looking just at Miss Gance, where she was geeked. You're not looking at the entire picture, Keebs. Sorry, Nininiru. Look at everything. Where all of 'em were geeked. And let me get a better look while you're at it. Let me see for myself."

She was wearing a padded longcoat, too warm for the weather. But it provided some protection from stray bullets, the rain, and helped hide Mordred and her other weapons. She'd brought him along on this return trip.

A glance at both ends of the alley to make sure no obvious eyes were on her, Ninn pulled a box from a concealed pocket in the coat and unfolded the weapon to its proper form—a Terracotta Arms Mordred model submachine gun that had been blued, the weight lightened, barrel clear as glass—one of a kind. It was enhanced with several vision upgrades, a safe target system, and smartlink, which Mordred chatted away through, his side of the conversation always carried on inside her head. The gun's software package included advanced AI, and boasted an artificial personality that while she sometimes found annoying, more often she considered it useful.

Ninn had accepted the gun as payment a year back from a Yakuza boss who wanted some snooping done on his "first mate." After a week in her company, Mordred revealed that his AI was a prototype from a megacorp, something they were developing for a military contract that didn't work the way it was supposed to. The AI was considered exceptional, but the personality too strong, and before they could switch it out, the weapon—along with several others—had been pinched by a band of runners that inadvertently ran afoul of the Yakuza gang...the new owners of the stolen arms.

From hand to hand to hand, more programs added to its AI, this one weapon eventually became Ninn's closest friend. She guessed the Yakuza boss had tired of Mordred's banter, especially the old movie references, and was glad to be rid of it. She'd had the gun smartlinked the old-fashioned way, with induction pads in her right palm and index finger. The gun always seemed to know when she was about to "turn him off," and sometimes protested. More recent smartlink tech was available, wireless that would make the pads unnecessary. Easier, but hackable, and in her line of work she didn't want that risk. It was the one old-fashioned piece of tech she liked.

Ninn was usually careful when she brought Mordred out to play, fearing the megacorp still might be looking for its stolen prototype goods, or some banger might take a fancy to the blued foregrip and try to nab it for resale. There were "eyes" everywhere, but alleys in the Cross were an exception to surveillance, great places to buy and sell black market...and apparently fine spots to kill tawdry house singers.

She packed other weapons that she wasn't so secretive about—namely a Nemesis Arms Praetorian, a used heavy pistol she'd found from a dealer on Darlinghurst. She favored its reinforced recoil operation, which kept the gun reliable during the worst downpour, and the underbarrel blade worked great in close combat. Today it was strapped to her left hip, hidden by the coat.

And there were a few additional backups here and there as well. "Adoni—Ella Gance—was found here. Right here, Mordred. Victim Number Six."

"Six? Thought the lumpers claim the Cross Slayer has killed five."

"I'm pretty sure they missed one. We'll call Ella six."

"With Six You Get Eggroll."

"What?"

"Old old old movie."

"You don't watch movies because I don't watch movies." *Not anymore.*

"Trivia in my programming, you know that. Extensive encyclopedia of films. Can't help myself. It just comes out. Doris Day, Brian Keith, George Carlin. You fragging well know I am chock full of old vid information. Nothing after 2025. We're talking back when films were good. With Six You Get Eggroll *was released in 1968 and—"*

"You're full of *ancient* movies, not old movies. Bone-dust ancient in my opinion. I'd like to find out who the hell programmed you with nonsense, get that ripped out—" But she couldn't risk it, removing the trivia might damage his more useful qualities. Besides, it was sometimes endearing.

Ninn looked at the door to Cadigal's, spun to stare in the direction the singer had been running. "Smack in the middle of the alley, Ella died. She'd lost her shoes. Either in a struggle—"

"—or because she kicked them off. Heels would be hard to run in."

"We'll assume she was running, probably hollering, no one outside to hear her. Let's assume she couldn't get back into Cadigal's. So she was probably running toward the park. There's usually always people in the park."

Mordred hummed his agreement.

"Too much music in the clubs, walls high and thick here, would trap sound. No one heard her."

Another hum.

Ninn paced the length of the alley to the park, spotted tourists—their pasty skins marking them from colder climes—admiring the fountain, posing, laughing. She felt like somebody was watching her, and not casually, but she couldn't spot the looker. Ninn turned and walked a block to the alley where a bartender from the Beat Red had been killed two weeks ago.

"Victim Number Five," she said. He hadn't been listed in the police report as part of the Cross Slayer investigation; the victim she believed AISE had missed. He wasn't an impersonator, a cross-dresser, transgender, or a metahuman, but he was gay and had quite a bit of cyber- and bioware, most of which vagrants had removed before the coroner claimed the body. Because he'd been cut up so badly, an arm missing, cybereyes gouged out, a few internal organs gone, she figured no one had noticed whether he'd been sliced like the other Cross Slayer victims. Ninn considered the hapless, practically dissected victim part of the string. Seemed to fit the pattern, someone the Righteous-Right would go after.

"So, Nininiru, who was Number Five?"

"Sanu Grumman, forty-eight, human, worked in the Cross at the Beat Red as a bartender for four and a half years, lived in a one-bedroom on Clement in Rushcutters Bay. Must have known Ella, she worked at the Beat Red three years back."

"Mmmm. A connection," Mordred hummed. "The Lithuanian Connection, *2023, Johnny Rydell's first feature, Imperium Pictures."*

"Maybe a connection." A block and half later and in another alley where the traffic murmur was muted, Ninn said: "Victims Number Three and Four, three weeks ago. Killer likes alleys."

"Lots of alleys in the Cross," Mordred said. *"Who were they?"*

Ninn relied on her encephalon to pull up the information she'd scanned at AISE. "Marla Duncan, Halfway House choreographer, elf, fiberoptic hair, face sculpting, gill implants, well tanned from her afternoons at one of the nude beaches—good place to use the gills. Zane Tresman, stagehand, human, Marla's fiancé. Report doesn't give me anything else on him; I figure he was with her and was therefore collateral. From his picture, looks like he'd had sculpting, too. No obvious cyber or bio." She reached a spot near the end of the alley. "They were killed right here." She was two back doors down from Halfway House and near the back door of an all-hours bar where they were likely headed, their coworkers had said.

Ninn swore someone was whispering, looked around and saw no one. Maybe a voice trickling down out of an open window of an upper-floor apartment. Too often she heard whispers. Maybe they weren't real, figments of her substandard audio receptors or residue from a graypuppy slip. Maybe she ought to try to go clean. She reached into her pocket and put a slip on her tongue. *Just one,* she promised. Needed to keep her head straight to work. The graypuppy winnowed in, and she accepted the rush. Stood quiet a moment and let the alley walls breathe in time, let the graffiti dance a moment.

An elderly couple herding a quartet of children—probably their grandchildren—passed by the end of the alley. The woman paused and glared at Ninn, shook her head and waggled a finger to indicate she disapproved of the gun, and then kept going.

"So the killer was here on a—"

"Tuesday."

"If It's Tuesday, It Must Be Belgium," Mordred said.

"What?"

"Directed by Mel Stuart. Featured Suzanne Pleshette, Ian—"

"Enough."

"Okay, nothing significant with Tuesday. No pattern to the days. No pattern that I can figure out anyway." Mordred hummed again. *"So the killer was in this alley, waiting for someone to come out who met his criteria. Just like Ella Gance stepping into the alley behind Cadigal's. Waited until he found something he liked. Like Sanu."*

"Or rather didn't like."

"Definite thing for alleys."

"Darker, less chance of being seen. Haven't spotted a single surveillance camera in any of these alleys."

"They don't put surveillance in the alleys. It's the Cross," Mordred said.

"It is that."

"Next," he prompted.

Ninn struck off down Bayswater Road, cutting through the colorful throng on the sidewalk—people were out in considerable numbers for lack of rain. She chatted with anyone who would give her a moment, recording it all.

"Notice much RighteousRight activity? Protests? Placards? Rallies?" She asked again and again.

The answers yielded nothing she didn't already know.

"Don't like the RighteousRight."

"RighteousRight? You mean RighteousWrong."

"Been here and there in the neighborhood, the Double-Rs, flashing their tats."

"What's the Righteous Write, some religious magazine?"

"Rock on Double-Rs."

"Nothing too rude to get them tossed into jail. The RRs're careful, you know."

"Cross Slayer might be a RighteousRight ratbag."

"Spray paint. They love bright paint. Leave twin R marks on

the bricks."

"I've cracked a tinny with a Righter before."

"Arrrrrrrrrr, matey."

One notable: "It's a free country, and the RighteousRight can strut wherever the frag they want. They make some sense, if you think about it. Got a lot going on upstairs. You got a problem with it, Keebler?" Ninn got a close up of that woman, who had a ЯR tat on her forearm, and then she and Mordred went on their way.

Ninn stopped at the alley just before Ward Avenue. This was narrower than the others, blacktopped with heavy cracks in it. A service vehicle or garbage truck couldn't squeeze through.

"Bikes and foot traffic only," she mused.

"Could use a good coat of duracrete."

The alley sat right next to a bar that sent a shiver down her back. The place was called One Hundred & Thirty Proof, and there was a RighteousRight flyer taped to the inside of the front window.

"Never been inside there?"

"Hell no, Mordred," she said. Nor had she really noticed the place before. Her haunts for libations were conveniently closer to her office.

"Dezi Desire met her end somewhere down this alley, right?"

"Yeah. Victim Number Two." Ninn peered through the bar window. Only a half dozen men inside, all looked human, drinking and eating. She captured their images, saw one of them staring back, and then stepped to the alley. "Yeah Dezi Desire, Hurdy Gertie's friend."

Ninn jogged down the alley, noting discarded food wrappers and broken bottles along the buildings. The other alleys had been practically Better Homes clean compared to this. The place reeked, too, despite all the washing from the rain. *Probably serving as a dunny for the area's vagrants,* she thought. "Wonder why the hell someone would go down here so late at night."

"Pretty dark even now if you ask me," Mordred said. *"Dark Places, 2015, Corey Stoll as Old Ben Day."*

"I didn't ask you." But the gun was right. The cloud was darkening, the gap closing, and the day's precious sunlight had become a suggestion. Early on, she'd wondered how Mordred could see, since his sleek mechanical self was eyeless. He'd told her on their third outing that he had sensors that translated images, plus the smartlink connected him so closely he looked out through her eyes. After that, Ninn disconnected the link when she had close company over.

"Four weeks ago," she said when she found the spot Dezi was slain. "Right here, four weeks ago."

"Wonder if she was any good."

"No idea. Dezi Desire," Ninn said, rattling off what she'd learned from AISE records for Mordred's benefit. "Twenty-six, human, started singing as an impersonator in the Cross two years ago at Halfway House after going under the knife for a voice modulator and skin tightening, enhanced articulation, all paid for by a patron. Before that worked as a nurse's assistant in a retirement home. Lived in an upper efficiency off Victoria Street. Ahhhh—"

"What?" Mordred's thin voice sounded almost eager. *"What? What? Spill, Keebs!"*

"Dezi—Harold Naughton—must have used this alley as a shortcut to hit Victoria. Dezi's apartment wouldn't have been far from here, a block at most."

"A shortcut that led to the last cut, huh?"

Ninn went on: "A few arrests, shoplifting, bar fights, nothing major...and that was *before* Halfway House. No significant other except for the patron, belonged to a pagan enclave, volunteered every other Sunday in a soup kitchen. That had been a community service sentence that she'd been handed four years back, and kept up with out of the kindness of her heart. Doesn't appear she and Ella knew each other, but maybe they did because of Hurdy—"

Ninn waited for a trio of teens cutting out the alley door of a youth hostel, playfully jostling each other. The tallest, a boy with a ropy scar on his neck, pulled something out of his pocket and passed it around. Slips. The youngest-looking one declined.

Smart kid, Ninn thought. *Stay away from slips. Expensive habit if you buy the good stuff, deadly if you buy too cheap. Even the good stuff screws with your brain after a while, makes you need more and more and more of them.* She popped one in her mouth as if to prove her own point. The rush was good. The teens spotted her, and hurried along and out the other end of the alley. Like the one behind Cadigal's, this alley was coated in graffiti, though not quite as colorful, especially with the sun not hitting it. Eighteen ЯR tags here, some of them tough to see, one inside the "o" of *Joey loves Tamara*, another under a caricature of a hawk that resembled a Chicago Blackhawk logo.

"Chicago," Ninn purred, her voice thick from the graypuppy.

"Chicago. Toddlin' Town. Big shoulders."

"Yeah, you keep saying you want to go back there."

"I miss it."

"No you don't," Mordred argued. *"You just miss the memories."*

"I need a drink."

"What about victim Number One? Aren't we going to the spot of her demise?"

"After I get a drink."

"Not in that bar," the gun cautioned.

"Exactly in that bar." She folded Mordred back into his box form and stuck him in her coat pocket. "'Sides, I want out of this alley. Got that prickly feeling that someone's watching me."

The stranger hid in a crevice between buildings, looking out into the alley, pleased that the elf had not noticed him. The stranger was curious who she was talking to, not seeing anyone else after the youths disappeared. There didn't seem to be another soul in the alley. Who was she talking to? A ghost? An invisible man?

Interesting. He'd seen her before. Where? An alley? He preferred traveling in the alleys, hugging the buildings and embracing the shadows. Only the alleys, he'd been told, travel only in the alleys. And the sewers. Sometimes he broke with that, at night and when it was especially dark and rainy.

The stranger loved the storms, and he did not fear the pink lightning. The fancy lightning made the world a little more interesting...God willing, it might make his own self more interesting. The notion that a tiny thread of it might give him wings or a third eye set his heart thumping in anticipation.

He sniffed, picking out the awful scents permeating this particular alley. There was a restaurant side door directly across from his crevice, and he'd been waiting for something tasty to be tossed out. The lunch crowd was still feasting, so it was only a matter of waiting a little longer.

Where had he seen the elf? So familiar. Too familiar. Think think thinkthinkthink.

Where where where?

Ah! With the crowd that had gathered to gawk at his latest killing, the girl in the red dress he'd slashed. Was she significant, this elf? Something about her niggled at his brain. She'd went under the yellow strip, looked at the body. He would make a point to remember her, and if he saw her again, he would know she truly was significant, was a prier, a meddler, someone to be dealt with. Her and the invisible man she talked to.

The restaurant door banged open, and a thin Asian in a greasy white apron brought out a biodegradable box, which he carried to the trash.

Lovely, the stranger thought. His stomach rumbled in agreement.

SIX
RIGHT CROSS

"This is a bad idea, if you ask me."

"Good thing I'm not askin' you, Mordred." Ninn left the alley, pausing at the corner of One Hundred & Thirty Proof because she had that prickly feeling someone was watching her again. "See any eyes on us—human, metahuman, or otherwise? Anything?"

Mordred clicked and whirred, not a noise necessary for his scans, just something the AI seemed to do out of annoying habit. "Nada. Niets. Niente. Wala-lang. Ekkert. Netchego. Klum. Gornis-cht. *Nope. Why? You notice something I don't? 'Cause I'm seeing through your eyes, not mine while I'm a box, and so I've got zip. But if you'd unbox me, I could—"*

"Not happening." Ninn took a long glance in all directions, but saw no one or nothing that stood out, no obvious surveillance device. Still.... The feeling passed after a moment, and she went inside. "Guess I've got *wala-lang*, too."

"Bummer, *2024, starring Satchal Rotreguese, shot in 4D.*"

Overall, the place looked appealing and on the upscale side, and she wondered why she'd not bothered to visit before, as many years as she'd lived in the area and as much as she liked eating out. The RighteousRight flyer would have been a turnoff, though.

The main room was long and narrow, a polished wood bar stretching a full half of its length. Stools looked like real wood with padded leather seats, next to a brass railing. Mirror beveled at the edges, bottles arrayed on shelves underneath, two big tappers visible. Booths along the opposite wall, also wood, padded red vinyl seats made to look like the leather ones on the stools, cracked along a few edges. Tables were wood too, or an approximation so close that a cursory glance didn't reveal them to be otherwise.

Instrumental jazz played softly from speakers that nested next to obvious surveillance equipment...meaning there might be more surveillance equipment she couldn't pick out. It smelled of floor polish, something pleasantly musky, and over all of that were the spices used to prepare the food. Ninn thought if she had those expensive nose filters she could have picked up far more.

The ЯR coat-of-arms at the back of the room, next to a sign with an arrow that pointed to the restrooms, was disconcerting. The size of a large platter, it was made to look like a medieval shield, crossed swords beneath the raised ЯR that was painted gold.

Only five men in the place, one of them the bartender. Two drinking at the bar, middle-aged, casual clothes, ruddy skin, looked local, sat one stool apart, no risk of touching that way—manly, phobic, whatever. They sounded local too, from the slang they were using: smackers, yakkers, dag, bludge, fair go. The two sitting at a table dined on fried shrimp and egg rolls, and they weren't talking. Nothing in the bar's appearance to hint that it doubled as an Asian restaurant, but it certainly smelled like it from the odor of oil and spices.

The two diners glanced her way, then returned their attention to their shrimp. Might be tourists, their skin fairer, both in jeans, high-end sandals, one in a muscle shirt—though he didn't have the muscles for it—the other in a T-shirt advertising a band she'd never heard of.

No obvious cyberware, no visible weapons on any of them. Food must be good, the way they shoveled it in. They were close to finishing.

"Bad idea," Mordred said. *"Being here is a bad bad bad bad bad idea."*

"What do you see that I don't?" she whispered.

"Box, remember? I'm looking through your peepers."

"What am I missing?"

"Reading your vibes, Nininiru. And that tells me this is a double-bad notion. I could see better if you took me back out, your Keebler peepers alone—"

"—are serving just fine, thank you," she subvocalized.

"Help you?" The bartender looked in her direction.

"Late lunch," she said.

"Menu's on the table." His accent was thick Australian, prob-ably legitimate, didn't sound feigned. The men at the bar looked up from their drinks, one with a wide face studying her longer than was comfortable.

Ninn glided to a table midway in the room, taking the far seat so she could watch the men at the bar and the two diners, while keeping the front door in sight.

"You're hungry? Really?" Mordred asked. *"You ate a big breakfast. A good eight hundred and seventy-four calories. You could've been an extra at* Breakfast at Tiffany's. *All the extras."*

"Huh?"

"1961. George Peppard. What about skipping lunch, not threatening the seams on your jeans, and visiting the spot of victim Number One's demise? Dinner after." "That alley's not going anywhere," Ninn whispered while eyeing the menu, pleased that the lunch specials were in effect until 2:30. She had a half-hour to spare. Hot Spicy Shrimp, Basil Chicken, Pepper Steak, Mongolian Beef, Mixed Vegetables, Zucchini Lamb, probably the real fare, judging by the prices. She ran a finger down the offerings, listening to the duo at the bar, boosting her audio receptor when the two at the table finally started talking, not recording anything...no need to take up memory with obvious tourist chatter.

"—That was good shrimp. Haven't had this good of shrimp since we were in Kokopelli's Cave Bed and Breakfast for our honeymoon," the one said. "Though that was cave shrimp, not sea shrimp. There's a difference." He had an overlong nose, with a scar on it like he'd had a skin cancer spot removed.

The other man snorted. "We never took a honeymoon. Didn't have the nuyen for it, spent too much on the fraggin' wedding, fed all the guests and put up the out-of-towners. Then the kid came. This's our first trip we needed a passport for."

"Ha! Ours was simple, the wedding. Spent our money on travel, you know. We like to travel. A vacation every year. Going to the zoo tomorrow," the long-nosed one said. "Wife will have enough of her shopping fix today, signed up for the whole package, ferry ride to the zoo, antique cable car. You zooing, too?"

Must have come in together with a tour group, seemed to know each other reasonably well, Ninn decided, but definitely not best friends. Both talked with an eastern States accent, maybe Boston. "Car" had come out "cah."

"Didn't sign up for that package, taking the one-day to the Blue Mountains, though. My son wants to hold a koala before they go extinct. Wife's gonna do more shopping."

"Guy on the plane said they don't let you do that no more, carry koalas."

Long-nose snickered. "If my boy wants to hold a koala, he gets to hold a koala."

"Chicken fried rice," Ninn said when the bartender came over. He was human, and as he set down the water glass and she spotted the ЯR tattoo on the inside of his wrist, she knew he would be tech-less. "No onions, extra egg."

"Haven't seen you in here before."

"Haven't been in here before," she replied. "Nice place, like the wood. Homey. Feels comfortable, you know."

He stood there, his face blank, but his dark eyes intense, made no move to write down her order. Maybe he had a good memory.

"Yeah, this place is comfortable. The neighborhood doesn't feel so comfortable, though," Ninn continued. "Heard there was another murder last night. Not too far from here. Know anything about that?"

"Hadn't heard," he said, eyes seemingly getting darker.

"I think the lumpers are looking at the RighteousRight. That's the talk on the sidewalks and—"

"They're not involved."

"They're," not "we"—interesting, his words giving him a little distance. "How'd you know that, when you hadn't heard about the murder?"

"That all you want? Fried rice?"

"No onions. Toohey's Bitter Red, too, and one eggroll."

"With Six You Get Eggroll," Mordred said in her head.

The bartender—Albert, according to his nametag—studied her a few seconds longer before heading toward the back.

"That tattoo is not good news for someone like you, Keeb. There's a reason only humans're in here. Did you see the ЯR on the shield? On his wrist? Well, of course you saw them. Are all the ЯRs tatted? Take me out of this box. It's—"

She disconnected the smartlink, not wanting the gun's distracting banter. She watched Albert walk into the kitchen, a few beats passed and he came back out, went behind the bar and leaned close to the two patrons. He nodded toward her.

They turned and slid off their chairs, the one with the wide face stopping at the tourists' table. "You should leave, mates," he said. "This is gonna get messy. Don't worry about your bill; it's on the house."

The pair pushed back from the table, nervously looked at Ninn, then headed to the door.

"Real messy," the man repeated.

Ninn tried to size them up, but it was already too late.

The wide-faced man was surprisingly quick, pulling a baton from his waistband. He was on her in two long steps, slamming it down on the tabletop and setting the condiments dancing. The other man, thin, tall, and with a bald spot that gleamed from the lighting, pulled an Ono Arms Steadfast from his pocket and held the weapon close. The pistol looked oddly small in his big hand, but was still fairly concealable. The way he stood, the surveillance system would have trouble catching it.

Which meant she better not draw one of her guns. It would only take six seconds to unfold Mordred, a lot less to pull out her Praetorian, but she didn't want to be snagged in a recording shooting one of these goons. AISE already had her in its crosshairs, the lieutenant had made that clear in the alley. Waller would use any excuse to lock her up.

"I'll leave," she said. "Don't need no trouble." *Want it? Yes.* She'd like to put these fraggin' drongoes in their place. The one with the Steadfast had a navy blue ЯR tat on his neck, the other had them on the back of each hand, but more obvious than that he wore a T-shirt with RighteousRight printed horizontally and vertically to form a big Christian cross. Apparently the members didn't mind broadcasting their affiliation. "Just wanted some fried rice with no onions and a Toohey's. And maybe a little conversation with the bartender over there."

"Like I said, she's the one that's been out on the street asking too many questions about the Right," the bartender called. "Trying to link the Right to the *entertainers* that got geeked. Trying to cause trouble."

Hmmmm, so news of her questioning some of the locals had bounced here already. Quite the lightning-fast network the RighteousRight had in the Cross.

"Don't like your kind," Wide Face said.

"What, elves?" Ninn noted the Steadfast had even scratches on its barrel. Victory notches? "Or you don't like people who ask questions about the Double-R?"

"Both," Wide Face said.

Ninn rose and took a step back to give herself room. "Where's my lunch?" She looked around them to the bartender.

"It ain't coming. Don't serve your kind," the bartender said. He'd picked up a rag and was wiping down the bar, but kept his eyes on her.

"Would that be elves?" she said, "Or would that be—"

"Both, you skankin' Keebler. We said both." The one with the Steadfast wrinkled his nose. "This place is sacred. Got no right to be here. Lookit her eye, Johnny. She's got a cyber—"

"And I'm keeping it," Ninn lowered her left hand and pivoted, a distracting move to take their attention from the follow through; a long swinging uppercut to Wide Face's jaw. It was a move she learned in a boxing class she took years ago in Chicago. Living in Kings Cross, she'd had reason to keep in practice. Her reaction enhancers helped, a few vertebrae that had been replaced in her spinal column made her quicker. It had been cheaper and less painful than the wired reflexes the doc tried to sell her.

She connected, feeling the jolt all the way to her shoulder, and his head snapped back and he wobbled, but he caught himself against a table and didn't topple.

"She's big trouble." The Steadfast was pointed at her chest. "Back off, Keebler. I'll plug ya and pluck out that cybereye. Gut you for whatever else electric's hooked up inside ya."

Ninn moved away, intending to leave and keep this from escalating. But the bartender had other ideas. He'd come out from behind the bar, blocked the front door, and thumped a baseball bat against his open hand. "She's not going anywhere, mates. Not until she's learned some manners. I cleared it with the cook. He says have at her. Toss what's left down the sewer."

"Right we will. She started it!" Wide Face had regained his balance. "You saw, Albert! She threw the first punch. You tell the cook it's all on her."

"I did start it," Ninn admitted. *Maybe shouldn't have done that.*

"I'll finish it," Wide Face continued. "Don't shoot her, Hank. I'm gonna tear this bloody blow-in from top to—"

I started it, Ninn thought. *I might as well finish it.* Her left fist slammed into his wide chin, a power shot crossed over her right. She drew back and jabbed again and again, keeping a left foot forward stance. It was a typical boxing punch, and she followed it with another jab, then a hook and an uppercut, all fueled by ire and aided by her muscle augmentation, cables woven to enhance her strength. She heard bone snap, and registered that she'd broken his jaw. Teeth, too, as several *pinked* against the floor. Then he fell, and took a table over with him.

The other man shot, but his hand was shaking and his aim was off. Ninn was on him before he could fire again. One good thing about RighteousRight members was they apparently eschewed anything like dermal plating or bone lacing, relying solely on what nature gave them...which was basically nothing in Ninn's eyes. She cocked her right hand back to provide extra extension, and then drove it forward in a wide, semi-circular hook fashion, all the power in her muscle augmentation behind it. Putting that much effort into one punch left her open, but she had nothing to worry about.

He dropped like dead weight, more teeth hitting the floor, another jaw cracked.

Ninn looked to the bartender. "Okay if I leave now?"

He held the bat down to his side and with his free hand opened the door for her.

"This'll come back on ya," he said as she passed by. "Ya'll pay for this and for pryin', for accusin' us. And it'll cost dearly, *elf*. We promise ya. It'll be expensive."

"We" this time. We promise.

Ninn laughed. "It'll cost me? Just make sure the Toohey's Bitter Red is cold the next time I stop in." She was convinced there was more than a good bet that the RighteousRight was behind the slayings in the Cross, and that she might be coming back to this hole to do more digging.

Out on the sidewalk, she felt a gentle rumble of thunder under her feet. Ninn turned on the smartlink.

"Keebs, what happened?" Mordred's questions tumbled through her mind. *"Where are we–"*

"We're going to the spot where Victim Number One was killed," she cut in. "Isn't that what you wanted to do?"

"Yes. And where is that?"

"Another alley. Behind a dance club called the Forum."

"A Funny Thing Happened on the Way to the Forum," Mordred said. *"Zero Mostel and–"*

"Yeah, well it wasn't too funny, my failed attempt at lunch," she mused, "not too funny to the choobs in that bar, anyway. I'm still hungry."

SEVEN
MANA FROM THE HEAVENS

She was halfway down the block when a thin bolt of bright pink lightning shot across the sky just beneath the cloud cover, accompanied by a wild, keening scream. Then there was silence.

Absolute silence.

She tried to ask Mordred: "Did you hear that scream?" Knew she said it. Her lips moved, but no sound came out. Her feet stomped against the pavement, nothing. She clapped her hands. Nothing. She tried shouting. John Milton had penned: "*Accuse not Nature, she had done her part...*" What if that part was to steal all sound from the world?

Wala-lang.

A few paces ahead, a woman who'd been shopping dropped her packages, looked up and appeared to cry out—mouth wide in terror, hands held to her head like the famous Edvard Munch painting. She whirled and darted into a store.

"*Keebs?*" Mordred's thin voice reverberated inside Ninn's head. "*I don't hear anything 'cept my awesome self talking.* Nada. Niets. Niente. Wala-lang. Ekkert. Netchego. Klum. Gornischt. Zilch. Squat. Nothing. El-zippo. *And since I'm using your expensively modified ears, I can tell you don't hear anything either. Not a good sign.*"

The sidewalk emptied. People darted into the nearest doors and pressed their faces to the windows. She saw a lumper take cover under an overhang and fiddle with a comm.

Never before had she heard...nothing. The absence of any sound—she couldn't even hear herself breathe—was eerie, and she shuddered with a fear that made her teeth hurt.

"*Get inside, Keebs. Now! Move move move!*"

Mordred's urging propelled her through the nearest door, a chemist's shop that already had a dozen people inside hunkering between the shelves of unguents and pills, nervously fidgeting and talking to each other—with no sound coming out. Ninn wedged herself between two middle-aged orks at the very front and looked out the window with them, seeing the sidewalk and the businesses across the street—a trendy clothing store next to a resale shop next to a spring rolls dive next to the most expensive steakhouse in the Cross. Not a soul within her sight remained outside.

Her ears might not work, but her other senses were fine. She smelled the warring colognes the orks wore, pine air freshener, a burst of foulness...someone had farted, a serious SBD. She felt the roughness of an ork's bare arm pressed against hers; he had some dermal plating. The other ork wore a flannel shirt, odd for the warmth of Australia's summer, but he appeared frail, like he might be a geezer that needed the extra layer.

The sky had darkened in the passing of a few moments, looking like midnight instead of mid-afternoon. Lights flickered across the street and in the chemist's. She looked up and saw a pattern to the flashes, like Morse code. Her smartlink sputtered and sent painful little jolts, and she mentally shut it down, cutting Mordred off in mid-sentence about *"bad mana rain."* Her cybereye throbbed, and she shut it down, too, relying on her natural eye. Fortunately, elves enjoyed low-light vision. It helped her pick out details in the dark.

She didn't need the gun to tell her Sydney's mana cloud was going to throw down something awful. The orks jostled for a better look, and she pushed them back, glaring and getting more breathing room. Ninn suddenly tasted peppermint and smelled ozone, watched as pink lightning flared and all the power went out. It was like being dropped into a very deep cave...she knew what that was like, visiting the Mark Twain Cave once in Hannibal, Missouri, when she was a kid. Blackest black coupled with the utter silence. So black her low-light vision was useless. Was this like death? Was she dead? Was she one more victim of Sydney's blasted magical storm and she floated along toward the afterlife? She pinched herself—she felt that. Not dead yet.

Then the lightning came in slow motion, illuminating the street outside with a dancehall strobe effect. The rain came heavy, she could *feel* that intensity in her bones, vibrations skittering through the floor tile and agitating her fellow lookieloos. Big, fat drops that shot down rapid like machine gun fire; hail in the mix now, hard enough to crack the bricks in the sidewalk, little pieces of stone shooting up. Some of the hail had shapes—serpentine like snakes, ovals, cylinders, polyhedrons, headless dolls, and fusilli twists.

Then a mist appeared at ground level, maybe fog, maybe smoke, maybe it didn't matter; it was pale gray and undulated seductively, dancing to music she couldn't hear. Dance? The Aborigines called Sydney's massive mana storm cloud their version of the Great Ghost Dance.

She called it hell.

Some of the misty tendrils slipped under a gap in the chemist's front door, and sent the people farther back into the store. Ninn shivered, and not from her escalating fear. The air seeping in with the mist was cold; she felt goosebumps sprout all over as she pressed closer to the window, which felt like ice. *Chicago*, she thought, *ice skaters in the park*.

When the pink lightning pulsed again and again it revealed the presence of wind, and if there were any sound, Ninn knew it would be piteously wailing. She felt the building shake from the blast of air, watched a man fly by the window, the lumper she'd seen earlier, arms flapping madly, like he was trying to gain some measure of control, careening into a lamppost and continuing out of range. Objects followed him, looking broken and garish in the flickering pink lightning—a bench, a few trash bins, a stray cat that cartwheeled out of sight, followed by a burnt orange Blitzen—a combat bike that must have belonged to a collector, and that was tossed as easily as if it were a toy.

The storm went on and on, minutes became what must have been an hour—or more. Her legs cramped from standing in one spot, so she shifted back and forth on the balls of her feet, did a few knee bends. As she did, she noticed the orks shuffling around in place, the old one rubbing his calf muscles. Her bones hurt, her muscles ached like she'd run a marathon...something in the mana was playing havoc with her augmentations.

The hail grew larger, bouncing up above the thickening layer of mist. A chunk the size of a troll's fist slammed into the chemist's window. The duraglass held, but a web of cracks raced through it, making it appear that Ninn was looking out through a child's kaleidoscope. The ache in her body deepened. The orks retreated, leaving her as the only soul against the window. She could feel breath against the back of her neck, realized somebody was using her as a shield.

Ninn held her spot, enduring the pain from her implants—like she'd gone under the knife without anesthetic—certain another hour had passed, and her muscles too sore to lift her chrono to see the time. *Chrono's likely fritzed, anyway,* she thought, *with all that mana playing games and doing an EMP boogie.*

Still, she remained transfixed by the horrid, arcane tableau. A small, uprooted tree shot by the window just as the rain and hail came sideways now, perfectly parallel to the walk. More lightning skittered, a chaotic rhythm of bright pink flashes that showed the cloud had turned blood red...something she'd seen only once before. The thunder was stronger, not that she could hear it. But the vibrations were more noticeable against the bottoms of her feet, and when she glanced away from the window as a particularly brilliant stroke flashed, she saw bottles of pills and boxes of powders topple off the nearest shelf and she registered the horror on the faces of her fellows. Most of the people sat cross-legged between the aisles, the owner sitting on the counter and cradling his cyberarm, which sparked like it had short-circuited.

Sweat ran down her face and arms, nerves, not from the heat—the air was even colder now inside the shop, and in the next lightning flash she saw her breath puffing out in a lacy fan that fogged the window. Ninn dug her fingernails into the palms of her hands, the added pain helping to keep her focused. She leaned against the icy glass to stay upright.

More time passed before softly sound intruded, whispered voices that swirled like the wind. Not from the people in the chemist's...the voices came from somewhere else, maybe somewhen else. Too often, she heard voices:

> *"–Get out of here, you fraggin' tusker!"*
> *"Got no right to live on this bridge. My bridge. SCRAM!"*
> *"Six million rivets. And you dumbasses disrespect every one of them."*
> *"Not a bowl? I'd drink soup out of it."*
> *"Honestly, Houdagh, you don't haveta grouch at me. I was just makin' conversation–"*

Ghost chatter? Ninn thought she could see vague shapes in the mist that rose and twisted and marched away. Ghost dancing? Music scored it, sounding tribal.

"–Old soul, old troll, big eyes the shade of charcoal."
"It's the bottom of the ninth, and I'm comin' up to bat."

The whispers grew louder, the music dissonant, and then it all turned into waves of thunder that made the fractured front window tremble. Ninn stepped back and heard the wind whistle under the door, more objects on the shelves behind her clatter and fall, glass break nearby. More voices, this time from the people in the shop.

"Pigs, but we're all gonna die!"

"Get away from that. You break it, you buy it."

"Mary. Oh my God. Mary was going to ride the ferries, Elspeth was with her."

"My comm is all static. Where's the lumpers?"

"My skin hurts. By the Old Ones, it fraggin' hurts."

"Saw a lumper fly past the window. Storm got him. Good riddance."

"Storm'll get all of us."

"Stop that! No stealin' the medicine. You need a prescription!"

The lightning stopped being pink and flashed yellow-white, thin tendrils that flickered like the lights that were coming on in this store and the ones across the street. The rain continued, but straight down now, the wind dying. No sign of hail, save the thick clumps of it melting on the sidewalk that was now clear of the strange mist. The lights finally brightened to their full intensity, and she heard the orks breathe sighs of relief, the frail one getting a hand to help him off the floor.

"Mary. My Mary."

"I ain't stealing no medicine!"

"Think it's safe to go out?"

"He's got brollies at the back."

"And you're not takin' 'em—you're buyin' 'em." This from the man who'd been sitting on the counter. "Shouldn't be out on the street without a big brolly anyway."

Ninn glanced over her shoulder to see the rabble making for the umbrella display. Umbrellas were no protection from a mana storm. But regular rain...if the rain was regular, she'd welcome that without an umbrella.

Sucking in a deep breath, she reconnected the smartlink and stepped outside in a shuffling gait. Her legs throbbed, and her chest felt tight. The rain was pelting, but warm. It would have relaxed her if she didn't have such a good view of the aftermath of the mana storm.

Mordred whistled. "That was bad."

"That was an understatement." She looked at her chrono: 5 p.m.—5:15 p.m.—5:30 p.m. It stopped adjusting itself at 6 p.m. The mana storm had lasted about three and a half hours—it had felt like forever. She'd suffered through longer ones, but usually when she was stretched out on the couch in her office, cruising to get through the mana deluge with some slips.

The businesses across the street were damaged to varying degrees. The trendy clothing store had been pitted and blasted, the façade crumbling like it was in a war zone. The resale shop had taken up the bottom floor of a four-story building...which was now a three-level building, the top sheared off and no trace of rubble from the missing floor. The spring rolls dive had changed from a brick front to glimmering blue metallic, a definite improvement. The expensive steak house's awning had turned from green canvas to electric white planks...Ninn shuddered. She saw a dozen patrons pressed against the window beneath that awning; the late lunch crowd had been watching the storm like she had. They'd all been turned to stone.

No doubt others in the city had suffered the same statuesque fate...or worse. Two months ago, Ninn had watched a pair of young, hand-holding tourists vaporized by a pink bolt. There were reports that outlying areas years ago had suffered great casualties—populations turned into koalas and dingos, the latter eating the former before another errant storm returned everything to normal and sent the survivors to shrinks. Fortunately, serious mana downpours like this one were usually months apart.

"Chicago," Mordred offered. *"Chicago, 2002, 113 minutes running time. You could get me through customs easy enough."*

Ninn glanced back at the chemist's storefront. The only apparent damage was the cracked window. No other customers had come out; through the spiderweb cracks she saw them clustered around the counter with umbrellas in hand.

Others were edging out onto the sidewalks—from the resale shop, the trendy clothiers, tentative, looking up, one woman tiptoeing to a corner, peering around it, and then sprinting away. Sirens echoed from many streets over, and Ninn saw the flashing red lights of emergency vehicles reflected in the now-pale gray clouds. The bank looked almost beautiful as it shifted to a silvery opalescent blue-gray with bands of pink, a big piece of mother-of-pearl stretched as far as she could see. Lampposts came on; the sirens grew louder and then retreated, the sound bouncing off the canyon of buildings.

Everything smelled of sulfur.

Ninn planned to watch tonight's news, take a gander at what devastation had been wrought citywide, reports of cleanup, eyewitness statements. Every so often, Discovery Down Under would splice together segments of video captured by tourists and locals and newsmen, call it "The Storm Part Whatever." And every so often, Ninn would watch it out of morbid curiosity. She bet there'd be plenty of footage from today's blow.

"Chicago," she said, picturing big fat flakes slowly drifting down, intact storefronts displaying after-Christmas sales, shoppers having no fear of being turned to duracrete during their excursions. Why stay here, in the Cross? In Sydney? Why did any of these people stay? Because it was home. Or they lacked the nuyen to go elsewhere. Because random magic from the storm, while dangerous, was also exciting and unpredictable and terrifying all at once, and let them live life on a razor's edge. Or they craved the safety the storm provided—the surveillance wasn't as plentiful under the cloud. Less law, a laxer government, easier to hide, easier to be nefarious, sometimes easier to find work because people were nefarious. Easier to not pick up and move.

Easier to do nothing but hunker down and watch.

"Keebs, uh, Nininiru, if we figure out who this Cross Slayer is—and take several days to do it—you'd have more nuyen, buy you that trip back to the States. Chicago, indeed, we could—"

"We could be quiet for a while, okay?" Her head pounded. Her legs and arms dully ached, only a slight improvement since the pink lightning stopped. Good thing the storm rarely tossed down mana that toyed with implants. She wondered if arthritis was like this. There were treatments and modules that didn't cost all that much, that would make sure arthritis didn't happen. She'd put one of those on her list.

Ninn shelved her plans to visit the spot where the first victim was killed. Tomorrow. When she didn't ache so much. After she'd drunk enough to numb her throbbing limbs and send her troubled thoughts spiraling into oblivion.

She ambled to the corner. Just inside the entrance to a building a young mother squatted in front of a stroller, sobbing. A small, struggling wombat was strapped in the seat; it had probably been a child. Nothing Ninn could do; she crossed the street to the spring rolls dive, seeing herself reflected in the shiny new façade. What a mess, she was. Not unattractive, but she needed some new clothes, something that didn't look like rumpled tourist attire. And she ought to have at least some of her wardrobe laundered...give her more options, since she was working a case. Put on a little makeup. Look professional, and be treated like a professional. Thanks to Cadi, she had the nuyen to do it.

She glanced down at the sidewalk in front of the spring rolls restaurant, where the chalky outline of a portly man in mid-stride stretched toward the door. He probably fell and had been vaporized in the storm, the tracing left to mark his passing. Not fast enough to reach safety. There were other similar traces of people around the city, Sydney's Vesuvius.

"You're hungry, Keebs? Didn't you eat at that Righteous—"

"No, I didn't, Mordred. I wanted fried rice."

"How about some Fried Green Tomatoes, 1991, Kathy Bates."

She started to click off the smartlink.

"I'll shut up. I'll shut up. Get yourself some dinner, by all means, Nininiru."

"I intend to." A little takeout was a good idea—or a lot of take-out; she was famished and had plenty of nuyen on her credstick. She'd use some of it to fill her belly. A trip to the resale shop for some duds was in order too, a quick stop at the liquor store on Darlinghurst to add more variety to her deep desk-drawer stash, and then she'd pass the evening in her office, eating and drinking, and anesthetizing herself with a slip or two or maybe three and mulling over the murders. Maybe ask Mordred to quote from old movies until she fell asleep.

"Hoi! Ninn! Ninninninnin!"

She groaned as a disheveled elf awkwardly galumphed toward her, sloshing through puddles and waving his arms. Where the hell had he come from? Her vision was acute, and whenever she spotted Talon—which she had been doing up until about four months ago—she'd duck into a business, disappear down an alley, do whatever it took to avoid him. Frag, but she'd let her rumbling gut and aching bones distract her. He was truly the last person she wanted to see.

To ever see again.

Hell, she thought he might be dead. Hadn't seen him for months. Had half-hoped he was dead, put out of his misery. How could he still be alive?

"*Hoi*, Talon." She waited as he skidded to a stop next to her. She smelled something other than sulfur now, though she couldn't put a name to the cloud of stench that swirled around him and settled like wet duracrete on her tongue.

He looked awful, and she knew it wasn't because of the storm, which continued to pour rain down on the Cross. Her hair, his hair, clothes, were plastered to them. What there was of his clothes, anyway. They were raggedy, as many holes as threads, faded, spattered with color from paint, food, and who-knew-what. The rain had probably washed away *some* of his stink, but what remained was close to making her gag. At least the storm had power-scrubbed some of the dirt off his face. She'd seen him far filthier before.

Lord, but he was still somehow handsome; startling blue eyes, long lashes, high cheekbones, and a strong jaw. A heartthrob face like a movie star. She would have called him beautiful but for the ropy scars on his arms and one trailing down from his knee, knew there were other scars, and he was much too thin to be considered a hint of healthy.

He used to be godawful beautiful...back when she loved him. And he didn't used to stink then, either.

"Haven't seen you for a while," she said, suddenly feeling sorry for him and angry at herself for avoiding him. Their past history should have been enough to make her act more respectful.

"I've looked for you, Ninn. Often and all over. Was at your office earlier yesterday, day before maybe, and last week, last month, last whenever. I get days mixed up. You weren't there. I figured you were either avoiding me, or you'd moved back to Chicago. I was praying you hadn't moved back."

She remembered that this past August he'd come knocking on her door, and she pretended to be out, though she'd almost caved. Maybe should have. Dear God, he still had that gorgeous face. She hadn't opened her door to him in...what...fifteen, sixteen months? And before that she'd opened it way too often—back in the days before he became the poster child for malnourishment.

"I'm working a case, Tal. I've been busy."

"A case."

"The Cross Slayer."

"Well, that's a holy-dooly. So, you have some nuyen, right?"

Fraggin' mooch.

Neither said anything for a few moments, letting the sound of the rain take over. It had let up a little, the drops smaller.

"Yeah, I have some nuyen," she said finally. "You hungry?"

"Starvin'. Starvin'! I'm so hungry, Ninn. I 'aven't eaten since—"

"Spring rolls do?" She gestured at the restaurant door. If she'd gone in the moment she'd thought about it, he wouldn't have noticed her on the sidewalk.

"Anythin', Ninn. Soooooooooooo hungry."

"You can order whatever you like, take it back to your place, and—"

"I...don't have a place, Ninn. Well, not a solid place right at the moment. And the homeless shelter.... Well, there was a problem there, and the guy that runs it said—"

The sidewalk trembled from a wave of thunder. What if the storm had more mana left in its cloudy innards? What if it still wasn't safe to be outside?

"So you're alley flopping?"

"Yeah."

"Don't have a box somewhere?"

A nervous downward glance. "Yeah, I got a box, sometimes. Not now, but sometimes. And sometimes I stay down by the bridge by the pilings. Don't need a box at the pilings, there's some dry spots. Stinky Stella lets me crash with her sometimes. But the gangs are getting worse, meaner, and—"

"You can stay in my office."

"Oh, Ninn, you're a lifesaver! I love you love you love—"

"For tonight. Only tonight, Tal. Because of the storm."

"One night only." He nodded vigorously, the snarled strands of hair wiggling like snakes, and then looked hungrily at the restaurant door.

"Just tonight, Ninn, I understand."

"Just tonight, Tal. We're going to the resale shop next door first. You're not raunching up my office with those rags. Shop first. Then we'll pick up some spring rolls to take back and eat at my desk."

"Whatever you say, Ninn. Been a long time. Too long."

Mordred whispered into her head, as much as it was possible for him to whisper: *"You got a history with this walking piece of refuse, Keeb? Or are you just being untowardly kind?"*

She wondered if the gun could see her glare.

EIGHT
LIKE OLD TIMES

Ninn sat in the high-backed chair at her desk, towel wrapped around her head, reveling in the strawberry scent from the soap she'd been so liberal with and imagining how much more intense the smell would be with the nose filter.

She'd washed up in the office bathroom and put on some new clothes—new to her via the discount aisle at the resale shop, a pair of gray linen slacks that were the perfect length but a hair too loose, and a black short-sleeved blouse that must have been pricey the first or second time it was on the rack. She thought she looked fragging nice in the ensemble—a multi-purpose garment she could wear for business or to a funeral. The other outfit she'd bought was more casual, could pass for tourist garb; just couldn't help herself for liking the style. She had the nuyen to buy new, but the resale shop was one of her favorite haunts. Besides, bargain hunting left her more to put toward enhancements.

She'd bagged up the clothes lying around her office, and paid a service to pick it up and launder it all. Her wardrobe would be back late tomorrow afternoon.

Talon had washed up, too. She hadn't given him a choice. If he was going to stretch out on her couch—which he was doing right now—he was going to be reasonably clean and as bug-free as possible. She'd bought him a pair of khakis and a long-sleeved shirt, both of which hid all the ropy scars...except for the one on the side of his neck. Dressed in the new clothes now, and under a light blanket, he snored soundly. His other clothes were history; the shirt had fallen apart when he took it off, and his shoes had been soleless. The loafers she'd bought him sat by the door, which she intended he leave by first thing in the morning. She had to get him out of here, before she started liking his company again.

The spring rolls had been surprisingly tasty, and they'd each eaten two full orders, washing it all down with a bottle of Shiraz. She had stronger stuff in her desk drawer, but she wanted to make sure Talon was indeed asleep, and not pretending. Ninn wasn't going to share old scotch or her slips. Talon had asked her a half-dozen times after dinner if she had slips—or anything else mind-altering or questionable. She said she was out, that she was cutting back, trying to quit. She didn't usually lie to him, but he also didn't used to be so pathetic. Besides, it wasn't *all* a lie; she intended to quit.

Maybe she should keep him around for a while instead. Not wanting to end up like him, he could serve as an incentive for her to get clean. Put him in her orbit again so she could climb out of the "lower deep." Milton's ancient words sprang into her thoughts: *"...And in the lowest deep a lower deep, still threat'ning to devour me, opens wide, to which the hell I suffer seems a heaven."*

"So, are you going to spill?" Mordred made a *tsk*ing sound. *"About this guy? Because clearly you knew him before we hooked up. And he's sleeping on your couch. Where are you going to crash, Keebs? Couch ain't big enough for both of you unless you get creative and have a naughty. So spill."*

"I've known him a while."

"Obviously."

"We were a couple once."

"The Odd Couple, 1968. Herb Edelman played Vinnie."

Her thumb went back and forth over a clear spot on the desk, like the surface was a worry stone. She looked at the clock: closing in on midnight.

"All those scars. Looks like someone practically butchered him, Keebs. You going to spill?"

"Talon just—" She turned off the smartlink.

Talon was her first real friend in the Cross, and her first and only romantic interest since leaving the States. Met him right after she'd been drummed out of AISE, moved to this neighborhood, and applied for a PI license. He'd worked part time in the clerical office, where she had to file her credentials. He'd asked her out.

She'd accepted.

He was beautiful after all, the most striking-looking elf she'd ever seen. And she needed a distraction after the AISE disappointment, and before that the crushing loss of her sister. Depression snowballing in her life, she was searching for something to lift her spirits, and he worked...for a time.

He was an incredibly beautiful distraction.

Talon had also been a great asset in her new line of work. He decked—or used to—and had a state-of-the-art datajack and could interface with practically any cyberdeck to trip through the Matrix like a dust mote riding the wind. A true wizard at surfing data streams in all the telecommunications grids, he'd tap calls for her, retrieve important files, sneak remotely into computer systems for vital tidbits, and make her life as a PI easier. He wasn't a "legal" decker with gainful and legitimate software employment. No dataslave. His part-time clerical job was a front where people contacted him for runner gigs, usually corporate espionage plays. He made his real money in the shadows. It was serious nuyen. *Had been serious nuyen.*

Ninn let herself get close to him, closer than she'd ever gotten to anybody in a decade, and she even entertained the "happily ever after" notion. But the longer she knew him, the more troubling aspects surfaced, namely that his shifting makeup of runner companions were a bad influence on her. Ninn came to covet the augmentations some of those runners had, and she started going under the knife to get them, a couple of times at street docs they recommended, but more often at reputable, licensed places, where the tech was more reliable and came with nuyen-back guarantees. She could afford the reputable places back then.

She'd never really been into drugs until moving to the Cross, fearing it might impair her police work. But Talon shared and she caved...Crystal Dream, Jazz, BTLs, Tempo, Deepweed, mood enhancers, performance enhancers, psychedelics...caved again and again, silencing random voices she heard and intensifying ghost sounds. Amazing. Was going to cave in a few moments, the slip of graypuppy sitting on her fingertips. *Addicted to slips? At least a little,* she admitted, got the shakes if she went too long without one. Graypuppy was her favorite. Might follow it with a scotch chaser. An alcoholic? At least a little on that account, too. A cyber-addict... hell, yes on that score, approaching a vatjob. She'd lost her sister, lost her AISE job, lost self-respect and self-control, lost Talon— dropped him actually—and gained one bad habit after another after another, collecting them like a spinster collects cats. The more she lost of herself, the easier it was to embrace bad habits.

Talon obviously had embraced a few more than she'd taken on. What was the phrase? "On the metho," that was it, and the elf had sunk so low he'd drink methylated spirit. She'd learned to identify a metho from the vague, glassy-eyed expressions, and the accompanying scent of a brewery horse's hind end. The more drugs he did, the fewer runner gigs he got...which led to him doing even more drugs to soften his hard times. To support his escalating habits, he'd started selling his augmentations and enhancements, going to whatever street doc paid the most for ripping out his parts, and eventually had to sell his jack. No more tripping through the Matrix. The long, thick scars showed that the street docs were neither very good nor cared what marks they left behind.

It was where Ninn had drawn the line; she wouldn't have some doc cut out anything she'd already had implanted—unless it was for an upgrade. She wouldn't sell herself to fuel her addictions...she'd been finding just enough work to cover the next new tech, a packet of slips, and a few bottles of booze. God, how far down this hole had she dove?

Did she have some kind of death wish? Everybody died sometime, eh? No one should live forever. Why not hurry the process along, see if there was something on the other side?

Did she care that little about herself?

Ninn certainly wasn't the same person who'd brought her sister to Sydney trying to save her, who'd joined AISE to stay in police work. Not physically. Not mentally.

Chicago?

She couldn't go back there, not like this.

A passage from *Paradise Lost* slid through her mind as she put the graypuppy slip on her tongue: "*Our torments also may in length of time become our Elements.*" Her curse and her pleasure were all rolled up into one little drug. Had she lost paradise by imbibing, or had she found it?

Ninn felt her senses deliciously twist as the drug took effect and the walls in her office started to breathe. Chicago drifted ever farther away.

She couldn't go home again, could she?

The voices started again, conversations that boogied through her brain.

Don't listen to them. Never listen to them.

In the back of her mind, she saw her sister; vibrant, beautiful, a dance student with aspirations of signing with a prestigious ballet company. The fire at the hall had scarred her—third-degree, full-thickness burns over eighty percent of her body. It had nearly killed her—maybe should have killed her right then—and the docs suggested Ninn consider a medical transport to Sydney, where a biotech corporation had made incredible strides in regrowing devastated flesh. Ninn's sister didn't have enough viable flesh left for the regrowth treatments in the States.

Ninn left Chicago Lone Star, used all of her savings on the transport and initial fees at the biotech corp, and then watched as some measure of success was achieved, hope was pirouetting in her brain, and then something went wrong and wrong again, and despite the technicians' best efforts, her sister died anyway.

All that pain—for nothing.

Her ties with Lone Star cut, her nuyen down to *wala-lang*, and so no ability to return to Chicago, she managed to get on with AISE and started rebuilding her life and finances. She lived in a high-rise down by the harbor then, her AISE salary enough to pay for a nice studio with an acceptable view of the once-impressive bridge. Ninn began exploring the city, learned which clubs had the best bands, and even got some culture by visiting trendy galleries. A hint of happiness had intruded.

Then the AISE gig was stripped away by charges of a bad collar that she stood by to this day. She hadn't liked seeing the AISE officers in the alley behind Cadi's, and fervently hoped she wouldn't run into any tomorrow while she was looking through Ella's dressing room, poking around Cadigal's. It was clear Lieutenant Waller would arrest her for even the slightest infraction.

Adding a second graypuppy slip on her tongue to chase away the bad memories, she saw the drab colors of the office brighten and shift, spin and glitter. The walls had a pulse now, and the paint cracks turned into veins that skittered in random patterns, like the storm's pink lightning. All the delicious flavors from Chicago's big summer food fair rolled across her tongue, the scents of the Windy City's arboretum filled her nostrils. The surface of her desk felt like expensive velvet, and she rubbed her cheek against it and inhaled more of the summer food.

Summer in Chicago had never been as hot as summer here. Ninn closed her eyes, and the colors intensified and cavorted, blue chasing green chasing red chasing a buttery yellow that melted to reveal a vibrant purple that took flight on magnificent butterfly wings. She opened her eyes and fished in her bottom drawer, her fingers coiling like baby snakes around the neck of the scotch bottle, easing the cap off, chasing the colors with a double shot. Or was that a triple?

One more slip.

When everything was gone, drank and inhaled, she'd quit cold turkey. But until then, she'd revel in this rush.

The ceiling light turned all silvery, slowly whirling like an antique disco ball to music that played in her head. Ninn drummed her fingers against the velvet desk in time with the rhythm, swore she could hear a woman singing, dulcet tones enhanced by vocal augmentation. It was Ella Gance crooning, floating across the stage. "Somewhere Over the Rainbow." Perfect pitch. Perfect face. The image shifted and still Ella sang, but this time out of the slit in her neck, her eyes vacant and dead dead dead, and her fingers stiffening with rigor.

Sometimes slips coupled with alcohol did that, transported her to an unhappy place.

Shouldn't have had two slips. Or was that three?

Shouldn't have had the scotch. One more swallow.

One more.

Drain the bottle; she could always buy more with Cadi's nuyen. No, she wouldn't buy more. Couldn't...

One more swallow...

Should stop it all and save herself. Lose and find paradise.

One more swallow, then toss the empty. Quit for good after the last swallow.

Quit.

The colors shifted again, all the shades of red in the world, running like blood, pooling on the floor and soaking the loafers she'd bought Talon, running up the couch and over his beautiful face, smothering him, swirling in the center of the room until they formed a whirlpool that sucked everything down.

Down.

Down...

NINE
STRANGER AT THE DOOR

Ninn awoke to a mammoth headache and a persistent tapping on the door. Her mouth was desert dry, and her head hurt like it was being squeezed by a very big troll.

Talon was up, sitting on the couch, looking slightly rumpled but handsome, hands wrapped around her best mug. A glance to the shelf—he'd brewed coffee. He'd found the real stuff, not the soykaf next to the machine. And he'd raided her larder; food wrappers were strewn across the counter.

"Should I get that?" His eyebrows rose. "Or are we gonna ignore it and hope they go away?"

We. Ninn hated the sound of that.

Her stomach rumbled. She felt so hungry.

The knocking continued.

She pushed up from the chair, her legs stiff from sitting in one position for...how long? A glance at the desk chrono: 5. Five hours she'd been out. Great. Who the hell would knock on her door this early in the...then the p.m. registered, as did the fact she'd soiled her new pants. Hours she'd been comatose, *seventeen hours* when she did the math. She should have spent the largest chunk of that time investigating the murders. Cadigal hadn't paid her to crash.

Definitely had to stop the slips or the booze or both. There were plenty of AA and SA meetings in the Cross, she ought to attend one before the addictions killed her.

Look up a meeting up after she solved the Cross Slayer murders—if she could keep her head clear enough to work the case. Not *if*. She'd have to stay clear.

What was in the big box just inside the door? When had it arrived? Sometime in the past seventeen hours. On top of it draped the hanging bags with her clean laundry; it didn't look like all of her clothes had come back. Maybe the rest would come tomorrow. Maybe they'd lost some of her shirts—again. The label on the box said MALDEN'S FINEST MAGNESIUM POWDER. Great, another wrong delivery. She'd been able to eat the last wrong delivery, a sub sandwich, cup of chili, and barbecue chips order from SANDWITCHES 4 U. Maybe Talon would snort the magnesium. Maybe she'd make a quick run to Sandwitches and quiet her stomach.

"Ninn...you all right? You look...fuzzy. You were out a long time. Almost thought you flatlined." He pointed to the big box. "I had to sign for that, for the laundry too, talked the laundry into billing you. I'm still pretty good at forgin' your siggy."

The knocking persisted.

"The door, you want me to get that, Ninn? Doesn't sound like he's going away." She frowned at Talon, who should have left hours ago. "Just one night," she'd told him repeatedly.

"Just tonight, Ninn, I understand," he'd said.

Her clothes sullied, she needed to change. Rather than reaching for her clean laundry, she grabbed up the second outfit she'd bought yesterday—faster than sorting through the clothes bags.

"Yeah. Get the door for me, will you, Tal? It might be the landlord." She was a month behind, and she'd be able to settle with him using the nuyen left from Cadi's payment. She retreated into the bathroom to clean up again. Frag, but she was stiff from sitting in one place for so long.

Ninn heard Talon open the door and exchange pleasantries: "Nininiru Tossinn Detective Agency. You lost it, we'll find it."

Ninn groaned and switched on the smartlink as the water splashed in the sink. Mordred softly hummed.

"The Awful Awakening," Mordred said. *"2020, Su Weng as Jarrod Wey."*

"Come in. Come right in. I'm Talon Kassar, Ninn's assistant, and you're one of the original people, right mate? A real Abo. Lost something we can find for you?"

"We Happy Few," Mordred said. *"2025, most recent film in my database. It was about failed relationships."*

We. Ninn ground her teeth. "Don't lecture me," she whispered to the gun.

"Lost someone we can find?" Talon continued.

"I am Barega Kogung."

"That's an interesting name. Does it mean anything, either the

Barega or Kogung?"

"My name means 'the wind.' I wish to see Nininiru Tossinn, please."

"She's, uh—"

Kogung, Ninn considered the name as she shimmied into burnt orange leggings and threw the beige kangaroo print slouch top over it—a little too long, it settled past her hips. A glance in the mirror to straighten her hair and wipe the drool smudge off her mouth. She had to stop the slips and booze. "Kogung," she whispered. "That rings a bell."

Mordred supplied it: *"Last name of Cadigal's dead singer. Victim five according to AISE. Six according to you. Ella Gance/Adoni Kogung. With Six You Get—"*

"—*Eggroll,*" she finished. Was that her head pounding? Or was someone pummeling the ceiling? Had to be her head.

"Is Nininiru Tossinn available? I have an important matter—"

Talon was talking again. "Ninn. Well, Ninn's...she's...uh—"

"Right here, Talon." Cleaned up, fresh towel draped over her arm, she slid out of the bathroom and closed the door behind her. "You were leaving, weren't you, Tal? Had someplace you needed to—"

"Nope. No place I need to be. I'll stay." He returned to the couch. "Maybe I can help. Assistants help, you know."

"Nice piece of sticky refuse you got with that one." Mordred's snide comment bounced around in her aching head.

Why the hell hadn't Talon left? Because he had a roof here. Was she going to have to physically toss him out of her office? A glance at the shelf confirmed that he'd eaten all her snacks.

"Good to meet you, Nininiru Tossinn." Barega bowed politely.

Ninn guessed the Aborigine was in his mid- to late seventies. He was barefoot and wore dark green pants that came to his knees, a loose shirt with a black and ochre design, maybe something tribal. He was thin, hovering near gaunt. Her encephalon brought up an image and superimposed it over his face. She'd seen him before, standing with the crowd the night she'd answered Cadi's summons. In the sea of white bodies, he'd stood out. Wearing the same clothes as he had then.

"Yes? Can I help you, Mr. Kogung?" If she hadn't heard the "Kogung" part, she'd have thought the old man had the wrong office, was looking for the Area Aging Group at the far end of the hall.

"Please, Nininiru Tossinn. You can very much help me." He shuffled past her and into the office proper, aimed straight to the client chair at her desk. "I desire to learn who killed my brother Adoni, and my meditations and dreaming indicate that you can assist. We can help each other." He settled in the chair, reached to his pocket and pulled out a cloth bag. "In fact, all of my dreams point to you."

Ninn hurried to the other side of the desk, giving Talon a thumb toward the door to indicate he should leave. He stayed put and drank more coffee.

"For payment. You will require payment, correct?" The Aborigine poured the contents of the bag onto her desk...a good-sized handful of rough opals. "Will this do? A deposit for your services?"

She laid the towel on her chair, sat on it, and hunched forward so her face was even with his. God, but her head pounded. Did she overdo it last night because of Talon? Depressed at seeing him... what he'd become...did that make her take the second slip? Or had it been three? And the booze chaser? God, she'd drained the bottle.

She rubbed her temples and studied her potential client. Seventeen hours she'd lost. Her stomach rumbled again.

His wrinkled skin resembled tree bark, and the hair that protruded from an odd, box-like cap was wispy like cobwebs, a hint of whiskers along his jaw line. Perhaps he was older than she first thought; her encephalon yielded nothing on Barega Kogung...maybe Ella Gance's grandfather, maybe someone from the tribe. Ella/Adoni had no known relatives, according to the AISE record and the reports from Cadi's girls. However, Ninn recalled reading that large sections of an Aboriginal tribe could share the same last name.

The old man's eyes shifted from pale blue to gray with silver flecks. Maybe she still had a hint of the drugs and alcohol floating in her system, and couldn't focus on him properly. Those eyes didn't blink...not once had she seen the old man blink. And the longer she stared into those eyes, the weaker she felt.

Ninn glanced down to her desktop, seeing dried drool where her head must have laid for those seventeen fragging hours. Was she that far gone in her addictions? Unsalvageable? Irredeemable? Had she sunk so deep she could only find work here in Sydney's armpit, following unfaithful husbands, retrieving stolen designer dogs, paid by a troll tawdry house owner, and now perhaps by an old man who looked like he stumbled in from the Outback?

"Will this down payment do?" he repeated.

She focused on the little hat on his head, easy to do because he was short. "I would like to take your gems, Mr. Kogung, but I'm already working this case. I am already being paid to find Adoni's killer." She suspected the opals were worth far more than the nuyen Cadi had forked over.

"Good for you, Keebs, you have morals. But that won't get you enough nuyen for Chicago." Mordred hummed softly and made a tsk-tsking sound. *"Those opals...that should be* The Sweet Smell of Success *as far as you're concerned. 1957. Burt Lancaster, Tony—"*

Ninn made a move to turn off the smartlink, and Mordred shut up.

"I am aware that you work the case, Nininiru Tossinn. You look for the—" His reedy voice trailed off, as if he was searching for the correct words. "—the one called the Cross Slayer."

"Yeah. That's what the people who live around here are sticking on him. The Cross Slayer. It's possible an organization called the RighteousRight is involved. I'm working that angle and—"

Talon waggled his fingers. "Hey, Ninn...about the Right? While you were...um, out...I called a decker I know. Had him dip into the Matrix, focus on the Cross and the Double-Rs. He owed me a major major major favor, and I figured I owed you for the spring rolls and the couch. He dropped a chip off a couple of hours ago. Said its chock full of Double-R stuff. It's on your desk. Said he ruffled tons of feathers getting that, probably made some enemies. Find someplace to download and—"

"Thanks, Tal." Why the hell did he have to go and do something potentially useful? She looked at the chip, labeled ЯR in blue ink, and then turned her attention back to Barega. "I'm looking at the Cross Slayer as a member of the Right."

"We will look together. My payment is for your assistance. I need to find out what happened to Adoni, and my dreaming alone will not be enough, my totem the galah reveals. My totem—"

"Like I said, he was killed by the Cross—"

The old man nodded. "I need to know what *happened* to Adoni to ease my soul, Nininiru. Beyond the killing, which I might be able to see through his now-dead eyes. I need the *why* of it. *What* happened to Adoni, and *why* it happened, things his now-dead eyes cannot tell me in full measure. They cannot tell me where this killer is. Perhaps you will be doubly rewarded for your time if we are successful."

Why had it happened, the killing? Because the RighteousRight hated anyone "different," and Adoni fit within their parameters.

Ninn let out a deep breath. The opals certainly had value, and with no record of the transaction she wouldn't have to report them as earnings. She always needed nuyen, went through it like some people went through hand soap. While more nuyen would get her the nose filter, more upgrades, it could also fuel her unsavory addictions, the alcohol and slips...

Dear God, she had to stop the spiral.

"I don't know," she said. "I'm already working the case. Taking payment from two sources just isn't—"

"*Ethical?*" Mordred hushed. "*Now that's a word I haven't heard you use.*"

"—ethical," she finished.

"*Chicago,*" Mordred countered.

Chicago, she thought. In the quiet that settled between them, Ninn listened to Talon snore. He'd fallen asleep within a handful of heartbeats. His head back, coffee mug cradled in his lap and threatening to spill. Was she going to end up like him? Was she really that far removed from reality at this moment? He woke with a start and smiled at her, raised the mug in a toast and drained it.

"Why me? Why pick me, Mr. Kogung? There are other investigators in the Cross, and—"

"Nininiru Tossinn, I said the galah and my dreaming led me to you."

"*Electric Dreams,*" Mordred said. "*Science fiction, 1984, Virginia Madsen. Not worth a repeat viewing. The Dreaming, 1988, low-budget horror, Arthur Dignam.*"

"Dreaming?" Ninn rubbed her temples harder.

"My dreaming and the galah. The galah is my totem. There is one in the window of this building, and I took it as a sign."

"*The galah is a sign.*" Mordred snorted. "*An antique fluorescent one.*"

"And I do not mind that you also work for someone else at the same time, Nininiru Tossinn."

The first floor of Ninn's building was a dancehall—Pella's Rosy Parrot—that had, Mordred was correct, an antique fluorescent sign of a galah hanging in its window. Maybe the old Aborigine was tripping on slips too if he considered that an omen.

Maybe she ought to play along though, as the opals could probably pay a year's office rent—at least. She stretched out a finger, stirred them, reached over and touched the ЯR chip Talon's decker friend had dropped off.

"All right, Mr. Kogung. I will work for you, too." A pause: "But I can't guarantee success."

Talon softly applauded, and Ninn glared at him and gave him one more thumb gesture. He got up and poured himself another cup of coffee.

"I will accompany you on this investigation," the old man continued. "When we are concluded, I will give you twice more that amount of opals. All that I have, as I am an old, old man, and do not need such things weighing me down any longer. The more one knows, the less one needs, yes. The treasure is worth the attempt on your part, isn't it?"

Ninn was going to protest, not the opals, but the "accompany you" part. She worked alone, didn't want anyone crowding her life; Mordred had just enough upside to be allowed. Talon, she wouldn't go down that road again. She didn't want to drag an old man—

Mordred whistled in her mind. *"My appraisal program tells me the quality of those opals are—"*

"No guarantees," Ninn repeated. But her eyes on the RighteousRight, this investigation shouldn't last more than a handful of days...if it was solvable. It had to be solvable, didn't it? The promise of more opals for success was making her mouth water. She'd asked enough questions about the Right yesterday, poked her nose where the fanatics certainly didn't think it belonged. The bartender had threatened her, a clean signal she was onto something, right? So something might surface soon. There might be something telling on the ЯR chip. She could put up with the old man's company for a few days.

"Let's start with Adoni—Ella Gance—who was she to you?"

"I told you. Adoni was my brother, Nininiru Tossinn. My *older* brother."

The sentence hit her like a punch. *Not possible,* Ninn thought. Adoni—Ella Gance—was young, and though medicine in Australia was advanced, it could not freeze or reverse the clock. The old man must be mad.

"My brother...the coroner will not let me see him until tomorrow, she says the police have not released his body yet. Tomorrow, you and I can go there. Even in death, Adoni will help."

Four shades of nutso, Ninn decided. But those opals were valuable. She could play along, ethics be fragged. Ninn could well pretend that this old man wanted to find his "brother's" killer. She was investigating all of this anyway. Those opals...they just might be her ticket out from under the storm.

"All right, Barega. Cadi has an early show tonight. We've got enough time to get something to eat and get over there when the curtain rises. I want to take a look around."

TEN
VICTIM NUMBER SEVEN

The big stranger crouched in the shadows. The park and the beautiful fountain—all awash in yellow-blue lights—was across the street and smelled remarkable. He loved the scent of water, and it hung heavy in the air, suggesting it would rain soon. The cloud overhead was especially dense today, the color of lead; it pressed down like a weighty blanket, smothering the city.

He studied the milling people. There weren't many nearby, as he could count them on his fingers. Some drinking, some laughing, four humans, three elves, an ork wading with her skirt pulled up around her waist, two dwarfs amorously engaged. He'd eaten a dwarf once, shortly after he went away from the complex the first time. He'd found it peeing in an alley, and it had put up no real fight. It was old and stringy, not especially tasty, and there were metal pieces in some of its bones that had proved bothersome. Since then, he'd discovered that food left outside restaurants in trash receptacles was much more appealing. And cats, when he could sneak up on them.

He slipped into the alley when the dwarfs dropped their liplock and one of them glanced in his direction. He doubted anyone could see him, what with the clouds darkening and the night starting to deepen, but he didn't want to take chances. He didn't want to kill the dwarfs, as they weren't on his list.

The stranger had another target tonight, and work always came first. Isn't that what he used to say: "Work first. Always, work comes first."

"You sure you want to do this—" Ninn barely stopped herself from calling him "old man," "—Barega? There are better places to be than this alley. You sure you want to tag along with me?"

"This is where the galah sent me, I told you." He sat on a crate in the alley, directly across from the back door to Cadigal's Corner. "To find you, and to assist in your search for the slayer of my brother."

"And how is it that your older brother looked at least fifty years younger than you?"

"I do not know. Perhaps you will discover this for me, too. I had not seen him in a long while. We did not always get along."

"Then how did you know he was dead?"

"The galah told me. The galah directed me to you, so I can help gain justice for my brother."

"And how will you do that?" Ninn hadn't meant to say that aloud. "Help me?"

"I am *talmai*."

Ninn didn't find the reference in her encephalon.

"*Wirringan*," Mordred supplied.

"What?"

"*Mekigar*," Barega tried again. "*Koradji*." He looked perplexed that she didn't understand.

"*A shaman.*" This from Mordred. "*A mystic. Booga booga booga and all that.*"

"I see things, Nininiru. I dive down into the sky and—"

Yeah, well I hear voices, she thought.

The old man continued explaining his spiritual gift, and Ninn pretended to be interested. She could, and often did, see plenty of weird things without an old Aboriginal spell. All it took was too much gray-puppy and an alcohol chaser. She'd left her dozen remaining slips back in the office, inside her soykaf box, knowing Talon would leave it alone because she had a good supply of real coffee. That walking mass of scar tissue hadn't left yet, and Ninn didn't want to toss him out in front of Barega, especially after he'd been sort of helpful. She hadn't gotten a chance to get the RighteousRight information on the chip downloaded into her encephalon yet; that was on the agenda for tomorrow, and it was safe in her desk drawer. She'd put the opals in her pocket—making sure Talon saw her so he wouldn't go digging for them, and then left with the old man.

"I don't want you here when I come back," she'd whispered while slipping him a little nuyen in exchange for the chip.

"No worries," he'd replied. "I'll be gone."

Ninn suspected he was still there, stretched out on her couch. She'd give him the boot when she was done at the end of this evening. Couldn't afford to have him around. Too many bad memories, too much temptation. And that's what he'd be—temptation, not the poster child of Clean Yourself Up, Ninn. Besides, the couch had been her bed since she'd had to let her flat go. Every few seconds, her aching neck and back reminded her that the desk wasn't a viable sleeping option. She dug her fingers into her palms, and noticed the old man had stopped talking.

"Barega, we'll stay out here a while, watch the back door. Then we'll scoot inside, between shows. I want to—"

"Nininiru, I will stay out here and watch the back door, all the back doors here that I can see. Divided, we can cover more ground. That is how I will help you." Barega crossed his arms and leaned back against the bricks. "I will be all right here. Resting my feet and being useful. Old men lie if they tell you their feet do not hurt."

Ninn scratched her head. "Fine. Stay right here and watch the back door. I'll scoot inside, take a look at the patrons, see if there's any RighteousRight here tonight, poke around for anything that might be worth knowing about, and then I'll be back. Like I said, Cadi has a double feature. If nothing gets my hackles up here, we'll check another alley behind a different tawdry house. Maybe come back for his second show. Always the Cross Slayer—"

"—kills in alleys," Barega finished. "I know."

"Your galah told you that?"

He shook his head. "I listen to the news."

"If you don't feel safe here—"

"I said I will be fine. Best if one of us remains here in the event the Cross—"

"Here." Ninn pulled Mordred from a fold in her longcoat.

"I do not use—"

"This gun and me, we're...connected. It can 'see,' so to speak. If something goes down out here while I'm gone, I'll know it, and I'll come running."

"Not even going to introduce us?" Mordred's thin voice seemed testy.

Ninn was glad the gun's banter was mental, and that Barega couldn't hear it.

"I'll be back soon, Barega."

"And soon it will rain," the old man said, raising his head up to the gunmetal-gray cloud. "I can feel it gathering."

The stranger edged farther into the alley, peering at the familiar elf on the far end. His eyes were large and keen, and they divided the shadows so he could get a better look at her face. Worn-seeming, she hadn't bothered with makeup, nothing fancy about her hair, dressed in something a tourist might wear. But the stranger knew the elf wasn't a tourist. She was a problem.

He could smell her, even this far away; always he liked to smell his quarry. Sweet like fruit. He used to enjoy fruit. The elf hadn't been on his list, but her very presence festered, and it had put her there. Three times now he'd noticed her...how many times had she been nearby and he hadn't paid attention?

The stranger slowly crept closer, careful not to step on something that might snap or crunch, always touching the outer wall of the buildings where it was darkest. He peered more intently. The elf was talking to someone, this person difficult to see because the shadows cast by a stack of crates hampered the view. That person smelled like rich earth.

Who was it? Another elf? Someone small.

The stranger's lips curled back. He'd come to dislike elves. Too fast, hearing too fine because of those pointed ears.

Closer so he could get a better look. Closer.

The back door of the nearby Chinese restaurant opened, and the light that spilled out more clearly defined the elf and also let the stranger get a good look at the man. Old like the peeing dwarf had been, dark-skinned, fragile-seeming, not familiar. Puzzling. In the alleys behind the tawdry houses, the stranger usually saw beautiful women, sometimes with men who paid them. Maybe the little old man was waiting for a beautiful woman that he could pay. The elf wasn't beautiful; she was a bother.

Perhaps he would kill this elf *and* the old man, drop them in the sewers where the rats and worse would devour the evidence. He'd dumped bodies there before. They were not crucial to the Cross killfest, and so did not need to be discovered by the authorities.

He moved closer.

Closer...

He could see the wrinkles on the old man's face.

Then he watched the elf hand the old man a gun. The back door to the Chinese restaurant closed, taking the light with it. The elf hurried away.

It was just the old man now, and whatever tasty treats the kitchen worker from the Chinese restaurant had tossed into the garbage—those scents were teasing and coaxed his stomach to rumble.

The old man wasn't on his list. But...

He inched closer still.

The early show had already started. Ninn stood at the back of the theater, noting only about a third of the seats were filled. She hoped the later show would have more, both for Cadi's income and so she could search for RighteousRight members. This audience wasn't likely to yield a lot of possibilities. But she was here and so she'd take a good look, record some of the faces. Come back for the second show, go to another tawdry house or two in between, maybe go back to that RighteousRight bar, definitely download into her encephalon whatever information was on the chip in her office. Frag her to hell and back for losing all those hours to alcohol and slips! Cadi wasn't paying her to black out.

Sticking to the far aisle, she padded toward the front, scanning the sparse crowd as she went. Most of the people here were human—and senior citizens. *Naturally,* she thought, *a blue-light special for the blue-haired ladies. They'll be home and tucked in bed by eight.*

Hurdy Gertie was on stage, belting out "We Are What We Are," from *La Cage Aux Folles*, a vid reference that was no doubt in Mordred's database. Gertie wasn't half-bad, but certainly no Ella Gance. Maybe the audience was sparser because Cadi's headliner was gone.

She captured some of the faces in the audience—those few who couldn't yet qualify for AARP. Her encephalon pinged, a match from someone she'd seen earlier. Ninn stood against the wall, waiting for the image to appear behind her eye. Male, human, he'd been behind the AISE barricade when Ella was found, that's where she'd seen him before.

She looked closer, focusing on the man on the far side of the darkened theater. Despite her low-light natural eye and thermographic cybereye, it was difficult to get as many details as she'd wanted because only part of the audience was visible from this angle, but she noted a smudge on his neck that could be a tattoo. Maybe RighteousRight. She slipped toward the front of the auditorium, finding another familiar face. This time she didn't have to check her encephalon; he was the smaller of the two men she'd fought with in the ЯR bar. Definitely worth pursuing the Right angle.

Hurdy Gertie finished the tune, and as the crowd applauded, Ninn went through a narrow door. Up a short staircase, and she was backstage. A trio of elf tap dancers toddled past; she'd seen them once before. Cadi needed to get some better talent. She found the troll in the wings.

"Anything?" He kept his voice lower than he needed; the music was loud enough to cover an elephant trumpeting. The troll said something else, but she didn't understand it, some sort of slang tuskers used.

Ninn gestured for him to accompany her, and they went into the hall. "You've at least one RighteousRight in the auditorium. I've been following that."

"What? Following that choob out there? Is that why I haven't heard from you all day? I saw him. In the middle. He's a regular."

"I'm following the RighteousRight angle. There's some activity in the Cross. I think the Slayer is a Right."

"I think it's a fraggin' Righter, too." He snorted. "Good you're following that. But did you follow the news feeds at five?"

That was about the time when Barega had come knocking at her office. She'd been out cold before that.

"I was...busy. So no, I—"

The music upped tempo, and the elf dancers tapped in time with the snare drum.

"Tattered Cat lost a singer. Summer Peacock, a little slip of a thing, but she had a big voice. Ace visited just before it came on the news. Told me about it."

Frag it! "No. I—"

"Somebody found her in a Dumpster in the alley behind the Cat, when they looked in it this afternoon to see what was smelling so bad. Ace named...oh, something Draye, he'd been here for Ella, too. Draye said Summer'd been dead several hours, killed late last night or early this morning. Said she'd apparently left the Cat alone after her last number, didn't use the buddy system. Victim Number Six, according to Draye."

Victim Number Seven, Ninn corrected. She'd have to visit the spot of Victim Number One *and* where Summer Peacock died. Maybe tonight. Maybe she could get Barega to go back to the office and wait; she'd work faster alone, travel faster. But if he insisted on tagging along, fine, he was putting up the opals for the privilege.

"That Ace guy...Draye...said it's a serial killer for sure, said keep the girls out of the alleys. The girls, Gertie, wants me to close tomorrow. Guess they all knew Peacock. She was Jewish, they have funerals fast. Her funeral—they're not gonna show her, from what I understand—is tomorrow at six."

Six. With Six You Get Eggroll, Ninn thought. Nothing from Mordred; she checked her smartlink to make sure it was still active. She was liking the idea of putting the Aborigine and her prized weapon in the alley less and less with every passing minute. She'd met Barega only an hour ago. Why the hell had she trusted him with Mordred?

"Don't let 'em go anywhere alone, this Draye said. An' said I should hire extra security. Gave me a card for a firm, off-duty Aces, I'm thinking." Cadi kept talking, and Ninn recorded it, as she wasn't giving him her whole attention, was thinking about alleys and Mordred and why the hell she had handed her prized gun to the Aborigine, a stranger. "Tattered Cat's at the edge of the Cross. Draye said maybe the Slayer is widening his range. I think the lumpers are worried he'll start killing singers in the rest of the city."

Ninn stared at a spot on the wall over Cadi's shoulder. She'd been a good cop in Chicago, had been doing fine with AISE, was a decent private investigator when she was coherent. This Cross Slayer business was serious, and maybe she was in over her head. But she'd taken Cadi's nuyen and Barega's opals, and it wasn't her style to back down from anything. Her skin itched; a slip would fix that, smooth her rough edges.

"I'm gonna look around here for a bit," she told him when he'd stopped and took a breath.

"What for? Inside my place? Draye and his partner did that yesterday. Isn't an alley—"

"I need a better feel—for this place, for Ella, for all of it. Then I'll hit the alleys again. I'll find—"

"What I need you to find is the Cross Slayer," Cadi said. "You or the lumpers. Just do it quick." He turned and headed backstage.

"That's what I'm paying you for. Please, do it quick, Ninn. I want my girls safe."

Ninn waited until Cadi was out of earshot. "Mordred. Mordred." She tapped her foot. "Mordred!"

"What, Keebs?"

She looked down the hall. "Anything in the alley?"

"Do you mean other than me and the Koori*?"*

She bristled. The gun had a fondness for derogatory slang.

"Barega," she said. "Anything in the alley other than you and Barega?" She held tight against the wall as the tap dancers scurried past, their number finished.

"A little while ago there was a big homeless lug scrounging through the garbage behind the Chinese restaurant."

"I'll be out in a few," she said.

"Oh, and there's graffiti. There's lots of graffiti in this alley. And I saw a cat. Maybe you should get a cat, Keebs. The big homeless lug wandered off after the cat."

Ninn walked through the dressing rooms, the air thick with sweat, cheap perfume and cigarette smoke. She took a long look through Ella's things, finding a slip and putting it on her tongue. Crystal Dream, not as good of a rush as graypuppy. Still, it made her fingers stop itching. There were a few empty boxes; someone would pack up her dresses. "I should've brought Barega inside, had him go through this, see what he might want."

"You'll have to tell him that, Keebs. I can only talk to you."

"I know that, Mordred."

"Hey, Keebs. There's something else out here."

She stiffened and turned, intending to dash out the back door.

"Bricks," Mordred continued. *"A couple of empty bottles, and–"*

"Shut your gob." A pause: "Just let me know if some*one* comes out in the alley."

She didn't see any microcomputer in Ella's dressing room, no data directory, no comm, but that wasn't surprising if the singer was living off the grid and staying SINless...or if AISE had taken it all. The RighteousRight holocard wasn't here, probably in evidence. Maybe some of Cadi's girls also got the cards. She'd check with Hurdy Gertie. Clothes, all with ribbons and sequins, expensive and over the top, and looking undisturbed. Makeup, perfumes, several pairs of high heels, a wig. Draped over a chair was a pair of jeans and a pink T-shirt...probably what she'd come to work in. Another slip in the jeans pocket; she took it and put it in her own.

"I screwed up." Ninn sat on a stool in front of a beveled mirror, but she glanced down, not wanting to look at herself. She should have gone through this room yesterday or earlier today, went to Ella's flat. She shouldn't have been so wasted that the hours had melted away on her. She'd lost time...time Cadi was paying for. "*I'm* screwed up." She'd throw out the dozen slips tonight, try to go cold turkey, maybe give them to Talon as a parting gift, as no doubt he'd still be there, and she'd have to bodily toss his bony ass out on the street. Throw out the one in her pocket. She could handle the shakes, couldn't she? She'd been meaning to hop on the wagon.

The ceiling creaked, and she looked up, her audio receptors kicking in. Someone was walking—pacing from the sound of it—in a room on the second floor. *What's upstairs? Storage? Offices?* No. Cadi's office was on this level. There was a side door to the building, and that probably led upstairs. Maybe a way up from down here. Could get a good view of the alley from a higher vantage point. Worth checking out.

Ninn recorded images from the dressing room, using her magnification to zoom in on the details, and then paused in the doorway as the hall filled with a chorus line waiting to go on, the air saturated with the warring scents of a dozen different perfumes. She held her breath. A door near the end of the hall was locked, but it was an old door and an old fashioned lock, and it took her only a heartbeat to pick it. The stairs beyond looked old too, iron railings, wood steps, a spiral case—one curl leading up, the other down. It smelled old, better than all the clashing perfumes.

She felt goosebumps sprout on her arms, and the back of her neck tingled. *A good sign something's worth looking at upstairs,* she thought. A good PI always played hunches, relied on her proverbial sixth sense, listened to the voices that sometimes whispered in her head. Or maybe it was the jitters, her body begging for some booze. There was some sort of metabolism bioware she could have installed, way too pricey at ten thousand nuyen, but it would keep her from getting drunk, from wigging out on slips. Would it cure the addictions? Booze was a lot cheaper than the bioware. Frag it all to hell, she'd drained the rest of her bottle last night, hadn't saved a swallow.

But she had a slip in her pocket if the itching came back again. Probably Crystal Dream. It would do. She could buy more booze if she really really needed it.

The bottle as it empties, empties me. How hollow have I become? She started up the steps. *Maybe I should have been a philosopher.* The iron rail was rough against her palm and felt cooler than the air around her. Every step squeaked like she squeezed a tiny rodent.

Whoever was on the second floor was going to know company was coming, especially when her pick broke off in the door lock and she ended up forcing it open.

ELEVEN
VICTIM NUMBER EIGHT?

"That door...that door was locked, and you didn't use no key to get it open. You busted in here." The speaker was human, sharply dressed, and with a face all angles and planes, probably had some sculpting work done. "So if you'd be so kind as to turn your patootie around, slap on some makeup, and get ready for your next number—"

"I'm not—"

"You're not a regular up here, that's for certain. And you're not very pretty. But you might clean up all right." On the short side, but with broad shoulders, he took up half the hallway. He had a gun stuck in the waistband of his trousers. "Get gone. Now."

"Listen, I—" Ninn tried to use a polite tone.

"Doctor Siland isn't expecting you. Get gone, I say."

"No. I don't know who Dr. Siland is." Ninn held up her left palm. "I'm a registered private investigator—"

"Don't care if you're a registered Labrador Retriever, you can—"

"I've got permission to be here," Ninn pressed. "I'm investigating the Cross Slayer, Cadi Hamfyst—"

"Doesn't own this building. He's just a tenant. You might have permission to toddle through the tusker's burlesque house on the first floor, but this is off limits." He took a step closer and puffed out his chest, the movement causing his jacket to fall open. He had a holstered Nitame sporter dangling under his armpit. "Last warning before this gets bloody. Get yourself gone, dandelion eater."

Ninn hadn't realized Cadi was a renter, figured he'd owned the building. He'd been here for a dozen or more years.

"So he rents from *you?*" Ninn looked past him. The hallway was long, running the length of the building, but there were only two doors off it. What did they lead to? Apartments? And was this fellow the one she'd heard pacing? Above that, did it matter? Shouldn't she be out in the alley with Barega? Taking her valuable gun back and heading to another tawdry house? *"You own the building? You?"* *Or are you just hired muscle?*

He drummed his fingers on the grip of the pistol. His fingers were big like sausages, manicured, a clunky gold ring on his left index finger had a green shield symbol dotted with stars—a cricket team logo. "I'm not going to ask another time, dandelion eater. Turn around now and—"

The farthest door opened, and the big man looked over his shoulder. "Dr. Siland, the elf ain't one of the tusker's girls. She was just leaving."

"Not one of Hamfyst's girls? I'm expecting an elf, one of the new—" The speaker glided down the hall, stepped around the big man, and shook his head. "No. I don't know this one. Did Hamfyst send you?" The man looked Ninn up and down with an appraising eye and frowned. He was thin, well-dressed, handsome face, high forehead with thin hair, stylishly cut and long at the temples, probably in his early thirties. Could pass for a lawyer in the business suit. He smelled of expensive musk cologne, had dabbed it on liberally enough that she didn't need the nose filter to detect it.

"She broke in," the big man cut in.

"I'm working for Cadi," Ninn said. *Was the troll pimping out some of his entertainers, in the joygirl business on the side?* "Private investigator."

The man smiled warmly and extended his hand. "Looking into Ella's death. Hamfyst told me he'd hired someone from the neighborhood, doesn't trust lumpers much." He laughed. Ninn thought it was a good laugh. "Doesn't *like* lumpers, I should say. Sometimes Hamfyst's business wanders into gray areas."

Ninn heard thunder, the building trembled, and Mordred intruded. *"Singing in the Rain, 1952, Gene Kelly, Donald O'Connor, Debbie Reynolds. Had a two and a half million budget and pulled in almost eight. We're gonna be singing..."* She didn't turn off the smartlink, but pushed his banter to the background.

"You own the building?"

Siland smiled, perfect teeth. "I own a lot of things, Miss—"

"Nininiru Tossinn."

He gestured to the door. "Come into my office, Miss Tossinn. Max here will get us something to drink. I'd like to hear about your investigation. This Cross Slayer...it's not good for the neighborhood. I hope you're getting somewhere with it. AISE isn't saying much. But AISE doesn't like the Cross. Max...those drinks?"

Max growled low in his throat, but nodded to Siland.

The office was incongruous to the building. Where the first floor resembled an antique boxcar, this looked elegant. Thick carpet, walls painted burnt orange, pictures in elaborate and tasteful frames, furniture upholstered. The desk was real wood and gleamed in the light of an expensive-looking brass lamp. A certificate hung on the wall behind the desk, Ninn's optic system magnified the fine print: Hudson Siland held a doctorate degree in biophysics from the University of Canberra, couldn't read the date on it. Another certificate showed a doctorate in physics, and one more a doctorate in veterinary medicine. What the hell was a biophysicist-physicist-veterinarian doing in an office above a tawdry house in the Cross? There was a framed image on the wall of Dr. Siland presenting a clear case with three platinum credsticks in it to a woman in front of a red cable car. Another framed image showed Dr. Siland posed with three men in front of the Sydney Aquarium. A small, framed image was of Siland and a young woman near the El Alamein memorial fountain. In all the pics, he was well dressed and impeccably groomed. There were other pictures, antiques, showing someone with a resemblance, some ancestor.

"Look, Dr. Siland." Ninn stood near the chair across from the desk. Siland sat in the high-backed leather chair behind it and smoothed a wrinkle in his jacket. "No offense, but you seem out of place here, and—"

That warm and wonderful laugh again. "Oh, I am indeed out of place, Miss Tossinn. And yet I am right at home. Aren't we all out of place in the Cross? My great-great-grandfather Hudson owned this entire block, eventually passing it along to my father, who kept most of it and passed it on to me when he died. I have an office building near the harbor, but I find I can get more work done here in this neighborhood. The Cross is...oddly quaint...by comparison to Sydney proper, and pleasantly quirky. Besides, I can catch Hamfyst's shows...any of the shows along this strip...any time I please. I love a good song and dance routine. Don't you?"

Ninn leaned forward to get a closer look at him—no obvious tech, and his eyes appeared real. But the expensive stuff ranged from difficult to impossible to spot. An armored longcoat hung from a hook inside the door. A pressed leaf from a Chicago Grey, an Awakened marijuana plant, was displayed under soft lighting in a shadow box. A smaller pressed leaf—Hellhound's Tongue, an Awakened plant from the Milwaukee area—hung nearby. She was familiar with the plants from her time with Lone Star. On a corner of his desk sat an old-style photograph of a man resembling Siland, perhaps that great-great-grandfather he mentioned, standing in front of a pristine Mercury Oort sedan. Out of habit, she recorded everything.

"I was devastated over Ella," Siland continued. "I've rented to Hamfyst for a dozen years, and Ella...she was the best vocalist he'd ever signed. Her loss will hurt his business. Perhaps impossible to replace."

"How well did you know her?" Ninn cut in. "I'm trying to get a good picture of her life."

"Not as well as I knew some of the other girls. But I was a fan." Siland's eyes twinkled. "I prefer elves on a more personal level, Miss Tossinn. But I liked Ella nonetheless. I knew she was one of the original people, an Aborigine, that she enjoyed the company of men *and* women, and that she occasionally took trips to the Blue Mountains; she went with me once. I enjoy the scenery there. Had she been an elf...who knows...we might have been *very* close friends."

Ninn felt her skin crawl.

"I spoke with her after shows from time to time, went out to dinner with her and some of the other singers once or twice. Beautiful person, beautiful voice. Such a waste." He shook his head. "Such a terrible waste."

A silence crept between them, and in it Ninn realized she couldn't hear music from the theater downstairs, as if the floor was soundproofed. But not the roof. She heard thunder rumble faintly, a siren keened softly in the distance. "And not just her death that makes this all a waste. The other entertainers...Dezi Desire comes to mind, beautiful Summer Peacock. Artists silenced by some disturbed killer. If the RighteousRight is—"

"I'm looking at all of them, Dr. Siland. Cadi only lost Ella, but he hired me to find the Slayer, and that means I'm looking at all of—"

"Good for you, Miss Tossinn." He glanced to the door, seeming impatient. "I told Max to bring drinks."

"I don't need anything, thanks." But Ninn thought she did need something—alcohol, a slip; she was feeling jittery, and something to smooth her edges would help. Shouldn't have left all her slips in her office. Wrong time to go cold turkey. She did have that one slip of Crystal Dream riding in her pocket.

"Tell you what...I will financially reward you, Miss Tossinn, if you can catch the Cross Slayer. If you are successful—"

"Cadi's already paying me, and—"

"That's fine. But if you are successful, I will give you a bonus. I have more nuyen than I know what to do with. And if you can put an end to this killing blight, I will compensate you...no doubt more than what Hamfyst is able to. I am, as I said, a patron of the arts, and quite fond of elves. This is my neighborhood, and I'd like it kept safe."

"We're in the Money," Mordred cut in softly. *"Directed by Ray Enright, 1935, Joan Blondell, Glenda Farrell, whopping sixty-six minutes. Chicago here we come. You better solve this case, Keebs."*

"Thank you, Dr. Siland. But I can't guarantee success. Apparently the Slayer took another girl last night, and—"

"I know. I heard. Hamfyst told me. That was Summer, as I said. Beautiful Summer Peacock. At the edge of the Cross." He spread his hands on his desk. His long fingers were manicured, no rings. "Have you made any headway? In all of this? What can you tell me? I've talked to AISE. They have nothing...that they're releasing in any event. But you, Miss Tossinn, what do *you* have?"

Not much, I've not been working on it that long. And I spent a chunk of time passed out from overindulging. "Well, I—"

The big man from the hall came in with a silver tray, a brandy snifter, and two glasses on it.

"Thank you, Max," Siland said.

"Your girl's waiting in the hall, Dr. Siland. Says she can't hang around too long, says she has another number coming up. I could tell her to come back between shows."

"No, don't do that. I can see you're busy." Ninn stood. "We can talk some other time, when I've some solid information to share." The brandy looked inviting, and she almost caved. Would have caved if she had liked the man. "I need to get back to work."

"Another time then, Miss Tossinn." Siland stood and escorted her to the door. "But on that future occasion, please knock first."

Thunder boomed again, and the building quivered. The distant siren was joined by a second. She stepped into the hallway and saw one of the elves from the tap-dancing trio.

"Knock, you hear?" the big man said, as he thumped the stock of the gun at his waist and pointed to the stairwell. "Dr. Siland says knock if you want to keep eating dandelions."

Ninn hurried down the stairwell...and kept going into the basement. *Might as well take a little look down there as well,* she thought. It was dry in here, and it wouldn't be in the alley. Might as well put off going outside for a little while longer. "Raining hard, Mordred? Mordred?"

"It's raining, Keebs, and we ain't singing in it. Good thing it's warm tonight, or the geezer'd catch his death." A pause: "Death Wish, 1974, Charles Bronson. Death Becomes Her–"

"Death'll become you if you don't stop with the antique vid trivia."

The basement was black as pitch, and the light in the stairwell was too high to reach past the bottom step.

"Frag. Frag. Frag it to hell and back again." At least Ninn had the thermographic vision in one eye, which meant she had to close the other and deal with the initial dizziness. Maybe she should cave and get the good eye replaced...right after the nose filter, and right after she netted enough from this contract to afford a visit to a legitimate doc. Maybe she should switch the order of her future surgeries. Or maybe, if she didn't spend her spare nuyen drowning her senses in graypuppy and whiskey, she'd have enough to buy—

"Frag it." She shut down the thermographic module and relied on her low-light vision. The dizziness stopped.

Mordred had a TAC flashlight attachment, but a world of good that did her, with the gun being out in the alley. Ninn felt along the doorframe and then the wall, finally finding a light switch and discovering that tripping it did nothing. Her skin itched...did she need another slip already? Probably. Too long without slips and alcohol could make her feel dizzy. Shouldn't have left her remaining graypuppy in her office. One itty-bitty slip of that good stuff would hit the spot and last a while. Helluva time to try to sober up. Wrong time.

What the hell had nudged her down into this cave? She should leave; Barega and Mordred had been sitting in the rain long enough. Didn't need to be nosing through Dr. Siland's basement. Go to another tawdry house and poke around, get one slip, go—

Her audio receptors picked up something ahead in the darkness. Shuffling? Was someone down here? In this ink? Rats? The Cross had them in its old buildings, some of the pests the size of a wombat.

Ninn reached for her Renraku Sensei commlink. It had a software app to make it glow like a flashlight. It yielded just enough light to complement her natural vision and chase away the closest shadows. She crept forward. Racks of dresses, most covered with a protective film to keep them clean, stretched away from her. A palm tree leaned against a wall; its leaves looked to be dyed ostrich feathers. Stools, vivid overlarge watering cans, freestanding coat racks, stuffed animals, plywood lollipops the size of garbage can lids, music stands, boxes of colorful garland—all of it props for Cadi's shows. Crates were stacked to the rafters in a few places, all of it a jumbled crowded collection of stuff that held a tinge of dampness.

The floor was earthen, evidence that this building was probably two hundred years old. It dipped in places, but felt as firm as duracrete.

"Mordred, I'll be out in a few. Still nothing in the alley?"

"Rain," the gun said. *"Bricks. Me and the geezer. He's dreaming, Keebs. Wonder what I'd see if I was smartlinked to—"*

"So, nothing?"

"Nothing, 2003, 49th Parallel Productions, directed by Vincenzo Natali. Nothing."

Nothing here either, she thought. "*Gornischt. Ekkert. Wala-lang.*"

She smelled the fustiness of the place, traces of old cologne clinging to some of the garments...and she detected something else. Ninn had been without work for a time, and had spent too many hours on Sydney's nude beaches. A very familiar scent teased her—saltwater. Odd.

"*Wala-lang,*" a deep voice whispered from beyond the edge of her light.

Ninn wondered if she was hearing things again. Were her audio receptors playing dirty tricks again?

"*Wala-lang,*" he repeated, liking the sound of the word and the way it rolled off his thick tongue. "*Wala-lang.*" He wondered what it meant.

He watched the elf glide past the feathered palm tree, many steps beyond the bottom of the stairs—the familiar elf, the one he'd seen a short time ago above in the alley. Had she followed him down here? Not through the tunnel; he doubted anyone knew about the tunnel he'd dug and concealed behind the crates. He had several tunnels under the Cross, all secret, all his. But she had found him nonetheless.

Elves were special. Perhaps this one was magical. Why else would she come into one of his secret caves? It looked like she was following the sound of his voice.

She had a light with her, and was shining it at all the glittery feathery treasures of this place, at the pretty dresses and the fake flowers, the mound of stage props he hid behind.

He had someone on his list tonight, not this elf...but now indeed this elf. Did she know he was the Cross Slayer? Was that why she followed him? Prying into his doings? Was she trying to stop him? He would, instead, stalk her. He would catch her and drag her body through his secret tunnel and into the sewers, let the rats and worse nibble away until all that remained were bones. There were things in the sewers that would eat bones, too; it just took a little longer. He would erase her from Sydney.

"*Wala-lang*," he said, louder, again puzzling at its meaning. Maybe it was the name of some object in this basement. He added a snarl to it and again raised his voice. "*Wala-lang. Wala-lang. Wala-lang.*"

He saw the elf stiffen, alert, a trace of fear mixed with curiosity. He had keen senses and fear was the easiest emotion to smell, even amid the scents emanating from this clutter of treasures. He savored the smell of fear, and he sucked it in deep; it made him happy.

"*Wala-lang!*" He moved closer, disturbing a rack of dresses that made a *shush-shush-shushing* sound, knocking over something that clattered against the hard floor—an interesting sound. He circled to the right, picking up a shoe and tossing it to his left, where it *thunked* against the wall. The elf shone the light in that direction. He threw another shoe and she started toward that.

Easy prey.

Silent, he edged up behind her. The Cross Slayer drew the blade and flicked it so the edge crackled and made the soft humming sound he cherished.

"A heater—" the elf whispered as she whirled.

The Cross Slayer put his head down and drove into her, striking her squarely in the chest and sending her back into a pyramid of hatboxes, her light dropping and the beam playing crazily against the wood beams of the ceiling. He punched her with his free hand, flattening her, shared her breath as the air rushed from her lungs. The fingers of his free hand closed on her throat. He squeezed lightly, and watched her eyes widen.

It would be so easy to crush her neck.

Kill her fast? He should, then be about the business of slaying the soul on the top of his list tonight. But the scent of her fear was too delicious to hurry. He leaned in close and licked her cheek, put a knee on her stomach to keep her down.

"Stop wiggling, *wala-lang.*"

"Get off me!" she hollered, kicking with legs that seemed surprisingly strong for her size. Elves were tricky. And this one might be magical. *Or mechanical,* he thought; one of her eyes didn't look right. Bet she had metal in her.

But so did he. Bet he had more.

The Cross Slayer snarled, drool dripping in a string over his lower lip and plopping on her face. "*Wala-lang,* elf. *Wala-wala-wala-lang.*"

"No! Yousonofabitch!"

Foul language. His mother had told him never to curse. But his mother was long-dead, and so her manners did not matter.

The elf twisted one way and then the other, unpredictable, fast, reaching for something, shooting! A gun! He'd seen her give the old man a gun in the alley, hadn't counted on her having another one.

It hurt. It hurt. It hurt. Pain danced a jig in his stomach.

She shot at him again, higher. It hurt. It hurt. It hurt. It hurt.

Furious, he swept the knife back, the edge crackling and humming, the dust floating in the air around it looking like baby fireflies. He brought the heater down, but in the same instant she'd freed one of her legs and rammed her knee into his crotch. More pain danced and threw off his aim. The knife pierced a hatbox, not the elf, and sparks set the antique cardboard on fire. She rolled out from under him and jumped to her feet, but she dropped her gun in the process.

He was up a heartbeat later and coming at her again, slashing right and left, lunging, cutting her arm as she brought it up to ward him off. Cutting both arms, one slash deliciously deep; he'd found bone. There was another, smaller gun in her other hand. How many guns did the elf have? Was that her magic? To summon guns from thin air? He hurt. He hurt. He hurt.

She took aim and shot, grazing his cheek. The pain was hot this time, and it added to his anger.

The fire his heater had started was spreading to other hatboxes, the air smelled smoky, and he heard a crackling that sounded both ominous and interesting.

She shot again, striking his chest, the agony burrowed. This hurt worse than the other stings. He gritted his teeth and felt tears forming.

The Cross Slayer stumbled, howled, and slashed faster. Erratic because of his wounds, he managed to knock this new hated gun into the darkness, slicing her again. He smelled her blood, a better scent than the burning things in this basement. Too bad the heater cauterized wounds so quickly. Another thrust as she came at him, and the blade sunk into her shoulder—not where he'd aimed, but he was feeling woozy, and his blade arm wasn't working the way he wanted. Nonetheless, the sound of her scream was pleasing. Her scream and the sound of the fire played like a song. He yanked the blade out and pressed his attack, but withdrew as he heard someone racing down the stairs.

"Fire!" the intruder hollered. "Pigs, we got a fire!"

His real quarry? Was that his real quarry come to this basement lair?

More feet tromping. More people. Maybe all the singing women were coming down the stairs.

Too many.

The elf spun toward the stairs, and the Cross Slayer retreated into the shadows, tipping over a rack of dresses to buy him some space, then slipping behind the crates and lumbering into his secret tunnel. Knocking out a support, and then another, he collapsed the entrance.

He hated fire. And he hurt.

There were other tunnels and other caves.

He had a target tonight, business, one more name to cross off his list. That name could not wait until tomorrow. He would have to circle back after he healed. It would not take long to heal. He would come back through another tunnel.

Always the target came first.

He hurt badly. If the elf was still at the tawdry house when he returned, he would kill her too. *Kill her slowly,* he thought. Slow and agonizing would be a good way. A very good way. It gave him something to look forward to.

Wala-lang.

TWELVE
A DREAM IN FLAMES

In his mind's eye, Barega saw the galah. His totem was trying to tell him something, but at the moment it only tantalized him, all gray and rosy pink, the color of the great, angry cloud. The spectral bird was sometimes like a trickster holding a sugary piece of candy just beyond the fingers of a begging child.

Barega was used to waiting; he knew the treat would eventually come closer. The bird had led him here, after all, to the Cross, hinting at justice for his brother and that he should nurture another of his kind before his years were done. Two missions, one totem, everything tied together by a dark soul slaying people in this neighborhood. Barega had patience; he would wait on the galah.

Sitting on the crate behind Cadigal's Corner, he'd been listening to the sounds of the city when he had caught the galah's oh-so-faint call. Every noise was muted here, even the parrot's; the world kept at bay by the garishly painted walls over which the growing darkness looked like layers of ashen-hued shadows stretching to heaven. There were tiny spirits in the bricks, and he considered summoning one to speak with. That conversation would pass the time while Nininiru Tossinn searched for clues in the tawdry house.

But the tiny spirits could be distracting and sometimes overly playful, and he needed to be alert in this alley.

Dreary, but he could get through this. He could find peace in tedium.

There'd been a man searching through the garbage behind the Chinese restaurant, retrieving discarded food, stuffing his hooded face with it, looking in Barega's direction, then retreating to the other end of the alley following a stray cat. It was too murky here to make out the details, other than that the man was very large and clearly hungry. Barega had no food to offer him. There'd been an argument from an apartment above that restaurant, the deepening night doing nothing to diminish the hate-filled ranting. An irate man and woman volleyed unkind words back and forth, neither winning, the volume rising; they stopped when a baby started wailing.

The air was foul here, tinged with pollution the often-rains couldn't obliterate. The alley was worse than the streets, as it smelled of trash and urine and shattered hopes, everything close like a damp, clinging garment. He would rather be elsewhere, but more pleasant surroundings would not bring justice for his brother, and so would not mollify Barega's soul and satisfy the galah. The killings happened in alleys, and so Barega would help Nininiru by keeping watch.

The gun in his lap did not feel as heavy as he'd expected—no doubt because of the materials and craftsmanship. Barega knew little about weapons, but he guessed it was quite valuable, and that Nininiru Tossinn had honored him by entrusting it into his care.

His fingers played across its smooth surface. The gun somehow felt as if it was more than just the sum its parts, beyond the metal and plastic and whatever circuits some keen-minded weaponsmith had added to it. The gun felt like it had a presence.

Barega pushed a small button and a bright flashlight beam shone forth, stretching to the back door of Cadigal's Corner. He marveled at that and experimented gripping the stock and sweeping the barrel from left to right, illuminating the rear entrances to the buildings. There was a streetlight at the opposite end of the alley, but its light didn't reach far enough to be of any use, and the light that spilled from the hate-filled apartment above was diffused through a set of limp curtains. The gun's beam was therefore helpful to his old eyes. What else could this weapon do?

He let the light play across the graffiti, strange and colorful, some of the images beautiful, and others hurtful. Barega noted several ЯRs, and knew from the news and his previous forays into the city that the symbol served as the signature of prejudiced, ill-thinking folks. There were more of the symbols now than in the previous years he had visited Sydney. Those prejudiced fools would not have tolerated his brother, perhaps were indeed responsible for Adoni's death.

Barega had come into the Cross nine summers ago, searching for Adoni, an effort to renew brotherly ties and deliver the news that their sister had died. That year, the galah had led him to another tawdry house, the Forum, where Adoni had performed a song composed by Harriet Abrams a hundred years before the Commonwealth of Australia was founded:

"The frozen streets in moonshine glitter,
The midnight hour has long been past,
Ah me, the wind blows keen and bitter,
I sink beneath the piercing blast

In every vein seems life to languish,
Their weight my limbs no more can bear,
But no one soothes the orphan's anguish,
And no one heeds the orphan's prayer."

Barega had sat in the back row, watching with wide eyes, hardly recognizing the beauty Adoni had become, drinking in her mournful song that filled the auditorium.

The young woman who should be an aging man.

Adoni had gone by Gin-Anne Tonic then.

Barega knew there were many things in this world that altered the human condition—bioware, cyberware, drugs, magic. And though he was curious what Adoni had done to himself to reverse the years, Barega did not speak of it when they met, instead relaying the sad news of their sister. Adoni said he would not return to the Outback for the funeral ceremony, that his life was here now.

"Do you still swim through the Great Ghost Dance?" Adoni had asked. "Do you dance with our ancestors? Have you danced with our dead sister?" He laughed lightly, but it lacked humor. "Dancing has added wrinkles to your skin, Barega. It looks like bark. Dancing has smoothed mine. It seems, you and I, we live in reverse."

They were in a large dressing room full of lights, mirrors, padded stools, and racks of gaudy clothes. Feather boas hung from hooks, every color in the world's paint box on display. Sequins and rhinestones glittered like false stars, the air was thick with sickly sweet perfume, and Barega had trouble absorbing it all. Adoni sat on a stool and rubbed at his makeup.

"I should get something permanent," he had said. "Makeup tattoos. They're not expensive. But then I'd be stuck with my face, wouldn't I? It would be easier, though." He'd looked at Barega and displayed a wistful, crooked smile. "Easier isn't always the best, isn't that what you'd told me after one of your many walkabouts? The more difficult the climb, the more beautiful the view, isn't that what you'd said? I think I rather like putting all this old fashioned goop on and off. I am my own beautiful view." Adoni plucked off his wig and put it on a stand on the counter, ran his fingers through his short, curly dark hair. He took off his shiny dress and wiggled into pants and a T-shirt, still looking impossibly young, his face free of blemishes, all smooth and even-toned like his voice.

Barega had wanted to ask Adoni about it—why he'd done things to his body, maybe why he'd done things to his soul. The galah had circled higher in his mind, suggesting he leave that conversation for another time. They went out to dinner at an all-night spring rolls restaurant and just enjoyed each other's company for a time.

"Do you still go walkabout, brother?" Adoni had asked.

Barega nodded. "And I still dream. I still feel the Rainbow Serpent's anger manifested in the clouds. I still run with the rain."

"There is a lot of rain in Sydney," Adoni had replied. "Give my best to whatever remains of our family, brother." Adoni had finished his meal, grabbed his satchel, and headed out the door, looking back over his shoulder and waving. "And thank you for bringing me the sad news. I would like you to come visit me again someday."

They'd never spoken again.

Barega blinked the past away. Looking at the graffiti, made more interesting in the flashlight beam shining through the soft rain, Barega wished he would have talked longer with his brother. The tears he shed now for Adoni and that missed opportunity were lost in the summer shower, the memory bitter and thick on his tongue.

He continued panning the light around as the rain started coming down harder, clicking like the taps on a dancer's shoes. He wondered what Nininiru Tossinn was discovering inside Cadigal's Corner. Perhaps he should have gone with her and looked inside the place where his brother apparently thrived, not been so resolute that splitting their forces would be the better course. It would have been a drier plan. Fortunately, this was a warm summer.

He'd seen the placard on the side of the building, a framed one showing Miss Ella Gance in a beaded gown that was all the shades of an Outback sunset. His brother looked happy in the image, yet haunted; looked the same—*as perfect*—as when Barega had come into the city nine summers ago. Perhaps appeared even younger. Yes, younger.

The galah cried louder in Barega's mystic mind, rousing him. He pushed aside the muted sounds of the city and the steady rain and listened to the ephemeral bird. The shrill cry sounded again, and he felt the bird flying above the alley, circling, dropping lower and holding out that treat-of-a-message. Still beyond Barega's reach, but seductively closer. The bird banked, the rain passing right through it as it flew out of the alley and around the corner of Cadigal's building.

Follow me, its wings whispered.

Barega eased himself off the crate, gave a last look at the back doors in the alley, and then thumbed off the gun's flashlight. He stuffed the valuable weapon into a deep pocket in his pants and sloshed through the puddles. Nininiru Tossinn was a detective, and so should be able to find him.

Follow me, came the bird's whisper. *Follow—*

Then the galah's song was lost in the cacophony of sirens, and Barega's vision was filled with neon patterns reflected in the puddles on the sidewalk, electric rainbow snakes writhing in the storm.

THIRTEEN
WALA-LANG WITH A SIDE OF *EKKERT*

Ninn's arms throbbed where the Cross Killer had stabbed her. *Might need a doc,* she thought. *Might not be able to shake this off.*

She started recording with her thermographic eye, cursing herself for not doing it right away. But she'd been caught way the hell off guard, and for want of a slip hadn't been wholly thinking straight.

Charging after the hulking figure, her feet got tangled in the dresses on a rack the Slayer tipped over. She saw him lunge behind a stack of crates, and just as she freed herself, she heard something rumbling. *Should get out of here,* she thought, *the place is on fire.*

"I fraggin' hate fire," she said. "Go. Go. Go. I fraggin' hate—oh, hell." Her left arm stopped hurting and went numb. And useless. She couldn't move it, couldn't make a fist; it was a dead thing hanging from her shoulder.

Smoke billowed from burning cardboard boxes, forcing her to hold her breath. She couldn't see a fragging thing beyond the edge of the crates, her one real eye watering like a faucet, and her bioware and cyberware not helping much; she lacked the correct compensators—something else to put on her shopping list. She stumbled forward anyway, stretching her working arm out, feeling beyond the crates and finding a mound of dirt and rocks where a hole in the wall must have been. She hurled a string of curses that was drowned out by Hurdy Gertie yelling "Fire! Fire!"

"No drek there's a fire." Ninn hated fire, hated hated hated it. But this was a small fire, right? All smoke and no substance, and the sprinklers should kick on anytime now and douse it. Her prize was too near to quit. Couldn't use her thermographic for sure, even with the flare compensator it would mess her up.

Forget the fire, she told herself. *Focus!* Ninn furiously dug at the rocks with one hand. It was the Cross Slayer she'd fought, had to be, heater, slashing, trying to kill her right here in the basement of Cadi's tawdry house. He'd caught her off guard and so got the upper hand, was abnormally strong, even given his size, and he could have geeked her if he hadn't tried toying with her first. Clearly, he'd been playing with her. Had he played with all his victims?

Forget the fire. But she could tell it was getting bigger, threatening to swallow the contents of the basement—and her for good measure. It had saved Ninn from the Slayer, had forced him to retreat, but if the sprinklers didn't kick on soon, she'd have to retreat, too.

Where's the fraggin' sprinklers? She should get the hell out of here, before the smoke could take her down. Fire. Dear God, she hated fire. Still she dug at the rocks, gaining only inches and realizing that bravery and foolishness were first cousins. Finally taking in a much-needed breath, Ninn instead sucked in a lungful of hot smoke that only made things worse. She didn't have the tools for digging, nor any such useful cybernetic attachments in her fingers to help, and her right arm still burned from where he'd cut her. What the hell had that knife done to her left arm?

She held her breath again and somehow managed to work faster. But for every handful of dirt and gravel she pulled out, more replaced it, filtering down to take its place. Milton wrote: "Death is the golden key that opens the palace of eternity." She'd be waltzing into that palace in the next few minutes if she kept this up.

Dizzy. From the smoke, dust, the throbbing pain in her one good arm and shoulder. Light-headed, despite her adrenal booster. *C'mon, dig faster, you drekking dandelion eater! Go after the sonofabitch!*

"*We're on the move, Keebs!*" This came from inside her head, Mordred talking to her. "*The geezer is leaving his post and going somewhere. On the Road, 2012, Viggo Mortensen as Old Bull Lee. Can't tell where we're going. I'm riding in his pocket. In My Pocket, 2011, David Lisle Johnson director, drug addiction spiral. I don't think you'd like that particular movie. Too close to home.*"

"No!" She couldn't lose her gun! One of a kind, valuable, her companion! Irreplaceable! Idiot to have left it with the Aborigine. A stranger! What the hell had she been thinking? That was the problem, she hadn't been thinking at all. And if Barega moved too far away, the smartlink would cut out. The Cross Slayer or Mordred! The Cross Slayer or—

So dizzy!

Fiery hot!

"Moses on a pogo stick!" Her longcoat had caught fire, and she shrugged out of it. That'd been rather costly and had great pockets for concealing her weapons.

More rumbling, farther away but significant enough to send a tremor through the floor of Cadi's basement. Whatever route the Slayer had used to get here, he was probably collapsing all of it, and that made the decision for her. Ninn turned, woozy, tried to retrace her steps, bumping into another rack of clothes and knocking it over, the smoke everywhere, fire crackling. Tripping and struggling back on her feet.

Where were the fraggin' sprinklers?

There was a *WHOOSH! WHOOSH!* And some of the smoke dissipated. *WHOOSH!*

Hurdy Gertie manned a honking big fire extinguisher that *whooshed* white powder in an arc and cut the flames. Behind her were two performers Ninn had not seen before, their tall, wide hats taking up the stairwell, one manning a fire extinguisher too, the other simply panicking. Within a few heartbeats, they'd knocked the fire down to small, manageable hotspots.

"Did you do this?" Gertie glared at Ninn as she *whooshed* with the extinguisher. "Did you set this fire?"

Ninn coughed and shook her head, bent, and felt like she was hacking up a lung.

"She's hurtin', mate!" This came from one of the hat girls. "All cut up, she is. Look at her."

"You're gettin' it, Gert," said the one with the other extinguisher. "Fire's almost out. Over there. Get that little bit over there, and I'll get this. Ain't big enough to call a truck over. It was mostly smoke, all noise and no worries. I think we're gettin' it all. Fire department would probably let a place like ours burn anyway."

Gertie continued to *whoosh* with the extinguisher to make sure, *whooshed* until it was empty. "Let's get some water on this, just to be sure," she told the tallest girl behind her. There's a hose under the sink in the dressing room. Long enough to reach. Water ain't going to ruin what's already ruined. Pigs, what a mess you caused."

"I didn't start it," Ninn gasped, finally getting some air into her lungs. "The fire. I would never start a fire, you drekhead. The Cross

Slayer started it. A heater. He sparked it with his knife, and—"

"Pigs!" Gertie dropped the spent extinguisher, the fire out but the thinning smoke still filling the empty spaces. "Pigs, he did! Pigs, the Cross Slayer was—"

"Pigs yourself. He was here. Maybe he was looking to geek you this time." Ninn brushed past her and squeezed by the other two. "I gotta talk to Cadi. Keep blathering, Mordred. I'll find you." Then: "Cadi! Cad—"

She didn't have far to look. The troll was upstairs in the hallway, the wide-shouldered thug from the second floor close behind him. Concern, shock, ire playing on both men's wide faces. Ninn was fast to recount her tale, pointing to her injuries, coughing to clear the last of the smoke. The size of the Cross Slayer, the hole in the wall where he'd maybe come up from some sewer, the heater, the words tumbling out so fast and furious that Cadi and the muscle couldn't get a question in. The entertainers filled the hall behind them, and Gertie tromped up, muttering: "Pigs. Where's the hose?"

"The Slayer.... Should probably tell AISE," Ninn said. She tried to move her arm, twitch her fingers, anything...nothing, still useless. Needed to get to a doc. "He was big, Cadi. Friggin' big, almost troll big. But he didn't sound like a troll, didn't feel like it. And he felt...evil. Your girls should go home in bunches." A pause: "Make sure they're armed."

Mordred intruded in her head: *"Geezer's moving fast, Keebs... well, for someone his age. I'd probably hear him gasping for breath if there weren't all these sirens. Gonna be out of your range soon, its feeling like. I think we're just about—"*

The connection broke.

"Elf looks like hell." This from the wide-shouldered thug.

She could hear sirens, too, the building muffling some of the sound. Cadi started asking questions, but she whirled, pushed open the back door with her good arm.

"And put in a sprinkler system," she sneered over her shoulder.

She stepped into the alley, the door banging closed behind her. For once she considered the rain a blessing. Ninn had a level one adrenal pump, and that gave her a boost to kick off the fatigue and effects of the smoke; it didn't help her wounds, though. It didn't make her left arm work. The sirens were louder out here, and she followed the racket, feet slapping in a rhythm through the alley and right arm swinging. She needed a doc, but she wanted to regain Mordred first. Ninn rounded the corner and headed up the sidewalk.

Frag, but she'd dropped her comm in the basement, and her spare guns, leaving her weaponless. Her longcoat, credstick in the pocket. Frag and back again. She'd return to Cadi's basement, after she caught up to Barega and got Mordred back. The gun was irreplaceable. An old man like that, he couldn't have gotten too far. She'd get Mordred first. Then she'd see a doc, a street doc nearby if she had to, cut as badly as she'd been it would be a good idea to get checked out as soon as possible. At least she knew she wasn't bleeding; the heater had cauterized the wounds it made.

She still couldn't feel her left arm.

Frag! She'd had the Cross Slayer! Or rather, he'd had her. So close! If she'd been more alert...if she hadn't been fragging jittery for another slip...but who the hell would've thought he'd be caving it in Cadi's basement?

Get a shovel, that's what she'd do. Pick and a shovel and wail away at the wall until she found the tunnel the Slayer used. Maybe no one had gotten a look at him before because he traveled in tunnels, maybe lived in the sewer. Ninn shuddered. There were bad things in sewers. Too bad she couldn't've gotten a real good look. She'd recorded him, maybe the image could be enhanced into something recognizeable.

Two blocks and she swung left, seeing a crowd at the end of next block, fire trucks, and a building wholly engulfed—the building her office was in. The sirens stopped, but the lights on all the vehicles danced and spun and bounced off the restaurants, bars, and trendy shops.

"Oh God." Ninn froze.

The fire was a thing of special effects—bursts of bright white erupting from windows, flames dancing up the exterior walls, the rain doing nothing, the water from the fire trucks doing nothing. Rather, the jets of water and the persistent rain seemed to somehow encourage it.

She could feel the heat from a block away, and the sounds were a crashing wave: people shouting, crying, cheering, music blaring from somewhere, an ork fireman standing on a truck bellowing orders through an amplifier, the hum of aerial drones working to keep the crowd back, the blare of everything so confusing that she couldn't make anything out. The air smelled of sulfur, and overhead lightning flickered.

Drenched, Ninn shuffled forward, mesmerized and horrified, Mordred, the Cross Slayer, and her dead arm temporarily forgotten. It was a four-level building, an old one, like most of the structures in the Cross, each story with twelve-foot ceilings. It was one of the stumpier buildings in the block, but the flames made it appear much higher. White-hot eruptions pulsed skyward in defiance of the rain. The stench was awful. Despite its age, Ninn knew the building had state-of-the-art sprinkler systems in all the halls and offices; one hung above her desk. *Had* state-of-the-art. She'd *had* a desk. And it *had* her spare slips and that chip with RighteousRight goodies on it.

A fire had brought her to Australia...her sister Kalin burned so severely in Chicago, in a conflagration where the building did not have state-of-the-art extinguishers. It had been a dance club down by the lakefront, a converted warehouse with a large stage that often coaxed in popular techno-metal-fugue groups on the cusp of "making it big." Once the concert started, the doors had been electronically locked to prevent gatecrashers from getting in—that was the normal practice.

The fire had been arson, Chicago Lone Star confirmed, carefully planned by the lead singer's jilted lover, the firebomb going off as he appropriately started belting out their fast-rising hit "My Heart Burns for You."

Ninn's sister had been right up front, pressed against the stage, waving her arms, fingers brushing the singer's shoes. Ninn had watched it unfold hours later on the security cam's footage she'd managed to get a copy of—she was still with Lone Star then. The firebomb had been planted under the stage, and so the band, stagehands, and the lucky fans in the front rows got the brunt of the blast.

In the maddening seconds that followed, people were trampled as the hysterical attendees rushed for the doors, which took three minutes for the press of bodies to force open. The sprinklers had eventually kicked in, and coupled with the fire department saved some of the structure, but the initial burst did the damage the arsonist had hoped for. In the three minutes it took for the doors to open, the fire took lives...everyone in the band, ninety-eight fans, and eventually claiming Kalin Tossinn when the biotech efforts failed.

Ninn was afraid of fire not just because of what it could do, but because of the memories and loss it evoked.

The ork on the fire truck continued issuing orders. The firemen were in silver bodysuits and full-face breathers designed to protect against high temperatures—but that didn't make the wearer immune; even the latest technology wasn't that advanced. They worked with precision, the firelight reflecting off their shiny bodysuits and adding to the colorful, horrid tableau.

As she pushed through the crowd, Ninn could tell the majority of the firemen were concentrating on the nearby buildings, wetting them down in an effort to keep the inferno from taking the block; her building had obviously already been declared a loss—none of the firemen were going inside it, and no hoses led in through the front doors. She started recording everything, reflex. There were five ambulances, lumpers holding back the crowd; she spotted the AISE Draye, and for some reason worked around in the opposite direction.

"So hot," she whispered, noting sweat beaded up on all the lookieloos' faces.

"Keeb, that's your place flaming." It was Mordred in her head; he was seeing through her eyes, the smartlink connection reestablished. She heard other voices, too, dissonant and making no sense, people with British accents. *"Towering Inferno, 1974, Paul Newman. 'Cept your building's not that tall."*

Barega must be near, but a quick glance around didn't reveal him. She'd home in on the smartlinked gun when she was done taking in the carnage and the gawkers. There were mostly humans in the crowd, the bulk of them locals by their clothes and speech. But there were tourists, too: a half-dozen Asian orks chatted in an unfamiliar language. Some gangers in the mix, a few wired gutterpunks, dataslaves on their way home from work, a cybered-out razorguy with a sword strapped to his back. She watched a young man with blue hair pluck something from a woman's shoulder bag and ease away. *Should do something about that,* Ninn thought, but instead she edged all the way to the front, the heat keeping people at bay as effectively as the barricade did.

"Your place is a bonfire. The Bonfire of the Vanities, 1990, Tom Hanks."

"It *was* my place, Mordred," she said. It hurt to breathe, the air so blistering and her chest so tight. It might have been more tolerable had she not stayed so long in Cadi's burning basement and already toasted her lungs, if she hadn't gotten wounded by the Slayer's heater. Still couldn't move her left arm.

"Hey, Miss, were you in there? Did everyone get out?" A human nudged her injured shoulder. "You all right?"

"Fine," Ninn answered, and edged away. She probably looked like she'd come from that fire, clothes singed, shirt and leggings ripped—maybe from the heater, maybe from snagging something in Cadi's basement. Probably looked like she'd been spit out of a food processor.

What the hell kind of a fire was this? That it defied the rain and the streams of water from the fire trucks? What could do that? More white bursts followed by more flames, everything bright white, glowing yellow, and sparks of red and orange that put the annual harbor fireworks display to shame.

"Magnesium!" shouted a fireman on the other side of the barricade. Ninn noticed that she had a handheld magnetic anomaly detector in her right hand and a low-watt mineral detector in her left. A small drone clinging to her arm manipulated the controls; the woman's gloves were too thick to manage the keys. "It's why the water's not working, Lieutenant. Should've figured it out right away!"

"Magnesium." Ninn accessed her encephalon and she found a reference to magnesium fires, learning that water basically made a magnesium blaze go ballistic, feeding it rather than putting it out.

"Magnesium," Mordred repeated. *"That was on the label in that big box in your office. Malden's Finest Magnesium Powder. Remember? Think that piece of refuse on your couch tried to smoke it and caused this?"*

Not possible, Ninn thought.

"Foam!" the ork on the truck bellowed. "Foam down the other buildings!" He called into his comm for another unit. "Bring a foam truck, the one with a powder vat. Now! Water's making it all worse!"

Foam down the other buildings.

They'd truly given up on hers. Everything she owned was in the office...everything but the cyberware and bioware riding around inside her, Mordred, which was somewhere in the crowd, the opals still in her pocket. Her graypuppy slips were ashes, her real coffee gone, the chip with the RighteousRight information, her comfortable high-backed chair, her precious view of the block, her clothes, and her home. The loss made her dizzy. Fire had again taken everything.

Could that box of magnesium powder mistakenly delivered to her office been at the heart of this? Could Talon have accidentally caused it? Did he get out safely?

The top three floors had been offices, the lower floor a dance bar. What office had ordered the magnesium powder that she got by mistake? Not the dentist or the area aging council, not the attorney or the actuary.

Hypnotized by the blaze, she set her audio inscribers to flag any crucial bits.

"So much for dancing the night away at the Parrot, mate."

"Think everyone got out?"

"You recording this, Lucy? You could sell the video."

"News vans're pulling up. Took 'em long enough. Look, Missy Zee is gonna cover this. That's my sheila."

One flag: "Arson, definitely. Magnesium," the same fireman said again. She was talking to Draye, and there was another AISE with them, someone Ninn didn't recognize. "But it needed an accelerant. Magnesium all by its lonesome wouldn't't've done that. Gas or diesel likely as a fuel line, set on the top floor and worked down so the arsonist could escape, the rain helping it spread like crazy. The setter was savvy."

Arson. But why? Talon wouldn't have burned her building. *He got out,* she told herself. He was probably somewhere in this crowd, gawking like everyone else. She'd find him later.

"Backdraft," Mordred said. *"1991, staring Kurt Russell, Robert DeNiro, and Jennifer Jason Leigh, directed by Ron Howard."*

Ninn couldn't take her eyes off the flames. The crackling of it became white noise.

"Blaze, 1989. Paul Newman again. Vid has nothing to do with fires."

She kept listening to the people around her, but made sure the inscriber was keying in on the fireman's chatter to AISE.

"Best club in the block," a thin dwarf lamented. "The Parrot served the awesomest mojitos."

"You'd tink nothin' could burn in da rain." This from a troll in jeans and a strapless bustier. He tugged on his nose ring. "Must be magic fire."

Another flag: "Had to be magnesium. Seen it burn like this before."

That voice was ugly and familiar, and Ninn looked for that speaker, seeing Lt. Jacob Waller talking to a security guard-type, maybe a bouncer. The patch on the guard's shirt had a galah embroidered on it. He was from her building. Ninn focused her audio inscriber on that conversation and moved so she wasn't in the direct line of sight of either Waller or Draye. How many AISE officers were in the growing crowd?

A light flared behind her, and she turned to see a news station's spot, hooded for the rain, aimed at Missy Zee. That wouldn't be worth recording, Ninn decided; she detested listening to that particular insipid anchor.

Another flag: "Yeah, I've seen magnesium fires before," Waller said. "But it's been a few years."

"It started up top," the security guard said. "A dentist came running into the club, hollering, said it started on his floor. Then the detectors in the club went off, and I turned off the music and shooed 'em all out and called it in. Lots o' people were calling it in. Trucks got here fast, but not fast enough. The fire ate the building from the top on down. Floor to floor, flames like a bloody waterfall."

"Only two places in Sydney sell magnesium. We'll see who's been buying, track the deliveries," Draye said. He'd joined Waller.

Delivery. One box of Malden's Finest Magnesium Powder delivered to her office. AISE could track that delivery to her. Talon had even forged her signature to sign for it. Wonderful. She'd been set up, and AISE would be quick to accept the frame job, lock her away.

"Yeah, tracking magnesium shipments might help if the doer was sloppy," Draye continued. "I'll put Henepin on that, Lieutenant. And security feeds might have caught the perp."

The security guard laughed. "You'd think, right? Ain't gonna be nothing left of the video equipment. "Ain't gonna be nothing left of anything. It's gonna take the building next to it, too."

"Wala-lang," Mordred offered.

Magnesium. Ninn shuddered. Who had delivered the magnesium to her office? Who was framing her?

"Maybe a clubber caught sight of something, someone. They're always recording stuff, big into self-shots." The guard pointed a finger at various glittery-dressed women in the crowd. "Ask them if they saw somebody suspicious."

"Maybe they did. Someone leaving in a hurry," Draye said.

"Get on that." From Waller.

"Right away." Draye headed toward a gaggle of the glittery women.

"Don't know what I'm gonna do now," the guard added. "That was a good job. Music and sheilas. At least I got 'em all out, the clubbers. At least the fire didn't start in the club and kill someone. Just smoke hurtin' some folks. Nothin' more than singed lungs." He pointed to the ambulances. Three had pulled away.

"Started up top so whoever torched it could get out," Waller mused. "Double-Rs set a fire like that down by the harbor two years back, remember? Magnesium in a thunderstorm. Took down a building with a campaign headquarters in it; the Double-Rs hadn't liked the candidate."

"The Double-Rs, eh?" The security guard shook his head. "Just an old building with a dance club and dentist offices. Why the hell would the Double-Rs burn this down?"

"The Right has done this before, but I'm not liking them for this one," Waller said. "I'm thinking someone else."

Double-Rs. RighteousRight. Had they burned it down because Ninn had angered them, poking into their affairs, fighting with some of them in One Hundred & Thirty Proof? The bartender had said it would come back on her. If so, it had come back in flames.

"Think everyone got out?" a cybered-out razor guy asked. He was a bouncer from a club down the street, and now he'd moved up to take Draye's spot next to Waller. "Think anyone burned?"

Waller shrugged. "If they didn't get out, hope they didn't suffer long." He spoke into a comm: "Henepin, I'm pretty sure Tossinn had an office in this building. When I ran her financials yesterday arvo, it showed her behind in rent. Run that for me, will you?"

Great.

"Your associate did not get out, Nininiru." This came from Barega. Still caught by the fire, Ninn hadn't noticed him approach. "I dreamed in the flames, Nininiru Tossinn. In my dream I saw Talon Kassar die on your couch. He did not suffer long, but he did suffer."

"And it'll cost dearly, elf," the Double-R bartender had said.

"Not going to be anything left of the place," the cybered-out razor guy lamented to Waller. "Nothing."

"Ekkert," Mordred said. *"Nothing left."*

Wala-lang, Ninn thought. *Fragging wala-lang.*

The heat, the realization that Waller would look at her for the arson, her injuries from the Cross Slayer's blade—left arm still dead dead dead. Maybe she'd have to buy a new arm. And where the hell would she get the nuyen for that? The opals? A good cyberarm could run well more than that. She'd have to opt for used, from some back alley street doc. Dead dead dead. Talon dead—

All of it too much, she dropped to her knees and felt the shadows cast by the gawkers reach up and pull her under.

FOURTEEN
DOCTOR TARR

She sported stark white hair, gelled in short spikes and ringing a gleaming, tonsure-like bald spot. Elaborate cornrows beneath that were woven with colorful wires attached to ports on the sides of her thick neck. An aging dwarf with skin the color of just-washed coal, Ninn suspected the good doctor had Aboriginal rather than cosmetic roots—confirmed when Barega talked to the doc in his native singsong dialect.

And the "good doctor" wasn't really a doctor. Doctor Tarr was a former runner who had worked part-time at a street clinic, and parlayed that experience into hanging out her own discreet shingle in the heart of the Cross, operating out of the basement of a tea shop across from the park and the El Alamein fountain.

Ninn had met Tarr while running with Talon and his friends. They'd turned to the dwarf for various secondhand enhancements and to have bullets removed and cuts stitched up when they'd crossed paths with local gangbangers. Talon had used the doc so often he got an automatic discount.

Ninn didn't wholly trust Tarr, who'd installed recycled subdermal speakers in one of her chums. The electronics, which hadn't been properly sterilized, shorted out, and in the end resulted in a resistant staph infection and an agonizing death. Ninn had heard other assorted complaints about the street doc, and so had never actually used her services, but tonight she made an exception. Her wounds from the heater were too serious to ignore, and going elsewhere was not a viable option.

She'd mumbled the address to Barega, and somehow the old Aborigine got her here.

Ninn couldn't risk a visit to an emergency room or legal walk-in clinic since AISE considered her good for the arson fire, and by extension Talon's death—when they eventually discovered his body—plus whatever else they were going to pin on her. At least Tarr's office smelled cleaner than she'd remembered, antiseptic tinged with pine-scented cleaner. The stainless steel table she stretched out on gleamed under an outdated fluorescent light. She'd also not remembered the floor-to-ceiling shelves with real and artificial organs floating in jars of fluid, another shelf with bins labeled for various "pre-owned" cyberware, including that nose-filter she'd been coveting. She did remember the big refrigerator/freezer where the bioware was kept. It looked like the doctor had significantly expanded her clinic since Ninn had last been here.

Doctor Tarr poked and prodded, scanned the places where the Slayer had stabbed Ninn, and made a nervous *tsk-tsk*ing sound. "Deep muscle damage, some tendons cut all the way through. No wonder you can't make a fist or bend your elbow. Problem with these heat-blades, they cauterize, but they also burn. Very hot. The heat is so intense it warps the muscle. You've got some third-degree burns on the inside, not counting—"

"Can you fix it?"

"That's what I'm doing." Tarr leaned close. Nin swore there was spiced rum on the dwarf's breath. "But it will cost you. How are you going to pay for this?"

"I can pay."

"I don't let people run tabs anymore—"

"I said I'll—" Ninn swallowed the thought as whatever Tarr had used to put her under took effect.

Ninn floated, hearing whispers swirl around her like bees. She swam toward the loudest voices and concentrated, discarded high, thin, nonsensical chatter and found two people speaking in an Aboriginal dialect. It was one her encephalon could manage, and so it translated the conversation.

"I am from Djangadi," Tarr said.

"The New South Wales flatland," Barega said. "I am familiar with it. I am from Yuungai—"

"Buy the new Terracotta Arms Pup with optional silencer," a silky-voiced man interrupted. *"Lightweight, packs a punch."*

"Of the same people, you and I," Tarr said. "We share the same tongue, our tribes' grounds practically touching. Kindred, you and I, fate brought us together under the gaze of goddess Kamilaroi."

"Under the coils of the Rainbow Serpent," Barega said.

"The Pup features a blue smartlink and advanced safety. Your rounds are more likely to hit the intended target," the silky voice interjected.

"I have not seen my people in nearly thirty years," Doctor Tarr said. "My parents are not dwarfs, and they did not understand what I'd become. But in this city, it doesn't matter what I am."

"All of us become something," Barega said. "Differences unite us. It is when we embrace those unique—"

Ninn wasn't in the mood to listen to Aboriginal philosophy or the commercial of some arms dealer. She opened her eyes and took a deep breath of pine-scented, recirculated air.

According to the chrono on the wall, it was 10 p.m. She'd been out a little more than two hours. Tarr and Barega were watching a news program, a sportscaster droning about playoff soccer matches.

Mordred chattered too, she'd missed part of it, but he said something about Cadigal's Corner.

"Shush," she told him.

"Keebs, you really need to know—"

She made a motion to turn off the smartlink.

"Fine. Fine. Fine. Shushing."

Ninn eased up, swung her legs over the side of the table and sat, gripped the edge for support. She was woozy from whatever the doc had administered, her arms cold, but most of the pain gone. Her left arm was swathed in a fog-gray wrap bandage from shoulder to wrist...she *felt* the bandage; that was a good sign. Her right upper arm had a thick wound patch taped to it, another patch on her chest. She could curl the fingers of her left hand, the muscles obviously reconnected, sensations returned. She bent her left arm at the elbow, rolled her shoulder. Maybe Tarr wasn't so bad after all.

"Pleased to see that you are well, Nininiru Tossinn." Barega had been sitting cross-legged on the floor. He got up and handed Ninn a clean scrub shirt that was three sizes too big and a size too short—no doubt one of the dwarf's. She didn't see the tunic she'd worn in here. She still had the leggings, but they were in tatters. The pocket was intact, though, and it still had the opals in it. "I waited to make sure you would survive. Now I will return to the hostel for some sleep. An old man like me, I seem to tire easy these days. Late tomorrow morning I can see Adoni's body, the coroner said. I would be pleased if you accompany me."

"I've been meaning to discuss Ella...your brother...Adoni."
Ninn eased herself to the floor and tested her legs. She closed her
eyes, searching in the darkness for a way to approach this, mentally kicking herself for not going over everything when Barega
came into her office a half-dozen hours ago. But she'd been in a
bad state then, waking up after an over-indulgence coma, nervy,
not herself. She realized the itchy sensation of going too long
without a slip was gone. Must have been something really good
in whatever Tarr had dosed her with; maybe she could buy some
of it. "About your brother, Barega—"

"*Cue music,*" Mordred whispered in her head. "*Your tone is ominous, Keebs.*"

Ninn growled softly.

"Shushing again," Mordred said.

"I don't doubt that you're related, *were* related, you and
Adoni...Ella. I don't question it," Ninn continued. She did question it, but her client didn't need to know that right now. "And I
should have asked you about this right away." *But those opals got
in the way.* "Adoni...Ella...she could be your son, grandson, maybe,
but—"

"Adoni...Ella Gance...was my *older* brother, Nininiru Tossinn. I
told you before. I told you—"

"You're talking about Miss Ella Gance, right?" Doctor Tarr
clicked down the volume, turned her back on the sports announcer, and faced Ninn. "Saw her perform just last week. Amazing.
Amazing voice. Was terrible about her death. The Cross Slayer,
right? The Slayer got her. My favorite singer, the best tawdry
house in the neighborhood, and now it'll close."

Ninn and Barega looked at the dwarf.

"Cadigal Hamfyst dead, Ella Gance dead, who is there to keep
it open any more and—"

"Cadi's dead? The Slayer—" Ninn felt like someone punched
her in the stomach. Her knees were pudding and threatened to
buckle. She gripped the edge of the table harder. "That can't—"

"*I was trying to tell you about that, Keebs,*" Mordred cut in. "*But you
told me to shut up. Shut the Frag Up, 2019, low-budget horror flick.*"

"Slashed with a heater, just like the others," Tarr said. "It was
on the local, right before the soccer scores, came on right after
footage of the fire. Big old troll face splayed across the screen.
Apparently geeked while everyone was watching the buildings
burn."

"Cadigal…" Ninn was stunned. She'd seen him just a little while ago. In the hallway of his tawdry house. She'd talked to him, told him the Slayer had been in his basement, and then she went out the back exit and discovered her own building burning.

"Some lumper mouthpiece said Cadigal Hamfyst was Victim Number Six," Tarr continued.

"With Six You Get Eggroll," Mordred whispered. *"Except you're sure he'd be Number Seven.* Furious 7, 2015, Vin Diesel. Se7en, 1995, Morgan Freeman."

"Victim Eight, Mordred. Summer Peacock was seven. Cadigal—"

"Hamfyst," Tarr said. "You knew him?"

"A friend. Yeah, I knew him," Ninn said. "And a client." She reached into her pocket, pulled out four opals, and offered them to Tarr. "Will this cover all my repairs?" She hated to part with the stones, but the repair was far cheaper than a cyberarm.

Tarr's dark eyes widened. "Yeah, I s'pose that'll work."

"Gotta go," Ninn said. "Gotta—"

"Go where?" Barega looked frustrated. "To your office? It's not there any more. To Cadigal's Corner? He's not there anymore. To your flat?"

"I don't have one anymore." Ninn said. She'd been living in her office.

"The coroner said I could see my brother's body late tomorrow morning. I will go claim it. Will you come with me then? Adoni can still give us clues, even in death. I told you that before, too. We can find justice for my brother and for your troll friend. You can find yourself."

The Aborigine had not been privy to Draye's conversation with the AISE lieutenant on the street, didn't know Ninn was the suspect for the arson fire, and thereby couldn't show her face in a public place like the coroner's office until the real firebug was found…something she'd have to tackle very soon. She'd have to clear herself.

Cadigal dead.

She'd liked Cadi. Two fewer friends now…Talon and the troll. Her fault Talon was dead; she should have never allowed him in her office, should have passed him some nuyen and sent him away last night. Maybe her fault Cadi was dead, too. If she'd stopped the Slayer, if he hadn't gotten the jump on her, the troll would still be breathing.

Had the Slayer been waiting in the basement to take down another one of Cadi's girls when Ninn accidentally discovered him? Had he later come back through another tunnel? Had Cadi run afoul of him while looking at the damage from the basement fire? Had Cadi saved one of his girls, and the Slayer had killed him for that?

"Lumpers are probably still at Cadigal's Corner," Tarr said. "If you need to talk to—"

Ninn shook her head. She *did* need to go there, tell AISE about her run in with the Slayer in the basement. Her information—direct contact with the Slayer—would help their investigation. Maybe they could enhance the image she'd recorded. But if she showed up around any AISE officers, they'd lock her up for the arson, at least until she could prove her innocence. Hell, maybe she couldn't prove that she was innocent. That'd be just her luck, eh? Never have to worry about going back to Chicago.

So, she couldn't risk going back to Cadigal's basement...and she had two guns and an expensive comm unit she'd like to retrieve and that maybe could be traced back to her. A credstick in the pocket of the longcoat she'd shrugged out of. Maybe AISE would blame Cadi's basement fire on her, too, while they were at it. That'd be just her luck.

"No, I can't go there. I've some things—"

Tarr chortled, the wires hooked to her neck wriggling like worms. "Yeah, that might be risky. Saw your face on the screen too, but you looked a helluva lot better in that shot than you do now. Lumpers say you're wanted for the building blast down the street. Three buildings lost in the fire, a half-dozen dead. You didn't do it, did you? Not that it matters to me so long as you pay for—"

"No, I didn't do it." Ninn saw Barega glancing back and forth between her and the dwarf. So awesome that she'd been fingered on the news about the big fire. Barega must have watched the news too, so he knew she was wanted. "I didn't set any fire. I hate fire. I was set up, the RighteousRight I think. I irritated a couple of—"

"Ugh, the Double-Rs." Tarr made a face like she'd eaten something sour. "I hate 'em, I do. They keep dropping their hate lit in my mail slot. The New Amish are so old-fashioned they rely on paper. They give me the full-on creeps."

The sportscaster gave way to the weatherman, who was predicting a fifty percent chance of a mana storm tomorrow. There always was a fifty percent chance.

Barega's eyes were sad and weary. "I believe you, Nininiru Tossinn. I dreamed of flames, and you were not a part of that. In my dream, two men started the big fire. I will tell the lawmen what I dreamed. Perhaps I can describe the men if I dream again, but they were dark, in the shadows. My dream was dark. Sometimes dreams are like that. It will be difficult to explain, but—"

"Yeah, you going to AISE will help buckets. That and a couple nuyen will get us a spring roll to split. Guilty until proven innocent with AISE, at least in my case." Ninn caught sight of herself in a long, narrow mirror. She looked like hell. Hair singed on one side of her head like she'd slept on a barbecue grill. "AISE'll need proof I didn't do it...not proof that I did. And I'll have to worry about that later. Dreams aren't going to matter to them, Barega. Dreams aren't real."

"One is never truly awake until one dreams," Barega said.

"How about nightmares? This whole thing is a nightmare."

"My brother then," Barega persisted. "I must be about that." He headed toward the door. "Will you be with me in the morning, Nininiru Tossinn? I dreamed that you would join me with the dead."

"You don't get it." The Aborigine was clueless about society, Ninn realized. He apparently thought she could strut around out in the open with an arson claim hanging over her head. Murder, too, if six people died, Talon one of them. They'd blame her for all of that. "If I show my face, and there's any lumpers around, I'm gonna be grabbed."

"Maybe," Tarr said. "Maybe not. But it'll cost you."

A half hour later Ninn stood in front of the narrow mirror, hardly recognizing herself. The doc hadn't done any cosmetic surgery, but she'd shaved Ninn's head until it gleamed under the harsh fluorescent lights, shaved her eyebrows, fashioned big hoop earrings out of spare wire. She had added nanotattoos. Spotted green snakes arched where her eyebrows had been. A kangaroo bounced on Ninn's left cheek in shades of brown and olive. The artwork was an Aboriginal design comprised of thick lines, dots, and hash marks. As Ninn watched, the kangaroo straightened and morphed into a lizard that stretched and darkened, the tip of its tail resting on the center of her chin, the crest on its head reaching to the top of her bald crown, the claws of one leg dangled down to touch the bridge of her nose.

On her right cheek was a simple design, a black circle the size of golf ball with eight small circles ringing it—an Aboriginal sun symbol. It transformed into three wavy diagonal lines—the symbol for smoke and fire, then shifted to become a sun again. She could pass for a gogogo, or maybe a joygirl. She needed to find something different to wear to complete the facade; the scrub shirt looked like a shapeless bag. She spotted her singed and bloody tunic in the garbage can and decided to leave it there.

"People will see your tattoos. They won't really see you. Hide in plain sight, ya ken? You don't look anything like the elf whose sorry ass was dragged in here a few hours ago," Doctor Tarr pronounced. "Five thousand nuyen. It has the added benefit of monitoring your blood sugar."

It wouldn't bear up to close scrutiny with sophisticated scanners, Ninn knew. But she could avoid that kind of equipment, avoid AISE, go to the morgue with Barega, and get the nanites removed after all of this was done. The hair would grow back, or maybe she'd go for fiber optic implants like some of Cadi's girls had.

"Four thousand," Ninn countered.

"Five. Before I change my mind and make it six."

"With Six You Get Eggroll," Mordred whispered.

She reached into her leggings pocket and retrieved four opals. "Will this do?"

"Make it one more," the dwarf said.

"Fine." A thought flickered as she handed the stones over. "Adoni was SINless, Barega, no records. I got that much from AISE and Cadi. Do you have identification, anything to show you're related to him? Even an electronic image or a physical family photo might help."

The old man tugged on his beard. "Nininiru Tossinn, my word is good."

"Not good enough for the coroner." Ninn held out her hand. "My gun?"

Barega passed Mordred over.

Mordred sighed. *"Together Again, 1944–"*

"About your *brother*. You don't have ID, you have no way to prove you and Adoni are related, or that you have a legal right to claim the body."

"But, my brother. I must—"

"They're not going to buy that Adoni is your brother. Grandson...maybe. I don't know what your funeral practices are. But here's what's gonna happen." Ninn knew this from experience; from AISE and dealing with the coroner's office and working a few independent PI cases. It was also standard practice in Chicago. "The morgue attendants will strip out any potentially useful bioware, and Ella had some expensive stuff, Cadi told me about it. They'll sell all of that to cyberleggers or street docs like Tarr here. Maybe they have an arrangement with a local ghoul community, where bodies are sold as...meat." The last part came out softly. "If it goes the legal route, there are companies that come in and take remains, cremate or pulp them for fertilizer. Sometimes it all goes through a centrifuge first, siphon out any heavy metals for resale. SINless corpses are often targeted for research, partnering with DocWagon, a med corp. Recycle is the key here. Only the rich can bury someone. Cremation? Anyone can do that...if you have the right ID. But you're SINless too, right?"

Barega's mouth worked, but nothing came out.

"You have no bedside manner, Keebs," Mordred said. *"That came out pretty cold."*

Ninn was forced to agree with her gun. "Barega, I'm sorry. I'll still get to the bottom of this, Ella's...Adoni's...death. My friend Cadi's death. I found the Cross Slayer. Briefly." The tale spilled quickly about the basement, the fight, the fire, and the Slayer's escape. "He must have come back. Maybe another tunnel. Cadi must have found him, and paid for that. Hell, the Slayer almost had me." She stopped her story at the magnesium blaze that took down her building. The fires were not related. "That's how I got wounded so badly, the Slayer's heater. And I was so certain the Right was involved."

"They're not?" This from Tarr.

"The arson, yes. Killing the entertainers, no. The Righteous-Right wouldn't use someone like I fought in the basement. A metahuman, certainly, and tech, certainly. His pointed teeth looked stainless steel. The Double-Rs weren't responsible for Ella's—"

"I will see my brother's body, Nininiru Tossinn. I will make the coroner understand. I will—"

"Sorry, old man, but the elf's right," Tarr cut in. "SINless, Miss Ella Gance ain't going anywhere with you. But—" She let the sentence dangle like a biscuit in front of a starving dog. "—I can get you into the coroner's body stash tonight. Well...in what's left of tonight. I've got an arrangement with Serra and her night technicians. It'll—"

"—Cost me, yeah. I can pay," Ninn said. "For getting us into the stash." Her fingers, working fine now, reached for the opals in her pocket again. She had four left—but Barega had promised more if she was successful. She pulled out one opal and passed it to Tarr. "And for a couple of slips, a half-dozen slips...for pain... for when whatever you gave me wears off." Maybe Cadi's body would be at the morgue by now, too. She'd like to take a look at the troll.

"Make it one more," the dwarf said. "If you want the slips."

"*Easy Come, Easy Go,*" Mordred said. *"Elvis Presley, Dodie Marshall, 1967."*

"Yeah, that oughta cover it," Tarr said, holding the stones up to her cybereyes. "We better get moving. Before any organleggers—other than yours truly—get to Miss Ella Gance."

FIFTEEN
THE DEAD SING A MELODY

Passing on a shop that sold tourist attire, they instead stopped at SHINE, an all-hours glitter boutique so Ninn could replace the overlarge scrub that was drawing the wrong sort of attention. Two opals remaining, she spent one on a purple sequined halter-top, a matching pair of shorts that rode low on her hips, sandals with silver ribbon laces that twisted up to her knees, and a shimmery violet rain cape with a row of fringe on the bottom. She wore the cape askew to cover her bandaged arm. The cape had a pocket just big enough for Mordred. She thumbed a catch and the barrel folded back along the receiver, easier to conceal now. It took six seconds to open him out of his box form. She might not have six seconds, and so left him be and kept her hand on him as much as possible.

"Good thing you spent some time on the nude beach. No tan lines," Mordred said. Ninn was looking at herself in the boutique mirror, the gun seeing through her eyes. *"You look like a joygirl."*

"I do indeed," she snarled. But she also looked wholly unrecognizable. She was certain if she went nose-to-nose with Lt. Jacob Waller, he wouldn't know who she really was. Ninn had never used a disguise during her various private eye gigs—but if she got herself out of this current mess, she'd have to reconsider that. "I look—"

"Joyful?" Mordred mused.

Ninn was going to say "awful." She'd never considered herself attractive, rather plain-looking actually, in part because she never made any concerted effort on clothes, her hair, or with makeup. This get-up didn't make her look attractive either, despite the spangles and the tattoos. But she certainly was no longer plain.

And she was closing in on broke. The clerk refused to give her any change for the opal, and had to be persuaded to accept it as payment. That left her the one nested next to Mordred in her pocket. Ninn added a silvery chain belt, which was actually a necklace she'd spotted at the counter. It had glittery charms dangling evenly spaced—hearts, stars, shells, and half-moons.

"Joyful, no. Wrong word. You look unhappy, Keebs. And gaudy, gauche."

"You hide well in plain sight," Dr. Tarr pronounced when Ninn joined them on the sidewalk.

"You're paying for the ride to the morgue," Ninn told Barega. Her credsticks had burned up in her office, and she couldn't access her meager savings at a bank—not with AISE having her on their wanted list.

"Murders in the Rue Morgue, 1932, Bela Lugosi," Mordred said. *"A real classic."*

Doctor Tarr got them in through a back door off a deserted parking lot; the dwarf had a security card that let her in just like she worked there. Ninn noted no obvious monitoring equipment in the hall, and recalled she'd never noticed any on the few occasions she'd come here on AISE business. But she knew there'd be some security with the bodies—they were a valuable commodity.

A janitor was working the handheld panel of a radio-controlled floor sweeper. He gave Ninn a serious up and down and smiled slyly, and then nodded to the dwarf.

"A little late in the evening for you, ain't it, Doc? Shouldn't you be sleeping?"

"What hath night to do with sleep?" Ninn whispered.

"Quoting Milton again, Keeb?"

The janitor pointed to Ninn. "You got a CeeCee with you, Doc?"

"Corpse Cuddler," Mordred translated.

"You know the techs don't like it when someone—"

"Not your worry. She's with me, Curtis," Tarr said. The dwarf continued bantering with the janitor. Ninn thought they looked like old chums, talking about soccer scores and local politics.

"Craps game was last night," the janitor said. "Magualy made a haul. We missed you."

"Had an eye implant with some complications. Catch the game next week."

"Summer's going too fast, Doc."

"Ah, the days float by at their own pace, Curt-my-man."

"And the old man, Doc? What's his story?"

"In town visiting," Tarr said. "An old friend from a neighboring tribe. Showing him the sights."

"Ah, the joygirl's for your old mate, then."

"Something like that." Tarr played with one of the wires plugged into her neck.

"If he's sightseeing, there's better things to look at than dead bodies, Doc."

"Yeah, well, we'll be getting to that. I just had to make a stop here first."

"Not your usual night, Doc. You got an unscheduled pickup?" The janitor sent the sweeper down a side hall, its brushes making a pleasant *shush*ing sound against the tile. "Serra didn't say you were coming by. It's Victor's night for being the poddy-dodger, and he'll be by in a bit. So you better do your grabbing—"

"Haven't seen Victor for a while. He still running that clinic in Ultimo?"

The janitor shook his head. "Got a place behind a chemist's on Bathhurst. He fixed my brother up with a new leg a few weeks ago."

Ninn started tapping her foot. Tarr got the message.

"Just here for a few parts tonight, Curtis. Nothing major. Nothing Serra's gonna give a flip about. But I'm in a bit of a hurry. I want to take my mates here pub crawling on Clark." Tarr patted him lightly on the arm and strolled past, Barega and Ninn following.

"There's some sights to see on Clark, all right," the janitor said.

Ninn looked over her shoulder; the janitor idly scrubbed at a spot on the wall with his free hand and continued manipulating the sweeper controls with his thumb on the other. He didn't give them a second glance.

The "body stash," the room they headed to, had an obvious camera above the door and a secondary one across the hall from it. Ninn held back, Barega behind her. The dwarf tugged one of the wires free from her neck port and plugged it into a panel by the door, then touched a few keys on a pad.

The red lights on the cameras winked out. Tarr did the same with the cameras inside the room.

"Told you I had an arrangement. I'm a regular here."

"Obviously. And the call you made on your comm—"

"—was to get the night techs to step out for a time, look the other way so to speak. They don't need much encouragement to take an extended soykaf break. I figure we've got thirty or so minutes before they wander back. Not that they'd give me no never mind...but you and the old man? The old man would raise some eyebrows. Spent a bit too long jottering with Curtis. But he's a regular Nosey Parker, and if I hadn't talked to him, get the words out of his system, he would've followed us for some convo." The dwarf gestured. "After you."

Ninn plowed ahead, Barega so close behind her she could feel his breath.

AISE referred to this part of the morgue as Slab City. It resembled a city only in that its towers of cabinets of uneven heights cast shadows like a city skyline. They were refrigeration units, the older ones four and five drawers high. As the old ones broke down, they were replaced by new units a dozen drawers high, just shy of touching the ceiling, each drawer containing a stiff. A ladder on wheels allowed for access to the upper drawers. One bank of six had massive drawers for trolls.

Ninn recalled that the city policy was "no body rests for more than three days." Sometimes remains stayed only a few hours, but since Ella and Cadi were murder victims, they'd likely get the full seventy-two hour treatment. The corpses of vid stars and politicians sometimes got to stay longer.

"I should've come here before now." Ninn was angry with herself. She wasn't anything close to the investigator she used to be. Before she wandered into the dual realms of booze and slips and relying on her purchased enhancements to help with cases, she'd relied on her wits. In her sharper days, she would have come to the morgue as soon as Ella's body had been transported here, waited around to get a gander at the coroner's report, which would be impressively thorough and delivered quickly because of the latest equipment the department boasted. She would have checked the reports on all the Slayer's victims before traipsing around the Cross, so confident that the RighteousRight was involved.

She wouldn't have ruffled the feathers of the Right in the bar. Well...maybe she wouldn't have.

They wouldn't have put her in their crosshairs and firebombed her building. *Maybe* they wouldn't have.

Talon would still be breathing.

She'd devolved into a shoddy investigator, and her work-load lately reflected it...following spouses and exes, spying on competitors' restaurants, finding lost designer dogs, nothing of any great consequence, nothing that encouraged her to be better, and nothing that challenged her. Nothing that brought her a decent salary. Just enough work to pay for her addictions. But the Slayer case, that could change things. She reached into her pocket and pulled out the Crystal Dream slip, took it when Barega wasn't looking. Needed to save Tarr's slips; she was sure they'd be more potent.

Maybe if she could get her act together, return to her prior form, she could turn things around, maybe make a difference to someone. To herself. Maybe go back to Chicago with her head held high. Go back clean.

"This is a sad, sad place," Barega said, shaking Ninn out of her funk. He stood in front of one of the newer units, fingers touching a drawer. The holo label read: *Adoni Gance.* In smaller print she zoomed in on death date, weight, relatives/claimant: *none.* "Very sad."

Tarr shrugged. "There's worse morgues, places they keep bodies longer, refrigeration fails or is nonexistent, makes you gag at the smell. Ghouls prowl the alleys, waiting."

"There is no respect for the shells here," Barega said. "The spirits are sad. My brother sings, but no one has been here to listen to him."

Listen? Ninn thought she heard voices again. Maybe the Crystal Dream was bad.

"An old proverb of my tribe goes something like this: 'We are all visitors to this time, this place. We are just passing through. Our purpose here is to observe, to learn, to grow, to love...and then we return home.' Fits the morgue, ya ken?" Tarr rubbed her cheek. "See, I look at it this way, old mate. We're in the dead's realm here. This room belongs to them, and we're just visiting, observing, learning. We don't stick around here long enough to find out if any of 'em are singing. When they die out on the street, they're in our realm. Has a whole different feel to it, ya ken? This place to the street, it's all different. When they die, they're in our space, until they're moved here. Now we're in theirs. Like I said, half an hour."

Barega pulled open the drawer.

Ninn looked away, figured she'd give the old man a few minutes alone with the corpse. How could he possibly believe Adoni was his brother? Let him have his fantasy, he'd paid her...and had promised more.

She'd spotted a terminal with a lit screen, three files open above it. Apparently a tech hadn't signed off when he vacated the room for Tarr. Free and easy access to the coroner's—and maybe AISE's—records. She wished Talon was here; it would be effortless for him to dig through files. Easy as breathing.

"Which he isn't anymore," she said. Ninn sucked in a deep breath; the cool air was artificially scented with lilac.

Tarr and Barega talked softly in the background, and thankfully Mordred was silent. Ninn discovered she was familiar enough with the record systems; she wasn't that long removed from AISE. This wasn't going to be terribly difficult.

She found her way into their "murder books," they still called them that—reports meticulously logged about a victim, and started with the commonalities on those killed by heaters. She noted several shared traits.

The Slayer's victims—details on Cadigal Hamfyst hadn't yet been recorded, though his body was noted in drawer 112—were all killed between 11 p.m. and 2 a.m. And all in alleys.

Cause of death in all cases was a single slash to the jugular with a heated blade, with death coming almost instantly. The coroner believed the killer had at least rudimentary medical training, knowing where to strike so precisely.

Interesting...Ninn had thought there were seven victims, with Cadi being eight, but the records entered this morning by Officer Michael "Mickey" Dern showed a dozen. She accessed her encephalon, the microprocessor that helped her manage information. Dern was on the scene at Ella's death, the young lumper who'd made a reference to Billie Holiday. According to Dern's report, the first three Slayer victims were night security, and the fourth a biologist, all at the Sydney Aquarium, all killed around midnight twenty days ago. The latter seven on the AISE list were the entertainers in the Cross plus Cadi, who was no doubt collateral.

She found one of Draye's files that he'd entered a half-dozen hours ago, probably shortly before he'd been called to the Cross magnesium fire. It was separate from one of the murder books. He initially disputed Dern's belief that the aquarium deaths were related. Too far from the Cross, nothing in common with the tawdry house entertainers. Still, Draye said he would pursue this angle, as he agreed with Dern's notion that the Slayer was a sailor or dockworker, the killings committed on a night away from work, traces of seawater found at two of the Cross murders, a heater involved in all of them. Draye went on to speculate that it was a cybered-up dockworker trying to intimate the RighteousRight because he despised them; the Cross victims had all received Double-R "repent" materials, were slain in alleys where multiple ЯR tags were evident on the brickwork. Draye pegged the killer as a man because the angle and depth of the cut indicated a tall individual possessing considerable strength, likely a metahuman, probably an ork. Too, Draye pointed out that historically serial killers tended to be male, and the two most recent serial killers in Australia were orks. He'd begun to collect names of ship's complements in port during the various slayings for matches.

"He got that bit right," Ninn said. "Male, metahuman, considerable strength. I suppose an ork is possible, but it'd have to be a real big one. A man? Yeah, though I've known some awfully strong women."

It was the first two victims in the Cross that had a significant trace of seawater on their clothes, again hinting at Sydney's Darling Harbour—or maybe the Slayer was a fan of saltwater tanks and kept one in his flat. Ninn had smelled saltwater in Cadi's basement. "Or maybe he wasn't a dockworker. Maybe he works at the aquarium."

"*The Life Aquatic with Steve Zissou and Nininiru, too.*"

"So I stop looking in the Cross for a while," Ninn whispered, "and I go down by the bridge, poke around the docks, a change of scenery."

"On the Waterfront, *1954, Marlon Brando,*" Mordred said. "*Dogging the AISE Draye, eh? So he's a smart lumper.*"

"You seeing this, Mordred?" Ninn tapped the screen and dropped a hand into her pocket to touch the gun. The "screen" was a projection in the air above the surface of the desk. "These reports?"

"*Through your eyes, Keebs,*" the gun said. "*Seeing all of 'em. You want my take?*"

"Yeah."

"*That AISE Draye might be on the mark. Pretty clever for a lumper, ya ken? Looks like he's pretty thorough, too. But a dockworker? I dunno about that. I don't see a dockworker hanging out in tunnels and base-*"

ments. *I don't think that guy who tried to geek you was a common dock lug. Doesn't hit me in the this-feels-right, ya ken?"*

Great, he'd picked up one of Tarr's expressions—ya ken.

"Draye's not too shoddy. I agree. Not a dockworker, I agree. But maybe somebody who hangs around the docks. Maybe somebody who lives down there." There were plenty of squatters on and under the bridge. One of her first missing persons cases had led her to the bridge. Cadi had wanted his grandfather found, and Ninn had found the old troll—turned to steel on the bridge, victim of a mana storm.

Ninn made sure her encephalon was recording images of all the files. She skimmed a few more, pieces of each murder book, not really reading them—she didn't have time for that, but knowing she could call it up later when they were somewhere else and she had an hour or two to spare.

"Fifteen minutes," Mordred announced. *"Half of that half hour's up, ya ken?"*

Ninn restored the screen to the original files that had been displayed and joined Barega. Tarr had moved onto to another body and was picking through its organs for reusable parts.

"I wonder at humanity sometimes," Ninn mused, watching the dwarf work.

"The Inhumans, 2019, Marvel Studios, Joe Robert Cole, screenwriter."

"I think I actually saw the remake of that one," Ninn returned.

Miss Ella Gance was still beautiful under the pale yellow light that shone from recessed fixtures in the ceiling. She'd been sliced open and restitched, the autopsy long concluded. A tag listed that the body was scheduled to be picked up by SydbiTech tomorrow morning, a division of the Moon Corporation. Recycling, no doubt.

Barega's eyes were closed, his lips moving as if in conversation, but no sound came out. Ninn shut down her inscribers and took a step back, intending to open drawer 112 to see Cadi, and in that instant she heard singing:

"Love is where you find it, find it.
And if you find it, keep it, keep it.
Keep it close to your heart, where it's yours alone
'Cause if someone else finds it, they'll steal it, steal it."

It was Ella Gance, smooth and captivating, no instruments behind her, just that amazing voice, like she was crooning only for

Ninn.

"Do you hear that, Mordred?"

"Hear what?"

"Lover, won't you find me, find me?
I'm lonely, won't you keep me, keep me?
Keep me close to your heart, I'll be yours alone.
'Til another catches my eye and steals me, steals me."

In her mind's eye, Ninn watched Ella appear, naked like she was on the slab, the gash in her neck an ugly second smile. Mist billowed around her, swirling to form a gown, wrapping up her torso and concealing the cuts and staples the coroner had made.

"'Cause love is where you find it, find it.
And if you find it, keep it, keep it.
Keep it close to your heart, where it's yours alone
For when someone else finds it, they'll steal it, steal it."

Ninn watched Ella become as diaphanous as the mist, but her cloudy face loomed closer and larger, her staring eyes hot pinpricks, flaring and boring in. Ella stretched out her hands, and Ninn took them. The foggy tendrils impossibly strong, the singer pulled Ninn into the mist.

"In the mana storm, death will find you, find you.
It rains inside you, 'side you.
Your heart sings a melody, sings you'll be ever alone.
'Til another comes along and steals you, steals you.
'Til another comes and steals you away."

SIXTEEN
THE LOWER DEEP

Ninn whirled with Ella, like they were happy children at a playground, mist conveniently spreading beneath them to form a dance floor. Music started, not from instruments, but voices humming; some pitch-perfect, some off-key, the mix sounding dissonant, and reminding her of a tone poem she'd heard at an eclectic arts fair at the Sydney Opera House.

Ella seemed to have more substance now, color returning to her face, the rich dark brown flowing down her arms, stopping at Ninn's hands, which were pale in comparison. Their fingers interlaced like lovers would, and a chill scurried down Ninn's spine. The air was cold—as cold as a refrigerated corpse shelf.

She tried to blink, but found her eyes locked open. She tried to access her encephalon, and could not find it. Was this a bad reaction to one of the drugs Tarr had administered? She'd not taken any of the few measly pain slips the dwarf had given her. But this dance...it was like floating away on a double-hit of high-grade graypuppy, like when the walls in her office would pulse and breathe, and she'd embrace the sweet spot in her soul.

Shapes formed in the mist that rose up to ring them. The foggy tendrils became legs and arms, a hint of color intruding everywhere. A face emerged...Ninn recognized it from a file she'd flipped through in a murder book. Dezi Desire, Harold Naughton. He was in the ring, expression placid. She had no clue to the identity of the others; men, women, elves, young, old, some naked, with ropy, stapled patterns of Y incisions from autopsies, some clothed in fog, some wearing elaborate stage costumes. Dezi-Harold was in a long gown the color of butter, motes sparkling on it—maybe stars come to ground, maybe rhinestones. Suddenly Barega was in the circle too, the smallest of the watchers.

She and Ella continued dancing.

The accompanying music turned to conversation, nothing she could understand beyond a few scattered words that hit her like bullets coming at her from all directions:

"–Love–"

"–Song–"

"–Cross–"

"–Mother–"

"–Father–"

"–Slayer–"

"–Lost–"

"–Heartbreak–"

"–Cold–"

"–Hot–"

"–Pain–"

"–Free–"

"–Me–"

"–Free me–"

"–Freemefreemefreemefreemefree–"

Was she mad? Had she slipped into some nightmare? Had the booze and the slips and the injuries and the bioware and cyberware shorted out and nudged her mind over the edge into the lower deep? She half expected to see more people joining the misty ring—men and women in white coats who would pluck her from Ella's dizzying grasp and take her away to an insane asylum.

"Concentrate." That was Barega. "Focus. Let go of the physical world. It confuses you."

What physical world? She wasn't anywhere near the physical world. There was only the mist.

"Let go," Barega insisted. "You cling too tight to the earth, Ninn. Release your hold."

Another part of her nightmare, Barega? His words had cut through the strewn phrases, the cacophonous babble that made her yearn for the dissonant tone poem.

"Release the physical world, or you will be lost to this," Barega said, voice growing louder still, almost hurtfully loud. "Focus. Find something to focus on and dream about."

Dream.

Barega had talked about dreaming when she first met him.

Was Ninn dreaming? Was all of this a dream? Was she still unconscious in her office from the booze and slips? Was Talon still on her couch? Or had she fallen asleep in the body stash, amid the cabinets of corpses? Was that why she was refrigerator cold? Sleeping would be better than madness. She could wake up from sleeping, couldn't she?

"Focus."

Ninn stared at Ella Gance's perfect face and felt herself drifting forward, merging with Ella, turning and looking out through her eyes.

"I am...dreaming," Ninn said.

Ninn pushed open the back door of Cadigal's Corner, found an empty Toohey's bottle and stuck it in the jamb so she'd be able to get back in with time to spare for her second number of the night. There was no door handle on the alley side, and she'd accidentally locked herself out before. She trotted across the uneven bricks and sat on a crate, fumbled in her purse and pulled out a slip of graypuppy.

Oh dear God, she loved graypuppy. Take the world away for just a little while graypuppy. One thing she and Ella Gance had in common—graypuppy. She put the slip on her borrowed tongue. Ninn was hitchhiking, right? In someone else's head? Ella's? Or was she sound asleep in the body stash? A nightmare?

Dreaming, right? Dream or no, Ninn saw a man—huge, hulking, maybe a troll—interrupting her sweet graypuppy sensations. He removed the Toohey's bottle. Asshole. Now she'd have to go around to the front, tromp in through the little mezzanine to get backstage. Jerk. Ill-bred wacker. Dero. Cadigal would be furious if he caught her.

Ninn got up, closed her clutch, and talked herself out of a verbal jab at the big guy...who was coming toward her. She didn't have a weapon, not Mordred or her other guns. Dreaming, right? Sound asleep next to the city's dead? She tried to imagine Mordred in her hand, but it didn't work.

Screw this dream, she thought.

"Run!" somebody shouted.

Ninn didn't think that would be prudent—she wanted to face the pug, take him down. It was her dream, so she could do what she wanted, right? Nevertheless, she shot off toward the park and the fountain, where there'd be people and lights; the wacker would have to go his merry way. She was fast, but maybe the graypuppy had rendered her legs sluggish. Ninn couldn't match the large man's speed. Several long strides and the stranger came even with her, and then went past her, stepping to the center of the alley and flicking open a long-bladed knife that thrummed softly. He slashed the air with it, the thrumming growing louder and the knife's edge glowing pale red-orange.

A heater.

Just like the knife that the guy—the same guy, Ninn realized—had brought out in the basement of Cadi's. It was the same guy! The Cross Slayer!

"Please m-m-mate. Let's not have any trouble here." Ninn spoke the words, but they came out in Ella Gance's beautiful voice. "I'm not a woman. So if women're what you're interested in, you can look elsewhere." Ninn reached down the front of her dress—a beautiful dress, and she hated wearing them, didn't own any—and pulled out a piece of sweat-soaked foam. "See? I'm a false sheila. I'm an impersonator. Not a joygirl either."

But Ninn looked like a joygirl in her purple sequined getup. When had she changed into this beautiful dress and heels?

The big man took another step forward, and Ninn took another one back. She was sweating profusely, from nerves and the summer heat. It shouldn't be so hot this late at night. Shouldn't it be raining to cool things down? Why couldn't it rain when you needed it? Why was she backing away? She could take this man! She could flatten him like she had the RighteousRight goons in the bar.

A boxer, Ninn calculated what punches she could throw. Shouldn't have tried to run anyway. She shouldn't have let Ella's legs run. Ninn never ran away.

She drew back her right arm just as her heel caught in a crack between the bricks. She tugged her foot free of the shoe, and then kicked off the other one. Out of the corner of her eye, she saw the big man lean in.

Ninn got a good look at his face, tried to direct her encephalon to record it, but there was no link. Same man that went after her in Cadi's basement, but it had been so shadow filled she hadn't been able to pick out the details. The Cross Slayer. Draye's report pegged him a metahuman. She thought that a generous term.

Too bad she could indeed pick out the details here.

His visage was vaguely human, the head large and wide, but the eyes were too small for it—beads really. The skin was smooth and shiny black; not the black of an Aborigine, but black like pitch, like oil, like jet paint spilled and left to harden. His ears were holes, his nose flat and piggish, his mouth wide and lipless, his teeth pointed stainless steel—too many of them. He flicked his tongue against them; it was fat and rose-petal pink, looking like a bloated sausage.

His form was that of a man, but he was a monster, the stuff of nightmares and bad horror vids. Where was Mordred? Shouldn't he be making a reference to an ancient horror movie with actors so long dead their memories were dust?

Ninn felt her beautiful sequined purse slip from her sweat-slick fingers, heard the slapping of her own feet against the bricks... why was she running when she'd decided to punch him? Why did Ella's legs keep pumping? Then she heard a louder sound—the stranger's feet pounding behind her.

Ninn took in great gulps of the humid air. Shouldn't it be re-frigerator cold? Wasn't she in the morgue? Her lungs burned, and her temples throbbed like her head was going to explode. Let it explode so she could wake up! Her feet ran faster.

Slap slap slap slapslapslapslapslap

Ninn grabbed her aching side, then felt herself flying forward, her feet tangled in her long beautiful dress. There was a reason she never wore dresses! The ground rushed up to meet her, and she slammed hard into the bricks.

The Slayer bent—his throat oddly bright white against his otherwise blackest black skin—and his arm shot out, his webbed fingers closing on a slender ankle. Ninn defiantly grabbed at the cracks between the bricks and tried to pull herself toward the end of the alley—closer to the park and to the people who must be gathered there, who were always by the fountain late at night, drinking and laughing and wading in the water. Tourists and joy-girls and lumpers keeping them in line. Tourists and joygirls and lumpers, oh my.

Ninn was strong, and dragged the Slayer with her, and at last she saw faint light filtering into the end of the alley. The streetlight from the park. If she could pull him into the park, she could get some of the people there to help her. Dogpile him, beat the crap out of him, get the lumpers to haul his evil dero ass away and charge him with the string of murders. End the threat to the Cross.

Be a hero, and drown in nuyen and opals.

But the Slayer tightened his grip. *So strong. Impossibly strong.*

Ninn guessed he had some serious muscle augmentation, bone lacing, probably a top-of-the-line adrenalin booster. He leaned in closer still and ran his tongue against her cheek. The Slayer smelled strongly of saltwater and fish, like he'd just come from the harbor. A gull cried to lock that notion in her mind...no, not a gull. It was a screechy shrill cry punctuated with squawks. A parrot's screech.

A galah circled above the alley, right above Ninn, like a vulture circling a dead piece of meat. It looked electric, like the sign that had hung in the window of Pella's Rosy Parrot.

Ninn felt the bones in her left ankle break, then the bones in her right leg.

Her borrowed chest heaved as pain stabbed up from her shattered legs. The Slayer placed a heavy foot on her silk-covered stomach—no shoes, a wide bare foot. He bent over and she smelled...soy sauce? He drew his heater across her throat.

The galah circled lower and cried louder.

The heater slashed again—but this time Ninn looked out through Dezi-Harold's eyes. It was a different night and a different alley and the scents stronger...cabbage and fish and blood. Same blackest-black face.

A mask?

No, it didn't have that aspect to it; the face was real and horrible.

No wonder the Slayer stuck to the alleys and basements, tunnels, maybe the sewers. So distinctive, he'd be easy to see and apprehend. She should tell AISE what the monster looked like, how he smelled; that Draye was in part right, he'd come from the harbor, though he was no common dockworker. But she couldn't talk to AISE. Even though she looked like Ella-Dezi-Ninn-the-joygirl, someone might see through her tattooed and purple sequined disguise. She didn't want to be tossed away in a Sydney prison.

She didn't want...she was Ella again, pulled back from Harold's body by the strong, wispy fingers. The wounds were gone, the alley a memory.

Ninn was on stage, crooning. People cheered. Flowers covered the table in her dressing room.

"Lover, won't you find me, find me?
I'm lonely, won't you keep me?"

Then the scene melted and she was on a slab. ...not the one in the coroner's body stash, one somewhere else, gleaming, lights above it and around it, tubes feeding into her arms, someone working on her throat, the air smelled clean. A surgeon flashed a knife and held a small device. Must be that expensive vocal range enhancer she'd had installed.

The scene shifted, flipping like frames in an ancient movie. A different slab, different tubes. Then she was looking through glass at fish and rays, wanting to feel the ocean against her skin; Ella had loved swimming, Ninn somehow knew. Then she/Ella was floating in a vat, viscous liquid with no hint of salt. A vatjob? Ninn was practically that. Wrinkles melting, years seeming to wash away, time tamped down, skin so dark and smooth and unblemished.

More frames flipped, a different stage, smaller, still in Sydney—she heard the storm. Then a different stage; it was her first public attempt at female impersonation, beyond the quick displays at parties. More frames and Ella walked the streets, searching for herself.

Ella/Ninn regressed to her actual younger years. Sounds seeped in: traffic, sirens, birds, and the wash of the ocean against the shore, lightning, journos talking about political races fought decades past. More frames. And still more. Back and back, until Ella was only Adoni and was honestly young, not youth bought through chemicals and procedures. A child.

Adoni chattered in a sing-song language Ninn did not understand at first. But she focused, and then the words came to her, though not as a translation to English. They still sounded musical and foreign, but the meaning was understood.

"My blood filled a cup, brother," the smaller child said. It was Barega; Ninn recognized enough of the face. It was Barega as a child.

Barega and Adoni had indeed been brothers, the resemblance so close they could have passed for twins! But was that notion true or something fabricated by her swirling nightmare? She urged it to play out nonetheless.

"I barely noticed the pain." Barega-the-boy showed his arms with long fresh scars. Ninn felt the Adoni-child she resided in shiver.

"I painted with my blood, brother," the boy continued. "I painted lines and circles upon my arms and legs, and I painted symbols that came to me in a dream. And while my blood was still wet I pressed leaves against it and felt myself moving ever closer to the earth. I dropped so close and then I flew. I was walkabout, brother. I do not know how long I was gone."

"Days and days and days and days."

"I found the Rainbow Serpent, and he introduced me to my totem spirit, the galah. The Rainbow Serpent was wise and powerful, and he drove me down into the sky while he drank all of my blood and ate my flesh and then returned life to me and brought me back to this world. I learned new songs and met spirits. My heart sings a melody, brother. It sings that the world will be mine. I traveled through the hills and into the belly of the land where I rested on a bed of fire opals and listened to my heart."

Ninn felt the sun on her shoulders and the earth rough and dry against her bare legs. Her imagination couldn't be this vivid. This was indeed a dream...but it was so much more.

Adoni laughed. Ninn caught the sound of his voice, so like Ella Gance's, but not as rich or perfect as the adult version. More pure, though. "You make up stories, Barega. Father will scold you for running away. Heart sings a melody. Ha! Father will—"

"—understand." Barega's old-man face had superimposed itself over Barega-the-child. "I will tell him of the Great Ghost Storm that I swam through. I felt the anger of the Rainbow Serpent gathered in the beautiful, horrible, most magical clouds, brother. I ran with the rain."

Ninn thought she heard thunder, but the sky here was clear and blue. Ninn-Adoni stood and their shared mouth dropped open to see a galah circling slowly on an updraft.

"I am no longer a child, brother," Barega said. "I am *talmai, mekigar, wirringan—*"

"*Koradji,*" Ninn said in her own voice, eyes locked on the galah. "I believe you. *Koradji.*"

"Yes, and I can dream," Barega said. "And so can you, Nininiru Tossinn. You are *koradji,* too."

Ninn awoke to discover she was flat on her back on the tile floor of the body stash, shadowed by the extended drawer that held Ella's body. Barega kneeled next to her. Tarr leaned over her, fretting, reaching down and grabbing at her good arm.

"We need to be leaving," the dwarf said. "Half-hour's up. More than a half-hour. They called my comm, said I needed to scoot scoot scoot." She pulled Ninn to her feet, then shoulder-checked the body drawer to close it. "Don't want to be pushing my privileges. This place helps me earn a good living. I'd told the techs a half-hour was all I needed. I'm gonna have to make this up to them."

The dwarf ushered them out of the room, motioned them down the hall and paused to use her wires to restart the surveillance system.

Ninn hadn't imagined the thunder. It was storming again, and thunder gently rocked the ground. The rain was steady and straight, no wind to speak of.

"Good thing you opted for the raincoat, ya ken, Keeb?" Mordred had surfaced in her mind. *"So where'd you check out to? You really zoned out there."*

"I found a beast," she said, picturing the monstrous, inhuman face of the Cross Slayer.

"Fantastic Beasts and Where to Find Them, 2016, screenplay by J.K. Rowling."

"We part company here," Tarr said. "I've got to get some of these parts in my jars before they spoil." The dwarf hefted a duffel bag Ninn hadn't seen her bring to the morgue. "Next time you need some work done, look me up, ya ken?"

Ninn nodded and watched Tarr toddle away. She and Barega cut across the parking lot.

"*Koradji*, eh?"

"Shaman. Yes, Nininiru. The galah told me we were kindred. Your totem is the galah, too. It is why you rented an office above the Rosy Parrot. Without knowing it, you followed your totem. My galah led me to you. My galah told me you would awaken like the land awakened. My galah told me it was time."

Ninn didn't want to believe him, but after what she'd seen in morgue, she had to consider it a possibility. She'd heard voices on and off for years. Had they been spirits trying to talk to her...not drugs making her hallucinate?

"So if this is true, Barega, why did it take until now for me to—"

"Awaken?" The old Aborigine smiled slightly. "I suspect as a child you knew the secret...imaginary friends...faces on butterflies. But you lost your way as you grew. An old proverb of my people says 'Those who lose dreaming are lost.' You were lost, Nininiru Tossinn, and now you are found. But it will be a difficult path."

She raised a snake tattoo eyebrow.

"It's all that metal inside you, wires, the plastic and other bits. All of that suffocates your magical mind, your essence. I will teach you how to let your essence breathe."

"Guess that means no nose filter, ya ken?" Mordred cut in.

Ninn shuddered. Indeed she'd had imaginary friends as a child. And she'd heard voices, more often since coming to Australia, figured it was just the alcohol and slips, had never considered it might be something else.

"I saw things," she said. "When we were in the morgue. I saw your sister...brother...Adoni...Ella."

"I saw them, too. We dreamed together."

"I saw a monster."

"Through my brother's eyes you saw a monster. Adoni's slayer. It is a very bad man we hunt, Nininiru Tossinn."

"Ninn," she corrected. "Call me Ninn, remember? Yeah, a very bad man."

SEVENTEEN
BASSET HOUNDS AND OTHER STRANGERS

The raincoat worked, at least keeping part of Ninn dry. Her head and neck were soaked, though, and her feet kept slipping in the high-fashion sandals, threatening blisters.

"Go catch some sleep. I'm going to the harbor, Barega. I want to poke around the docks. See what I can find. There was saltwater—"

"I am an old man, Nininiru." Barega lagged slightly behind as they cut across the parking lot toward the street, the rain coming down steady like a sheet. His clothes were plastered to him, looking like a second skin. "I am tired, and need to catch that sleep. My legs are trees so heavy. They grow roots and do not want me to move. My feet hurt. I believe all old men's feet hurt. A few hours of sleep, then we will go to this place. My feet will be ready again."

There was a faint siren, then a second, blocks and blocks away. Always, Ninn could hear sirens if she listened for them. A city so big, someone always needed saving or catching. It was a police siren; she could tell the difference between the lumpers and the firemen.

"*You* rest, Barega. I'm going now." She'd lost too many hours to her drug and booze stupor, and needed to make up for that. Ninn worked better alone, anyway. The sensation of rain against her bald head wasn't unpleasant, no sodden hair clinging to her neck and shoulders. Maybe she'd keep it shaved. But she'd ditch the nanite tattoos if...when...she cleared herself of the fire. "You can drop off for a few hours—"

"And so can you, rest. Dreams can be exhausting."

Music blared from a Nissan Coda that glided past, a summer jingle. It was a food van of some sort, the sign on its side briefly illuminated by a flash of pink lightning: *SoyPro Frozen Treats*. Odd for it to be out so late, and during a mana rain. Maybe it was an AISE surveillance unit; food trucks worked great for that, blend into the neighborhood. Folks only got suspicious if they didn't have anything to sell.

"Me? Tired?" Ninn shook her head. But she was indeed fatigued, like she'd run a marathon. Maybe just a few hours wouldn't be such a bad idea after all. Maybe that would give her enough of an edge so she could think clearly, do a better job. Yes, she worked better alone...or thought she did. But maybe she shouldn't leave this old man who'd messed with her mind with all this dreaming and galahs and dancing with a dead singer. He had opened her up to a new world and new abilities—which she didn't yet know if she would embrace. Maybe she should be grateful to him. A Milton quote tickled through her head: "Gratitude bestows reverence, allowing us to encounter everyday epiphanies, those transcendent moments of awe that change forever how we experience life and the world."

The morgue and the spirits had definitely been an epiphany.

"We are in this, *koradji*. The galahs brought us together for a reason. To find you and to find this. My hotel room is in the Cross, and that is too many blocks away for my sorry feet." There was a glass and steel boxy building with YMCA flashing in yellow-orange lights. Through the rain, it looked like an impressionist's cubist painting. Overhead, pink lightning flickered in the clouds to add to the effect. The weatherman had been correct with his fifty percent forecast.

Ninn didn't mind the rain; you couldn't mind the rain and live under the mana cloud. But she didn't like the pink lightning.

"The Y looks high-end, but it's actually a cheap flop, Barega. And it smells bad, sweat and air freshener. If I gotta spend this opal, it's gonna be on better accommodations."

"I was not pointing to that building." Barega gestured again.

There was a vacant building next to the Y, a furniture store that had a GOING OUT OF BUSINESS sign stretched across the front window, maybe the oldest building in this part of the city. It looked beaten down and out of place. But it would have fit in the Cross.

It took Ninn only a few heartbeats to pick the lock on the side door. It didn't seem to have any security, as if the owner was saying: "I'm retiring, and if you won't buy my furniture, come and take it."

The offerings inside were pretty picked over—a half-dozen couches remained, scattered rocking chairs, a few end tables, mostly it was empty places where furniture had been. The place hadn't sold all its mattresses, though; there were several at the very back, which suited Ninn just fine. Nice and dark, not a bad place to nap.

"The spirits of the dead are not easy to conjure, Ninn. They taxed you...I can see that on your face."

"In the space between the tattoos?" She laughed.

"Clearly you have great potential. You saw many dead in the morgue. You shared my brother's lingering essence."

Ninn snorted. "There were plenty of spirits in the morgue. Too many. The trick was how not to talk to them. Guess there is no heaven...no place for them to go after the bucket's kicked. Guess they stick around in a misty limbo—"

"In time you will understand that some spirits are tied to something...my brother's spirit was tied to his perfect body."

"That he'd spent so much time and nuyen to gain," Ninn said.

Even cocooned by the building, they heard the sharp *crack* of lightning, followed by a rocking *boom* of thunder.

"His spirit was not ready to leave that perfect body. Other spirits there...they were also tied to something, but perhaps we can help some of them move on by bringing their killer to justice. Perhaps stopping the Cross Slayer will let them find peace. I pray that is the case with Adoni. The spirits of the earth—"

"Earth. Are there other spirits? Beyond dead people?"

"The Dead, *2010, zombie flick set in Africa,*" Mordred cut in.

"Many. Spirits in the earth and the rain, in fire. Spirits are everywhere, Ninn. In the bricks of this old building. In the wood of this old floor. Sometimes they want to be called; sometimes they want no part of us and this world. Sometimes they are helpful, imparting information, performing tasks. Sometimes they bind to you. Sometimes...ah, this mattress is wonderful. Most of the time they are benign. Most of the—"

Ninn took off the raincoat and stretched out on a mattress three away from Barega; she wanted some space. The old man was sound asleep, his last words a mumble about this being the softest thing he'd ever lay down on. Then he was snoring. She set Mordred next to her, needing the weapon within reach. Ninn yawned; maybe a quick nap would do her good—if she could sleep without thinking about Talon's crispy body and the slashed entertainers in the coroner's file cabinets. She would have liked to take a look at Cadi's body.

Of course, as she tried to drift off, Mordred started chatting.

"What do you smell, Keebs?"

"Furniture polish." She stared up at the light fixtures, domed things with metal rims and knobs in the center; they looked like breasts. "And something musty, dusty. This place has got some age to it."

"Think you need to do better than that. Still angling for that nose filter? Or are you gonna listen to the Koori and lay off the body additions?"

She shrugged.

"So, is he right? You a booga-booga? You going all shaman on me? Shaman, *1996, original title* Chamane, *starring Spartak Fedotov, Igor Gotsman, and Igor Gotsmanov. It had a budget of–"*

She turned off the smartlink and *felt* her surroundings. It was an old, old building with a painted tin ceiling. The tin panels were probably worth a good deal and would be sold when the rest of the furniture was moved out—probably worth more than the furniture or the building proper. The floor would likely be snapped up, too, a dark walnut that dipped in places from the decades; it could be restored. The building would be gutted for its antique treasures before some developer came in and modernized everything. Cookie-cutter condos, maybe. This'd be a good spot for middle-income accommodations; people who could afford high-end stuff wouldn't live next to the Y. Most of the buildings in this block had been reworked to modern tastes and to meet rigorous building codes. They looked shiny, just like the Y next door.

She liked the Cross better. It was outdated, yeah, but it was real and earthy. Unfortunately it would have a couple of brand new shiny buildings soon, courtesy of that magnesium fire.

Ninn listened to the *shush* of traffic out on the street, muted by the building, a faint siren hinting at an emergency somewhere, a whisper of creaks...was this old furniture store groaning with its years? Or was something trying to talk to her?

Focus, Barega had told her, so that's what she did, shutting down her audial receptors and listening with her own ears. Definitely a whisper, with a pattern to it that suggested conversation.

Focus.

The whispery sound grew more distinct and she imagined pulling it to her. Ninn's fingers worked like she knitted something in midair, dreamed she was fashioning a big spider web to catch whatever was making the persistent sound.

Dream, right? Barega told her to dream.

She felt a tug on her mind, a fisherman having caught something. Now it was just a matter of reeling it in.

She sat up, swung her legs over the side of the mattress, and put off the idea of a nap. She peered into the shadows. Only faint light crept in through the windows far to the front of the showroom. Flashes of pale pink from the worrisome mana lightning intruded. But way back here it was all a collection of blacks and grays.

Whisperwhisperwhisper...

"Where are you? What are you?" Whatever she'd snared in her imaginary web didn't feel like the dead spirits she'd danced with in the city morgue. "Who—"

The thing that materialized at her feet looked as if it had been pieced together from broken furniture. It had four legs like a dog, though none matched the others and so it was crooked, even with its straight wooden legs; likely from footstools, the right front one having a claw and ball foot with an embedded roller.

The body that rested on those was a small bolster corduroy pillow with stuffing spilling out along a seam. The neck was a woodworking tool, a curved gouge lightly rusted, and atop it sat an inverted kantharos vase, the handles resembling a basset hound's droopy ears. As she watched, a tail sprouted, a long whippy thing composed of nails, staples, nuts, and bolts. The collar that appeared around its neck was an antique light cord, tied in a bow, with the plug dangling down.

The creature growled softly and wagged its tail.

"What the hell?" Ninn said.

"Fetch?" asked the creature. "Fetch fetch fetch fetch fetch." Its tail wagged faster.

"What?"

"I'm a good dog. Good dog. Good dog. Gooddoggooddog-gooddogfetchfetchfetch."

"Uh..."

"Benzo," the collection of parts said. "I'm Benzo, a good dog good dog good doggie doggie dog. Throw the ball."

"Uh..."

"B-E-N-Z-O. B-E-N-Z-O. B-E-N-Z-O, and Benzo is my name, oh!"

"Benzo."

"Want to play? Want to play fetch? Throw the ball. Throw the ball. Throw the ball ball ball ball." The tail wagged so fast a couple of nails flew off into the darkness.

"I don't want to play."

The tail drooped.

"Maybe later."

It gave a low wag.

"Talk to me, Benzo." Ninn was at the same time amazed and guarded of the thing. What had she done? Had she created this? She'd been trying to pull the whispers to her. Why the hell was she practicing with her newfound booga booga when Barega was sleeping?

"Fetch. Want to play fetch? I can teach you."

"Persistent, aren't you—" This was indeed a spirit, right? Again she wondered why she was playing with this stuff without the Aborigine. What if she'd called up the essence of angry broken furniture? Or the sense of conciliation...something that had fed on the negotiations that had taken place in this store, and was now ravenously starving? A dog? Really?

Something else popped up behind Benzo, a mound of leather swatches with chair posts poking out of it. "Moooooo," it said, and then revealed that in life it had been a cow, the skin of which had been stretched across an easy chair.

Next to it was a swirl of dust that looked like a miniature tornado. Focus!

"Benzo. Just Benzo. Please! Only Benzo!"

"B-E-N-Z-O. And Benzo is my name, Oh!"

The mound of skins and the swirl of dust vanished. There was something else moving, another spirit...she could sense that...but it hung back where the shadows were thickest. And she didn't like the feel of it.

Benzo panted and continued wagging its tail. "I'm a good dog."

"Yes, I understand that," Ninn said. "You're a dog."

"I was a dog. A good doggie doggie dog."

"In a furniture store?"

"I lived here," Benzo said. "One dozen years I lived here. Good years. Two short of the 'years that nature permits,' according to Kipling. My friend Bernie had said that, 'two years short of what Kipling said I should have.' Bernie said I was cheated."

"Uh, Benzo—"

"Good dog good dog good good doggie. On a thick thick pillow in the back room. Good pillow. Good dog."

Ninn looked over to Barega; the old man still slept.

"What do you know, Benzo?"

"How to play fetch."

"Other than that."

For the next many minutes, Ninn listened to the spirit talk about the store and customers, the regulars who knew to scratch behind Benzo's ears, the cleaning crew that sometimes brought biscuits, the owner, Bernie, who died recently, and his son who had instigated the going out of business sale, pieces of furniture with big comfy cushions that Benzo would lay on at night when no one was looking. About the strolls along the sidewalk, the occasional trip to the vet and the groomer, about how marvelous and soft tennis balls felt against his tongue.

The thing in the thickest shadows inched closer. It was built of coat hangers and twisted pieces of plastic. An old smoking pipe hung from it.

"Do you know what that is, Benzo?"

"That's the bad thing."

Ninn pressed.

"It was here before Bernie. Slithered in before the first storm came." Benzo spun around, a ridge of corduroy rising on his back. He growled at it. "Slithered in years and years and years past, more years past than nature permits. Hasn't come out in a while, though. Hoped it was gone. Hoped it had slithered back out."

But Ninn had summoned it. Hadn't she?

"What is it?" she tried again.

"A piece of shadow," Barega answered. "A piece of darkness from some foul one's soul. Perhaps a collection of darkness given form."

She hadn't noticed that the Aborigine had stopped snoring. He was propped up on his elbows, and he started to chant, sing-song words that raised the hairs on her arms. The swirl of darkness and coat hangers retreated. After a moment, Barega lay back down.

"Be careful what you coax, Ninn." He started snoring again.

"Fetch?" Benzo asked.

"Later," Ninn said. She curled back up on the mattress and set her fingers on Mordred's grip. She turned on the smartlink and closed her eyes.

She felt the dog spirit jump up, turn around twice, and lay down at her feet.

Ninn took one of the pain slips Dr. Tarr had given her. It was potent and set her to sleep before she knew it.

When she woke a few hours later, the dog spirit was gone.

EIGHTEEN
SOMETHING IN THE WATER

The Sydney Harbour Bridge used to be called "The Coat Hanger" because of its shape. It used to be an engineering marvel; stunning, iconic. Featured on postcards, travel sites, and posters, it dared tourists to climb its span, and encouraged lovers to make promises beneath it.

It used to be shiny.

Six million rivets, seventeen thousand cubic meters of granite blocks, nearly fifty-three thousand tons of steel, it took fourteen hundred men eight years to build.

When the storm came eighty years ago, it took away the shine.

Now it was called "The Eyesore."

Ninn had attended a funeral service here eight months ago. Cadigal's grandfather had died on the bridge, struck by a bolt of pink lightning and fused forever to the railing. The old troll had bought an arsenal of guns, and mowed down dozens of squatters. More squatters had come to take their place. Cadigal used to drop off flowers every few weeks, bringing Hurdy Gertie with him to help fend off the rabble.

That's what the bridge had become since the cloud arrived— a palace for squatters. Humans and metahumans, most of them formed into clans or gangs that guarded their sections of the span, all of which was taken over in the early years of the storm when the lightning had gouged out chunks of the bed big enough for a semi to fall through...which had happened. The city was too slow to effect repairs, and so the homeless grabbed it. The politicians, rather than challenge the squatters, built a tunnel under a section of the harbor. Travel through the tunnel was safer on magically rainy days.

Hovels, looking like big insect nests, hung from some of the bridge supports.

Barega marveled at the collection of makeshift homes and people. It was a reasonable day to marvel at them; the cloud was so thin the sun filtered down bright, making the water beneath the bridge sparkle like big flecks of gold glitter had been tossed onto it.

"Amazing," Barega said. Ninn was unsure whether he meant the mismatched gaggle of people—some of who stank despite the rains—or what was left of the bridge. He waved his arm and turned, almost childlike. "Truly amazing."

Ninn just shook her head and asked questions:

"Seen a big man, black like oil, freaky face, favors a heater?"

"No, but I can sell you a heater," was the most interesting answer. If Ninn had had the nuyen, she would have taken the cybered ork up on that. She wasn't about to part with her last pearl for the blade, though. And she still had Mordred.

"Hear about the Cross Slayer?" she asked as they worked their way through the clans. She held the gun at her side, raising it when some of the toughs offered to answer questions in exchange for some "up close and personal time," clearly believing her joygirl disguise. She kept her back to the railing as she went, expecting trouble and pleasantly surprised when there was none. Maybe good weather made for good behavior. But she had noted two lumper foot patrols near the bridge ramp, and that might have helped. "The man killing singers down by Darlinghurst, heard anything? Anything at all?"

"Sure. Some Christian tusker, wot? Going all biblical, going after men who look like sheilas."

"No, that ain't it. Slayer's a RighteousRight. Putting the notright people out of their misery." This from an elf with an obvious cyberleg. "Doing a little cleansin', is all. Hate the Double-Rs, I hate 'em. But I don't mind the Cross getting cleansed. They're a buncha privileged throwbacks."

"On the news again last night." This from a human with bright green hair. "I saw the feed in the bar. Gacked a big troll, right? Gotta be nasty to gack a troll. Good thing he's staying in the Cross, the Slayer. The Cross can keep the wacker."

"Yeah, he's in the Cross now. He's stayin' in Kings Bloody Cross now." This from an elderly woman who drew out the now so long she had to take a gasping breath. "Started not far from our bridge, he did. Killed some folks not far from here one night. Three or four of 'em dead, slit, given a second grin. But that was some weeks back. Put more lumpers around here, so he had to go to the Cross to keep doing his killing. Heard they ain't got lumpers in Kings bloody Cross."

Ninn pressed the old woman for more about the first victims, but got nothing else. Just as well, it was past noon now, her stomach was rumbling, and the Sydney Aquarium was way past open. Time to act like a tourist—in joygirl garb—and take a look around at the fishes.

"Under the bridge," Barega suggested. "There are more people there."

"There's always people under the bridge," Ninn said. "We should be on our—"

The Aborigine gestured down the bank. "There are more people there."

"The aquarium closes at seven, doesn't sell any tickets after six."

"So we have time."

"Great." She was being thorough, might as well talk to the squatters down there. She was also jittery...been how many hours since she'd popped a slip? She had four, supposedly of the pain killer variety in her pocket, but they were different than the one she took last night. Their color hinted strongly that they were jazz...good for giving her an energy boost, but the side effects included paranoia and disorientation. Couldn't risk it right now.

"Keebs, I bet the AISE reports are filled with stuff from the bridge folk. You got some of that in your encephalon, right? Why not just go through that? Might save you some time."

Mordred had a good point, but she'd learned from working with Lone Star in Chicago that nothing beat going after the scuttle firsthand. Besides, the aquarium was nearby, and she was going there anyway. She'd dig through those files she copied out of the coroner's computer later.

She started down the embankment, taking it slow for fear the old Aborigine would struggle with the grade and break something. The wooden dog capered and pranced around her feet.

Ninn stopped halfway down. "Barega?"

"Yes?" He didn't look up as he answered, gaze intent on the ground in front of him.

"You can still see the dog, right?" She noticed it had lifted a stiff leg against a tall weed, as if peeing on it. Nothing came out.

"Dog *spirit*. Yes."

"I see the dog." This from Mordred. He'd been oddly silent on their walk to the harbor, no wry observations or movie references. He'd been so quiet Ninn had forgotten the smartlink was even open. She wondered if maybe she was too quick to disconnect the link when he chattered; too easy to close that door. She'd try not to do that so fast anymore. *"That's really an ugly dog, Keebs, ya ken? If I had a dog as ugly as that, I'd shave its—"*

"You can really see the dog, Mordred?" It "marked" another weed.

"Yes."

"Interesting."

The collection of furniture pieces stared up at Ninn, and a tongue lolled out from under the lip of the vase, a strip of rosy brocade fabric that maybe had been a man's tie. Its tail wagged, and the tongue retracted.

"Fetch?"

"Wonder why it's still following me."

"Because you have not dismissed it."

"Dismissed it?"

The Aborigine's eyes narrowed, a teacher about to scold a student.

"I didn't have to dismiss the spirits in the morgue, Barega. They didn't follow me. Benzo is following me." But she looked around, just to be sure, no misty suggestions of people from the corpse cabinets hovered. Benzo...God, now she was calling the collection of furniture parts by a name. It had disappeared for a while back at the furniture store.

"Those spirits were tied to something, I told you." He pointed at Benzo. "This spirit apparently had no such ties."

"But it was in the store."

"It had to be somewhere, didn't it, Ninn? And now it is with you. It has tied itself to you."

"Congratulations, Keebs. Bet you always wanted a pet."

Ninn gazed out over the harbor. There were boats lashed together—if you could call them that, a collection of floating hovels that the living detritus not accepted by or fitting in with the clans on the bridge called home. Had the Cross Slayer come from there? He hadn't come from the bridge...according to those she'd chatted with.

She continued picking her way down the bank. There was a

sandy stretch of ground at the bottom, bridge pilings rising from it, and more squatters had staked out parcels. *It'd be relatively safe from the rain,* she thought. Barega and Benzo followed her.

"So, you can teach me how to get rid of the dog?"

"Certainly, Ninn. All you have to—"

"I meant teach me later. Still got some digging to do before we can take a break for booga-booga." *And maybe for a piece of jazz.*

There were a few dozen people under the bridge, most of them even more talkative than the ones up top. And the last one they talked to, a woman sitting apart from the others, was actually helpful.

"The cats are coming back." She was a motherly-looking woman sitting on a cushion that had been ripped from a Hyundai Shin-Hyung sedan, and she cradled a big calico in her lap. She introduced herself as Stinky Stella, and wiped her nose on her grimy sleeve, and then petted Benzo. "They were gone for a few weeks, the cats, when the killing started."

Stinky Stella? Talon had mentioned sharing a box under the bridge with the woman. Small, smelly world. Ninn knelt next to her, and was instantly glad she didn't have the nose implant. The woman reeked. Bile rose in Ninn's throat. No wonder the other squatters gave her a wide berth.

"The cats were afraid, and that made me afraid, too," Stella said. "Normally the cats are only afraid of the rain...sometimes the rain. Normally I'm not afraid of anything."

"The lightning..." Ninn mused.

"Yeah, the cats don't like the lightning, especially when it's got a color. It's the lightning what really gives 'em the willies. That's when they cluster under the bridge. Except right around the first killings. The cats disappeared for a while."

"So, the killings—"

"Got something for me to eat?"

Ninn shook her head. "I'm sorry."

"I usually don't talk to folks, lumpers especially, unless they give me something to eat."

"I'm not a lumper."

"Really?" Stella smiled, showing she was missing several teeth, and the ones remaining were various shades of brown. "So, you're a hooker. Wait, got the word wrong. Don't mean to offend you none. A joygirl. I ain't got any nuyen to buy any of your joy."

"I'm not selling. I'm not a joygirl."

"Undercover lumper? No, you're not that, either. The elf lumper what was here earlier brought me something to eat." She proceeded to describe Draye and that he'd given her a bag of doughnuts. Ninn had a growing appreciation for the AISE; he did quite a bit of investigating, and wasn't a drekhead about it like many other cops might be. "The elf lumper wanted to know if I'd heard anything around here...people screaming, getting knifed. The elf lumper gave me food."

"Listen, Stella, I—"

"Kind woman." Barega moved up and squatted in front of her, apparently unfazed by the stench. "Stella, this man we ask about killed my brother."

"Sorry." Her face softened. "He killed cats first. Ate 'em, I think. I told the elf lumper I thought someone was down here killing cats. Lumper didn't seem interested in that. But the guy, he left the heads. Then he killed some folks by the aquarium one night. I know that 'cause I talk to the go go gos up top once in a while. They was nervous, too, about the guy. Afraid the guy would come and kill 'em. Maybe the guy did kill some of 'em. Nobody misses the bridge people. Nobody cares if a few bridgers get gacked. Don't matter to them none. The guy...they're calling the Cross Slayer now, all fancy the name, like Jack the Ripper...the guy moved on. See, the lumpers came 'round the harbor, and so the guy went away. Went where the lumpers weren't, I 'spect. Hope the guy's still killing people rather than killing cats. I like cats."

"Probably likes cats better than just about anything," Mordred cut in.

"Bloody oath, I do!" Stella continued, "I figure either the guy doesn't like lumpers or he's afraid of being caught, so he's hiding. Can't think of much he'd be afraid of though, from the looks of him."

Ninn's eyes widened. "You saw him?"

"Sure. Sure. Up close, almost personal. I forgot to tell the elf lumper that. But then, that elf lumper didn't ask directly. He just asked what I *knew*, what I'd *heard*. He didn't ask what I'd *seen*. 'Sides, I was busy eating the doughnuts. Realized I should have told him, but he was gone up the hill by the time I'd thought it. You tell him for me, will you?"

"Sure. Sure." But Ninn had no intention of doing that. "What did he look like?"

"The elf lumper? Already told you."

"No. The killer."

"Well, I think he's the killer."

"What did he look like?"

Stella's eyes twinkled. "He was big, but not a troll. I like trolls, used to have a best friend troll before the lightning took him. Troll brought me Chinese takeout and pressies once in a while. The big guy was a black man. Not black like you." She jabbed a crooked finger at Barega. "Not black like a dark-skinned man."

"Black like oil," Ninn said.

"Yeah. Black like that. Black like the harbor gets under the bridge at night when the cloud is thick and the lights go out. Black like that. Black like forever."

"Yeah, that's him." The woman's description matched what Ninn had seen in Cadi's basement, but in more detail.

"And he wasn't friendly, the guy. Didn't have much to say."

"You talked to him? A conversation?"

"Probably should have told the lumper that." She nodded, strands of gray-brown hair spilled out from under a stained baseball hat. "He was wading...right out there, like maybe he was looking for something in the water, little treasures. It was dark, and he had a light in one hand, shining it down and around. Sometimes people drop things off the bridge, little treasures. Pieces of jewelry, guns, soup bowls. Found me a little treasure just yesterday, I did. Something in the water that I think is worth a bit."

She reached behind her and brought out a pair of gloves hooked together with a rusty clip. Ninn recognized what they were; expensive, top of the line unarmed combat hardliners with a layer of densiplast set into the knuckles. "Don't know if he found any treasures, though. He had a cat in his other hand, hanging all limp. I knew it was dead. I asked him not to kill me."

Ninn waited for her to go on. A seagull cried, swooped low over the water and grabbed a tiny fish, flew up where another seagull tried to steal it.

"He said he had a kill list. Said I wasn't on his list, so he wasn't gonna kill me. And then he went away. I found the cat's head the next morning. Cats was probably on his list. Never saw the guy after that. But then, the lumpers started patrolling here the next night. They still patrol. Good thing, eh? But not many of 'em are around here now. Quite a bit more than a few lumpers early early, though."

"List? He told you he had a kill list?"

"Yeah."

"He said you weren't on his list."

"Yeah. Whatever that meant. I was glad I wasn't on it. I still got me some years left. I don't need to be on nobody's list. I didn't think to tell the elf lumper about the list."

"Thanks, Stella." Ninn glanced up, seeing a dwarf peering over the edge of the bridge, telescope fixed to his face. "C'mon Barega." She started up the hill.

"Sorry about your brother," Stella called. "And next time you come with questions, bring me something to eat, or some pressies all wrapped up pretty."

Ninn was tempted to ditch the raincoat—the day was that warm and rain looked blessedly out of the equation. But then she'd have no place to put Mordred, and she wasn't about to pass the gun back to Barega, and there was thse one remaining opal in the raincoat. Frag, but she should have bought a glittery outfit that had pockets. What was she thinking? She hadn't been thinking all that hard, had she? Just needed something to wear that fit the tattoos, her need to hide in plain sight and look one-eighty different than she usually did. The raincoat hung loose and when they passed by a big window, she saw her shimmering purple reflection. Benzo didn't appear in it, but he was at her heels.

"Hooker. Meh."

"*Happy Hooker, 1975, Lynn Redgrave. First of three films—*"

She didn't turn off the smartlink, she just thrust his running commentary to the back of her mind, and in so doing realized she hadn't used her encephalon to record any of the conversations on the bridge, hadn't used her cybereye to capture any images. Ninn laughed at going old old old school.

"*You are happy!*" Mordred hadn't realized what she was laughing about. "*Happy Hooker Goes Hollywood, 1980, Adam Batman West.*"

The gun talked about the screenplay writer, and again she let the words dissolve in her mind.

She didn't get as much nuyen for the opal as she'd have liked, and the broker made a jab at her: "Wot? Some sot gave you this for keeping 'im company last night, doin' the naughty?" But it was enough to buy her and Barega admission to the Sydney Aquarium, with two hundred left over on a credstick.

"It's probably the biggest one in the world," she told Barega. Remembering she had local facts stored on her encephalon, Ninn called up the aquarium. "The darling of Darling Harbour. A thousand different species, eighteen thousand creatures in ten million liters of water. Two dozen sections...swamps to rivers to—"

She noticed Barega was staring at the Sydney Opera House in the distance. Scaffolding on one side, drones buzzing around, probably doing repairs from the storm.

"I wonder if Adoni could have performed there? Adoni had a perfect voice."

Ninn realized the Aborigine wasn't really talking to her. She paid the admission, and they went inside, Benzo heeling. With the pollution from the city blocked, it smelled good; a tinge of saltwater, a little perfume from some of the visitors.

They walked through the Platypus, Rivers, and Billabongs exhibit and were coming to the Bay of Rays when she spotted Draye and two other AISE officers talking to someone who looked like she was in charge. Edging closer, Ninn kicked on her inscriber and recorded while Barega pressed his face against a tank of barramundi—sea bass.

"We are all visitors to this time, this place," Barega said. "We are just passing through. Our purpose here is to observe, to learn, to grow, to love...and then we return home."

"Nice," Ninn said. "Dr. Tarr said that very thing."

"It's an old quote." Mordred intruded. *"One that's hung around this country for well more than a century, Keebs. It's an Aboriginal saying. Thought you would've memorized that in school."*

"Chicago," she said.

"Yeah, we should go there, Keebs. Easy to get me through customs. Your new pet might be a problem, though."

She drifted closer to the AISE officers, one of who mentioned a "suspect in custody." Draye met her gaze and motioned her away. "AISE business, *girl*. Move on."

"The joygirl bit's effective," Mordred said. *"He didn't recognize you."*

No, he hadn't. And she'd been only an arm's length away. Ninn was pleased with the sparkly duds and nanite tattoos. She would indeed rely on disguises in the future. She turned a corner by the sea bass tank and pressed her back up against it, registering the delightful cool smoothness against her palms, and continued recording the conversation. She noticed Benzo clinging to the shadows, all his parts pressed up to a wall and practically invisible.

Draye was speaking. "Sydney Central took the suspect in about two hours ago. We're certain he's the one who killed your employees."

"Who?" The woman's voice was reedy. "Who's your suspect?"

"He has to be formally charged, of course. That'll come tonight, maybe tomorrow morning, and then we'll release it. No one you'd know. No one from anywhere around here. But I can tell you he's a dockworker from an Asian freighter, appears he's from Singapore."

"How did you find the man?"

"Persistence. Been talking to people on the bridge and located a couple of witnesses who'd been afraid to talk. They gave us a good description of him. One actually watched one of your guards get slashed, managed to get a picture of the doer...a cybered ork. We used the picture, found him on the docks. We had to use stunners to take him down."

Ninn scowled; she'd asked plenty of people on the bridge plenty of questions, and not one had given her that tidbit. Maybe the joygirl outfit wasn't such a good idea after all. Maybe the bridge people only talked to lumpers and bags of fruit.

"Freighter was in port twenty-one days ago."

"When my security guards were killed," the woman said. "And Dr. Elliott. It fits. Thank God it's over. It is over, isn't it? All of it?"

"Yes, ma'am. The freighter was in port other times that match the killings in the Cross. We're thinking he killed around the docks, maybe got some homeless before or after your security guards, then moved deeper into the city when we stepped up patrols around the harbor. So we're pegging him as the Cross Slayer. Fortunately, the freighter was still in port this morning, was just getting ready to pull out when we grabbed our man. We were lucky. Hell, this guy might have been killing people in ports all around the world."

Ninn heard the woman let out a breath of relief.

"Caught him with a heater, too," Draye continued. "Had the murder weapon on him."

"Guess we're done, eh, Keebs? Guess you can hang it up and look for more work. Gotta get some nuyen and a roof over your and Benzo's heads."

"B-E-N-Z-O."

"No," she whispered. "We're not done yet. Cybered ork? That wasn't what I saw. This ain't sitting right."

Ninn was glad the aquarium was reasonably busy; the *click* of visitors' shoes, their *ooohs* and *ahhhhhs* covering up her hushed, one-sided conversation with the gun. Even Barega didn't hear her. He was still mesmerized by the barramundi. "I think Draye was thorough. Just not thorough enough. I think he's too quick to close this."

"Spill, I say."

"Why would an ork from Singapore have a kill list that included security guards *and* female impersonators?"

"That's if you believe the line Stinky Stella doled out. If you believe the whole 'list' part at all. Kill List, 2011, Neil Maskell, Harry Simpson as Sam."

"I do believe her, about the list. And I know it wasn't a cybered ork." Once upon a time Ninn was a good cop in Chicago, was on her way to getting the gold detective shield before the fire changed her course. She bulldogged cases. She could bulldog this for Cadi.

Ninn tapped Barega on the shoulder.

"C'mon," she said. "We're going to the café for something tasty and no doubt bad for us. Then maybe we can find an empty office."

He raised an eyebrow.

"And if we can't, we'll find a closet until this place closes. Only got about two hours for that to happen because we'd spent so long with the bridge people." Maybe the timing hadn't worked out so bad. "Yeah, we'll sit in a closet if we have to."

"Because something's not sitting right," Mordred said. *"Sitting Right, 1946, educational film on posture."*

Ninn stopped herself from disconnecting the smartasslink.

NINETEEN
A STRAIGHT RIGHT

It wasn't a closet, it was an access tunnel, and she and Barega crept out of it a half-hour after closing time. She found an assistant administrator's office by accident, and settled at the computer, posting Barega at the door. There was a video feed, but it was easy to disable; that might make someone from maintenance or a security guard come looking eventually, but she didn't need long. She and Barega would be gone before company arrived.

The system was password protected and had a retina scanner, but it wasn't so defiant that she couldn't wrestle her way in employing a technique Talon had taught her. An older system like this was pretty easy, even for her. God, but she shouldn't have let him back in her life—he'd still be breathing and sheltered under the bridge with Stinky Stella. An awful way to die, that fire.

What was she looking for? Why even mess with the aquarium files? Barega had asked that, too, and she hadn't answered. She didn't know, she just wanted to take a look—felt compelled to, and knew she couldn't ask for AISE records—not with her in their crosshairs for yesterday's arson. Actually, she was probably at the top of their Most Wanted list now, since they thought they had the Cross Slayer locked up.

What was she looking for? Something. Because something wasn't sitting right; and that proverbial sixth sense kept twanging—maybe it was the *koradji* in her, if she really was all booga-booga—that was urging her to dig. But dig where? Here? Go beat the pavement? She called up employee records, getting the names of the slain security guards and the biologist by the most recent survivor benefit payout information, finding no common denominator other than that the guards were on the same shift—

different ages, backgrounds, residences, and years employed—and stuffing the tidbits into her encephalon.

She scanned the other directories...budgets, news, promotion, livestock, food inventory, ichthyologist schedules, and upcoming education seminars. All dead ends. *We should leave...*

A light on the monitor flashed, probably a reverse video feed, someone watching her. One more quick skim through. Nothing. Nothing. Noth—

"Siland..." She spotted his name as she closed out a file. Closed it too soon. What had she been looking at? What file? Accessing her encephalon with its microprocessor, she looked through the aquarium directory again. His name came up under financials...though that shouldn't have surprised her. When she'd met with him in his office above Cadigal's, he'd said he owned a lot of things. The Sydney Aquarium apparently was one of them. According to the records, he'd been the major investor when the city sold it, then three years past he bought out the other owners, leaving himself solely in charge. No wonder Siland was interested in the Cross Slayer—the thug had geeked the doc's favorite singer *and* four of his employees.

Small world, indeed.

She remembered Siland's office, the photograph with him standing in front of the aquarium. Must be nice to have so much nuyen you can buy one of the biggest saltwater galleries in the world. How rich was he? And no wonder he'd offered to pay her if she solved the crime, he could afford it...too bad. She could have used the nuyen; she was going to need a lot of it now that all she owned was Mordred and a skimpy joygirl outfit. Without cred, she'd be homeless and maybe living under the bridge next to Stinky Stella, swapping Talon stories. She'd need lots and lots of nuyen if she couldn't clear her name and had to flee Australia.

"What's this?" The board of directors of the aquarium had merged with the board of the Sydney Zoo, of which Siland was also a shareholder. The slain biologist had worked for both the zoo *and* the aquarium, spearheading a program called Renaixement...whatever the hell that was. Apparently the zoo had also been privatized some years back when city coffers were running on empty. Unfortunately, the databases weren't wholly connected. A trip to the zoo might be next on the list.

Renaixement...she'd heard the word before. Where?

"Moses on a moped," she whispered. The Moon Corporation

was listed as a significant contributor to the aquarium—and Elijah Moon, its owner, was *the* major shareholder in the zoo. The "livestock" file showed shipments of sea mammals to the Moon Corporation for "Renaixement Therapy." Maybe the zoo was shipping, too.

"So this Moon is buying research animals, right? I mean, you own a zoo, you can find a way to siphon off some of the critters." A practice publicly illegal because of animal rights laws, but certainly embraced in the shadows.

"What you thinking, Keebs?"

"I'm not, Mordred. If I was thinking, I wouldn't be sitting here." She skimmed another file. "Interesting, the sporadic animal shipments." But it was more the fodder for news reporters and animal rights champions. Nothing to ease her "not sitting right" feeling. So she'd cooled her heels in an access tunnel for *wala-lang*, and her sixth sense had yielded *ekkert*.

"And we're off," she told Barega.

"Now where to?" The Aborigine had been nose-to-nose with Benzo, who was wagging his tail.

Someplace where I can lean my back against a cool wall and pop a slip, take the edge off, stop feeling itchy. Aloud, she said: "Someplace where we can find out about the Asian freighter and the cybered ork they took off it. 'Cause I'm not sure he's the guy. But there might be clues there. So probably the docks. Can't go to Sydney Central. Don't think they've a prayer of recognizing me, but they're certainly not gonna share any information with someone looking like little joyful me. Hope your feet are rested. We're probably going to the zoo, too. Hell, maybe we'll go to the zoo first. It's just across the harbor. Your feet?"

"Rested enough. I've not been to the zoo. Is it open at night?"

"Maybe to us. So let's—" Ninn opened the office door and saw a heavy semi-automatic pistol aimed dead center to her chest.

"Don't move," the gun holder said.

It was an impressive gun; she'd used one with Lone Star in Chicago. The IZOM HP-49B was favored by military, police, and security. Smooth double-action, tactical flashlight, the upgraded caliber showed it would pack more punch than Mordred. Real impressive.

Security had arrived faster than she'd expected.

"Hands up, both of you."

Barega complied. Ninn was slow to copy him; she was listening, wanting to know if there were more guards out in the hall. Benzo clung to her ankles.

"Keebs, we can take him. Bring me out. Bam *and he's down and we're out of here.* Bam. Bam. Bam. *He's alone, by the way, not picking up anyone else."*

Probably wasn't the regular office feed she'd cut that had lured him. No doubt it was her prying into computer records, that red light she'd noticed. She didn't hear anyone else out there. Maybe Mordred was right; this guy was the only soul who knew about her trespassing. She shouldn't hurt him. At least not too badly.

"What were you doing in there?" The security guard was human with cybereyes that glimmered an unnatural shade of violet. He wore an earpiece with a comm extension lead. Someone was listening to this.

"Looking for the ladies dunny. I need to powder my face." Ninn knew it wasn't a convincing lie, but it was the first thing she thought of. She tried another one. "Looking for a place I could be alone with my...friend." She winked and pointed at Barega.

The guard's raised lip showed he hadn't bought it. "Trespassers in Hannah Granger's office," he said into the lead. "I got her. A joygirl and her handler, a goose and a gander, stealing something. They were on the computer. Any lumpers still around? Or you need to call them?"

"Oh, you don't need to call anyone—" As she spoke, Ninn stepped forward, shoving the pistol aside with a sweep block and delivering a straight right into his chest, discovering he had no protective vest. Benzo scampered out of the way. As much power as she put behind the punch, she thought she might have cracked his sternum. He dropped the impressive gun but stayed on his feet, air escaping from his lungs in a great, surprised *whoosh*. She pressed her attack, a straight left, then three more jabs, this time to his stomach. His shoulders hunched and he groaned. Still didn't fall, though; must have a little muscle augmentation or bone lacing or both.

She hadn't wanted to hurt him, and now there was no avoiding that. She'd make sure not to kill him, though. He was just doing his job.

There were basically four boxing styles, according to her instructor in Chicago: The out-boxer, who danced and kept a distance; the slugger...the brawler that relied on brute strength and classic moves; the boxer-puncher, a hybrid style her instructor favored; and the swarmer, who crowded the opponent with constant pressure.

In the close confines of the hallway, she used the last approach, bobbing and weaving right in front of him, reaching up and grabbing his headset and flinging it away, hearing the voice of whoever was on the other end of the comm saying lumpers were still in the director's office and were on the way.

"Don't need more company," Ninn growled. "Just need out of here."

The security guard gathered himself and tried to counter Ninn's attack, but she retained the upper hand. She hammered at him again, in the back of her mind picturing the ring where she trained, her instructor lecturing that swarmers have great stamina and conditioning, but short careers. The guard kicked at her and drove his elbow up, catching her on the chin. But it was only a glancing blow, and she evaded his next swing and followed through with a series of hooks and uppercuts, all her strength behind them.

"Oh my," Barega said. "Don't hurt him, Nininiru."

Great, the Aborigine had said her name. If the guard retained that...

"The Boxer, *1997, one hundred and thirteen minutes. Universal Studios. Strong sexuality, drugs, and violence, natch.*"

She bobbed and weaved, ducked an awkward punch and delivered another straight right. The guard finally dropped; his jaw at an ugly angle. She'd probably broken it...and regretted it, too, as she'd been the trespasser. But she couldn't let him take her into custody. Tommy Burns had been a swarmer, Jack Dempsey, Rocky Marciano, Cleegad Skamper, Vorgol the Fist. She almost mentioned "The Rock's" name, but knew that would draw a list of ancient movies from Mordred; she'd seen the remake of *Rocky XXI.*

"Let's go. This way." Ninn reached down and snatched up the HP-49B with her right hand.

"Hey, me! Bring me out, Keebs!" Mordred sounded insulted. *"Why you grabbing strange guns off the floor when you already got me?"*

"Can't leave him a weapon in case he comes to." She grabbed Barega's wrist with her left hand. "Move. We gotta move."

Ninn had looked at the huge map on the wall when they'd entered the aquarium, and so she knew roughly where they were. A right at the end of corridor and out through double doors put them in the aquarium proper, near the Dugong Island exhibit. The lights were dim and the tanks dark, and she hadn't expected that.

"What the—"

"Fish sleep, Keeb, if you turn off the lights and let them," Mordred said. "Sleeping with the Fishes, *2013, Gina Rodriguez, Steven Strait, comedy.*"

"Comedy? You reference a drekkin' comedy? This isn't funny." Ninn had low-light vision in her natural eye and kicked in the thermographic vision in her cybereye, the combination dizzying at first, but she adjusted; the effect like looking at a split screen of the same image. Her pause allowed Barega to catch his breath.

"All right, this way. This'll swing us back and around past the Bay of Rays, through their café; I saw an exit there."

"Run more." This from Benzo. Ninn had forgotten that the collection of furniture pieces still tagged behind. "Run is fun fun fun good good good dog."

"Yeah, run more," Ninn said. If Barega wasn't with her, she'd instead try to speed-stealth her way through the aquarium, lose any pursing guards, return to the access tunnel if she had to, and escape through an air duct. But the old man complicated things; he couldn't keep up with her if she moved flat-out.

"So dark," Barega said. "Can't see anything, Ninn."

Sucks to be human, eh? "Stay with me." Her hand went from his wrist, and her fingers interlocked with his. "Just keep up with me. Try."

He wasn't as slow as she expected...human, no body modifications, old, but he was reasonably fit, and matched the relaxed pace she set, his bare feet making a soft *slap-slap* in time with the *clack-clack-clack* of her fancy leather-soled sandals.

She turned the next corner and saw five men filling the corridor ahead, shoulder-to-shoulder, wearing goggles to compensate for the low-light. Three were human security guards armed with HPs—probably the entire security staff rounded up just for her. Two AISE officers were with them, Draye and a dwarf she'd not seen before. The dwarf had an Aphrodyte grenade launcher and was aiming it.

"Give it up," Draye shouted. "Drop the gun and you can get out of here with a B and E."

Breaking and entering? They'd tag her for more than that. If they took her in, a retina scan, fingerprints, swab, the spangly joy-girl revealed as Nininiru Tossinn—alleged arsonist and murderer. Assault and battery for the poor guard she'd mauled in the hallway, certainly...but that was the least of her worries.

She aimed for the dwarf's knees and fired a round, the HP

so smooth the recoil was hardly noticeable. In that same instant, she shoved Barega behind her and down, then dropped herself as she swung the gun around and fired a spray at foot-level at the security guards, who had all taken aim. Didn't want to kill them, shouldn't, only doing their jobs. And if she got out of this...and if she proved her innocence for the building fire...they'd put her away for this firefight, maiming all these men.

"Lose-lose," she said, as she swept the gun back and fired a second time, this time striking three of them. "Oops."

Either the guards had expected the elf in a sparkly purple outfit to drop the gun as ordered, or they hadn't counted on her shooting them. A third burst at knee level, and she hit all of them, except Draye—but she wasn't aiming for him, a good cop who didn't deserve injury. Hell, none of them deserved this. No padding on their legs, probably no armor, the guards had fallen and were hollering, one of them shouting into a comm to call for police and ambulances, had probably blown a few kneecaps all to hell.

Draye returned fire, but she was moving, shoving herself backwards, pushing Barega. "Move. Move. Move, old man!"

Draye was using a Colt Agent Special, a light pistol with a large caliber, known for inflicting a world of hurt, but also known for not being especially accurate.

Ninn was pleased it wasn't especially accurate. The rounds struck one of the smaller tanks and spiderweb cracks sprouted. She scrambled to her feet and took off, not waiting to see if it actually punctured the glass. Benzo raced after her, fabric tongue lolling out of its mouth.

Barega was up now too, running faster, no longer needed her prodding. A glance over her shoulder showed he was headed toward the softly glowing EXIT sign—the only light in the corridor; it was probably the only thing he could see with his plain old human eyes.

Draye fired twice more, one grazing her arm, the other putting a hole in her raincoat. His aim was getting better. She spun around, dropped to a knee and shot, noting that two of the security guards had recovered enough and were lying prone, weapons ready. One took a shot at the spirit dog. Benzo yipped, but kept running.

"Drop it, and you can still get out of this alive!" Draye shouted. In the background she saw that the dwarf was getting up—either she'd missed him, or he had some armor or dermal plating on his legs.

"Great. Why don't you drop it?" she screamed back.

Mordred said something, but she ignored him as she shot at Draye again. She was only looking to wing him, but her aim was knocked off because at the same time she caught a bullet in her shoulder—the same one the Slayer had wounded, and that Dr. Tarr had repaired. Fire lanced through her, and she fought to keep hold of the gun.

"Pull me out, Keebs!"

"Can't kill them, Mordred. Can't. They're doing their jobs." She spun and ran flat out, praying that if they continued to shoot, they'd miss. She wove right, then left, hearing bullets ricochet off something, hearing one of the security guards holler: "Watch the tanks!"

Then she heard an odd noise, barely noticeable above the racket. A loud *thunk*, followed by a brief whistle, followed by a *clank*, then a hissing release of smoke.

"Frag it!"

The dwarf had fired the grenade launcher. You didn't need a perfect aim with the launcher; you just needed to get in the general vicinity.

"Keebs, pull me out! Bam! *"*

"Run good good good dog."

"They're not villains in this, Mordred. Barega! Hold your br—"

Ninn watched the Aborigine fall, choking, grabbing at his chest. She'd not held her breath fast enough and had the sensation of twirling and being pulled down, felt her fingers stiffen and the HP drop, heard it clatter against the tile floor. Ninn had a fine trauma damper, a clump of receptors at the base of her thalamus that would trigger the release of endorphins and enkephalins to help keep her conscious. It had helped in Cadi's basement when she fought the Slayer, but it wasn't doing much here. Spin and twirl and down.

Down.

Down...

"Good good dog."

"Keebs!"

The gas winnowed its way deep into her lungs. Almost comforting. Certainly relaxing. Neuro-stun, she knew, not that she'd been on the receiving end before, but she'd dished it out during a Lone Star arms raid in the Loop.

"Crap..." was all she managed to get out before the tile floor reached up and smacked her.

TWENTY
SLAY ME

She heard every word, felt someone grab her wrists and pull—in the direction of the exit she'd been headed to. Good, maybe they'd toss her out by the bridge and be done with it. No, not bloody likely, she'd beaten and shot up the guards. B and E and assault and whatever else they might tack on. They'd discover she was Nininiru Tossin and add arson and murder to all that. She might qualify for the recently reinstated death penalty.

"A unit should be here in a few." It was a gruff voice, probably the dwarf's. Probably the dwarf's thick, stubby fingers around her wrists. "Throw the goose and her old gander on a bus to Central? Think they need a hospital first?"

The tile felt cool and smooth against the backs of her legs, her raincoat swishing as she was dragged across it.

"The ambos are for the guards." She recognized Draye's voice. Saw him looming over her, the HP she'd dropped was in his right hand, his Colt stuffed in the waistband of his pants. He had something in his left hand. Cloth. The Aborigine slid by when Draye moved—he had a fistful of the old man's tunic and pulled Barega. "The tunnel is for these two. We're not putting them on a bus."

"The tunnel? You daft? Aren't we gonna arrest 'em? Do this one by the book, dontcha think? Throw the book at 'em. Waller's already looking at us cross-eyed."

She'd told Mordred she couldn't shoot to kill because they were doing their jobs, that they weren't the villains in this.

"That joygirl? Saw her earlier today," Draye replied. "She was eavesdropping on me. Don't know her name or her game, maybe an undercover cop. Can't take a chance. And she was digging through electronic files. Definitely can't take the chance. Mr. Siland doesn't want any mention of his aquarium in our reports. So this one's off the book. Waller ain't gonna find out."

They were sounding like villains.

"But the aquarium was in the news when them guards was geeked—"

"That was weeks ago, an accident, and it was 'cause Eli didn't know any better. He was only supposed to take the one that night. Weeks ago. Old news. And Siland doesn't want any new news. Understand? He's made that very clear."

"Crystal."

Sounding a lot like villains. Siland. *Great,* Ninn thought. Taking her to a tunnel? She'd find a way out of it. It was fortunate they weren't going to take her to Central. The neuro-stun would wear off soon.

"So why the tunnel, mate?"

"Because I called Max, and he said to take her there."

"What about the security back there? They ain't geeked. They're breathing. Aren't they gonna ask questions? Aren't they gonna—"

"We're AISE," Draye cut back sharply. "They'll believe whatever we say...the sheila and her handler got tossed in jail all nice and tidy and forgotten...the sheila and her handler made a break for it and got away...the sheila and her handler are dead. We fried the goose and her gander. Yeah, I like that one the best. The guards don't know it was only a neuro grenade you lobbed. We'll say it was a frag. They'll believe what we say. And I'll do the talking. 'Sides, they'll be too busy licking their wounds to care about what happens to these two. Siland says just take these two to the tunnel, and I say shut your gob about it and do it, or Siland'll say put you in the tunnel, too. Now pick it up. Get them little legs moving."

"Good with me," the dwarf snorted. "I hate filling out reports anyway. But I'm just sayin' somebody might ask questions."

Yeah, me, Ninn thought. *If I could just move my mouth, I'd be asking a ton of them.* So obviously Draye wasn't quite as good a cop as she'd thought...he was on Siland's nuyen. That wasn't unusual, a cop on someone else's payroll. A little funding on the side.

"Keebs. Get up, Keebs. Do something."

She still couldn't move her lips and so couldn't answer Mordred. Eyes locked open, she couldn't even blink. At least they hadn't taken Mordred. But folded, they hadn't spotted him in her pocket. The AISE thugs didn't know she still had a weapon, thought the HP was the only thing she'd had.

"This ain't gonna end well if you don't do something, Keebs." The gun was honestly worried, Ninn realized, as he wasn't referencing ancient movie titles.

She was a little worried, too.

Draye was somewhere ahead with Barega, she heard the steady *click* of his heels and a *hush*ing sound the Aborigine was making against the floor. The dwarf huffed, like it was an effort to walk so fast; he was falling behind, and he tightened the grip on her wrists. Ninn concentrated, trying to move her fingers. If she could shake the neuro-stun toxin, she could take out the dwarf, and then go for Draye. She would shoot to kill this time. Should have when she'd had the opportunity before. Should've listened to her gun.

The dwarf took a sudden left turn, a door banged open. She heard a mix of sirens—ambulances and at least one squad car.

"Pick it up." This from Draye, obviously meaning the dwarf should drag Ninn faster still.

Then another door banged open, this one whacking her feet as they passed through it and it swung closed. She was being pulled down a slope, the cool tile replaced with a synthetic surface that smelled of old things and cleanser, the back of her legs feeling occasional seams in the floor...they were going down the people-mover, the ramp that led to only one place—the Plexiglas tunnel that ran under the harbor. "The Shark Walk," some called it.

That tunnel.

What the hell? Why take us there? A place to interrogate us? Away from the emergency crews coming to deal with the wounded guards? Certainly no reason for the EMTs to come down here...

Her stomach suddenly felt like a rock...they meant to release her into the harbor down here, let the sharks eat her and Barega, let her drown because she certainly couldn't swim. Probably would have thrown her in up top were it not for the sirens. Was there a vent down in the tunnel? Flush her and the Aborigine out through it like garbage. Chum.

The lights were off in the tunnel; it was like she'd been dropped in a barrel of ink. Her natural eye's low-light vision was useless, only helping if a little light was present—and there was none. Her cybereye, also useless, as the thermographic vision picked up heat sources, and everything within her limited range was the same temperature—save for the quick glimpse of the dwarf's wide face when he peered over her.

Draye and the dwarf must have infrared in their goggles, something she should add to her cybereye when she got out of here. *If* she got out of here. *If* she didn't end up as shark food. Focusing, she tried to blink, twitch.

Wala-lang.

Definitely a neuro-stun grenade, probably a VII because of the potency; even with her upped metabolism she couldn't shake it.

"*Do something, Keebs. Hey, Keebs, can you hear me? Come on, let's plug these choobs.*"

The dwarf dragged her a little farther. A muffled thump; *Draye releasing Barega,* she guessed. The dwarf released her, too. She saw his wide, hairy face again looming over her in thermographic vision.

"So now what?" the dwarf asked. He prodded her with his foot. "And what about that dog-thing?"

"Leave her," Draye replied. "Leave that pile of scraps, the old man...all of 'em." He'd been talking on his comm, but she hadn't caught it, and realized she couldn't mentally access her inscriber... any of her built-in tech. Must have been a tech dampener in the grenade, too. "I just called the boss again—"

"Again? Why are you botherin' him to—"

"Yeah, again. He brought Eli over. The big guy's on his way in."

"Then I want to be on my way out, mate. I don't want to be anywhere near him."

If Ninn's eyes could have, they would have widened. Boss, not lieutenant, or Waller or captain, or sergeant...not any of the terms a good lumper would use. *Boss.* Draye was in all the way in Siland's pocket. Shouldn't've surprised her, really; even in the states, a lot of Lone Star officers had two masters, or three or four—the department, plus whoever slipped them money on the side. Just the way the world works. She'd been above that in Chicago...but then she'd not been on the force all that long, and had never been approached. Would she have jumped in someone's pocket? Not all the way, but a side job here and there, sure.

Should've shot your ass, you son of a bitch, she silently fumed at Draye. *Should've shot you first. Right to the forehead.*

"So what'd the boss say? Why's he bringing Eli? That'll be a mess." The dwarf was all the way in the pocket, too. *Should've aimed for your face, shouldn't've missed. Should have plugged both of you right between the eyes. The HP would've punched a hole in your skulls and let the few brains you have squirt out.*

"Said Eli would take care of it, is all. But tidy this time."

"Eli don't know how to be tidy."

Ninn blinked. That was something, a blink. She swallowed, her mouth feeling desert dry, tried to move her jaw...that wasn't working yet, couldn't flex her fingers, but some sensation was starting to come back.

Heard footsteps retreating, the dwarf chuckling, Mordred still chattering: *"Keebs! Keebs!"* They still hadn't seen her gun. Probably thought there was no place to conceal anything in this skimpy outfit, hadn't bothered to search her. Thank God they'd been sloppy. *"Keebs! Keebs!"*

But Mordred wouldn't do her any good unless she could move her hands. Ninn thought she might have wiggled her toes. Couldn't be sure. Couldn't move her arms or legs yet, back flat on the floor, nothing but dark. *Frag!* Everything the same temperature. Can't see. *Frag frag frag!* She needed to move move move!

She needed to get out of here and wring some answers out of the high-and-mighty Mr. "I own lots of things" Siland. In an office above Cadigal's Corner he'd orchestrated...what? Something at the aquarium, definitely, something that involved the past death of the guards and the biologist, maybe had orchestrated Cadi's death...and thereby maybe was involved with the Cross Slayer. Maybe orchestrated the Slayer himself. And if that was true, why had he said he'd reward her if she found the doer? To help keep her occupied and out on the street? Away from Cadigal's building? Or maybe to doubly ensure that she stay focused on the slayings. Maybe something darker was involved.

The possibilities continued swirling in her head, while she envisioned squeezing Siland's throat and getting him to cough up the answers. Like why did Cadi have to die? Why did any of the entertainers, for that matter? What the hell did entertainers in Kings bloody Cross have to do with security guards and a biologist that split his time between the aquarium and the zoo?

Ninn replayed a conversation in her her head.

The dwarf had said: "—when them guards was geeked—"

And Draye had answered: "That was weeks ago, an accident, and it was 'cause Eli didn't know better. He was only supposed to take the one that night."

Take the one, the biologist. The biologist was "Patient Zero," the real Victim Number One of the Cross Slayer. So what did the biologist have to do with the entertainers in the Cross? What was the connection? Ninn had to get out of this mess to put all the puzzle pieces in place.

A door banged open, light momentarily streaked across the curved ceiling, confirming she was in the Plexiglas tube at the bottom of the harbor, shapes moving through the dark water. Then the door banged shut, the light gone. The neuro-stun continued winnowing into her system, deeper somehow, relaxing, and she was unwillingly accepting it. The drug was finding that sweet spot. It wasn't unlike the sensation of popping a slip and following it up with just a swallow of whiskey.

She couldn't move, might as well enjoy the muzziness, right? Embrace it just a little. Her head felt foggy, and she lost track of where she was. The muzziness felt pretty fragging good.

There was the loud hiss of someone exhaling.

It was the elf. The one in the alley, the one in the basement, the one that had hurt him in the fire. The hated elf. She looked different, no hair, no clothes...no clothes to speak of. With the little dark-skinned man that had been behind Cadigal's Corner. But she smelled the same. If she'd meant to hide herself with the scant purple sparkles and no hair, it had not worked.

Eli had keen senses. His vision was natural, enhanced medically, not electronically, and no simple disguise like the elf had attempted would fool him. He had other additions, though, to help; thermosense organs implanted in the sides of his thick neck, nothing that messed with his naturally perfect eyes. The organs helped him perceive heat in the dark, whether that came from electronics or bodies, let him find chameleons. Siland had said Eli could see things otherwise invisible. The organs told him that the old man was only flesh, but the elf had tech riding round inside her, electronics in her innards. She wouldn't be tasty, and the old man would be stringy and tough.

He hated hated hated the elf. She'd hurt him in the tawdry house basement. Might have killed him if he hadn't slipped into one of his tunnels and let his augmented healing kick in, cells regenerating, muscles repairing while the trauma damper released endorphins and put him in a happy state.

"Eli, kill them, my friend," Siland had said. "Eli, have fun."

Twisted fun with the elf, most certainly. "With pleasure, Huddy," Eli had said, almost adding thank you, but stopping himself. Made his throat itch when he said too many words in a row.

Siland had also mentioned not to make a mess, but Eli would tell him later that he'd forgotten that part. He indeed would make a mess, and revel in it, but he wouldn't eat them. The harbor was right here; Eli liked fish. He would dine after dumping what was left of the bodies.

"Eli, put them in the harbor when you're done," Siland had said.

Thanks, Huddy, Eli had almost said in return.

"Then come home. Don't stay out too late. And stay to the shadows."

Eli liked the shadows. But maybe he'd pretend he hadn't heard the bit about not staying out too late.

His heater was gone, taken by Draye, who'd said he needed it to blame the Cross slayings on some mug they'd grabbed off a boat. Plant the heater on the unfortunate tusker. Eli didn't need it, as he was perfectly capable of killing with his hands, but he liked the way the heater's handle warmed against his palm. He liked the sound it made, and more than that he liked the look of terror in his victims' eyes when they saw him flick open the hot blade.

Eli wanted his heater back.

Like pitch in this tunnel, the elf and the little dark-skinned man would not be able to see their deaths coming, and so Eli would miss the beautiful expression of fear on their faces. Maybe he should turn the lights on. Yeah, he'd do that. Let them see him. Let them be terrified. Eli loved the scent of fear.

Good to have this work to do for Siland, he knew. He was perfect at his job, as he'd slashed everyone on the list Siland had given him. Eli was a good friend. He'd always been a good friend. Best mates.

"The Cross Slayer's work is done," Siland had said, explaining that there'd be no more throats that needed cutting, that the lumpers will mark the serial killings case-closed. "But not Eli's work. Eli's work will go on. I will have other tasks for you. Like tonight's work. Eli, kill these two."

Eli liked being called the Cross Slayer, it made him feel important. It was a more powerful name, spoken with hate and fear and awe all along Darlinghurst. It was on the lips of journos and lumpers and tourists.

Eli would make Siland reconsider. Eli would ask for his heater back and would ask for another list to slash. Eli would ask for the

Cross Slayer to come back with a vengeance, for the case to be unclosed. But first, the elf and the little old man, to make Siland happy. Killing the hated elf would make Eli happy, too. Maybe he'd tear apart the thing that looked like a dog.

He palmed the control by the door and the lights came on. He palmed them again and they dimmed. *That's better, all shadowy around the edges,* Eli thought, *nicely moody.* Shadows down under the surface of the Sydney harbor just for him. And the shadow he cast was the longest and most frightening.

He shuffled forward, making as much noise as possible and disappointed that the elf was still on her back and that the old man was in a crumpled heap. The mechanical dog skittered away into the darkness.

"Eli, have fun," Siland had said.

But there would be no fun unless they put up a little fight.

He growled deep in his throat, the sound like the rumble of an antique furnace kicking on. It was a pleasant sound. He shuffled to the old man, bent, and prodded him with a foot. Eli growled louder, wanting to see the old man tremble.

Eli was careful when he poked the Aborigine. Impossibly strong, stronger than most anything, he had to be careful to keep his power in check. Otherwise the night would pass too quickly, and his quarry would die too fast.

"You die first," Eli told him, drawing each word out. "S-l-o-w and f-i-r-s-t. The elf last and even s-l-o-w-e-r. My best mate said I could have fun."

All the words, they made his throat itch. But he saw the glimmer of terror in the old man's eyes; the words had helped birth that.

TWENTY-ONE
A SLOW SPELL

Barega wished the man would have kept the lights off. His heart raced, seeing the wide visage looming so close. And "man" was not perhaps accurate. Man*like*, with skin as black as oil, oddly shiny in the dim lighting; it looked wet, but was not. Wide, lipless mouth; pointed teeth made of metal; round, dark eyes resembling those of a wild pig. When the man turned his head and sneered, Barega saw the tiniest of ears, practically flat against the sides of this head. Thick neck, bulging arms, long fingers with two joints, not three.

This was the awful man he'd seen in the morgue when he shared a dream with Adoni's spirit and Ninn. The one who'd killed Adoni and the other entertainers in the Cross.

The Cross Slayer, they'd called him. Eli was the name that the bad police used, a Hebrew name meaning high or ascended. The priest Eli in Biblical times watched over the young prophet Samuel. There was nothing good or high in this Eli. Barega sensed only palpable evil.

The dwarf's voice had quavered at the mention of Eli.

Good reason to be worried. Barega had passed worried the moment the light came on and went straight to terrified. Good, perhaps, that he could not yet move, as he could not run fast enough to get away. Better that he rely on his mind. *Calm,* he told himself. It only worked a little.

"We are all visitors to this time, this place. We are just passing through," the ancient Aboriginal saying went. "Our purpose here is to observe, to learn, to grow, to love...and then we return home." *Just passing through,* Barega thought. *But let me linger a while longer. There are things I still need to do.*

He had spent plenty of decades on this earth, but he wasn't ready to return home just yet. The galah had sent him to Nininiru Tossinn to awaken her, so that together they could find justice for Adoni. *Things I must do. A student to teach.* A shaman, he dealt with spirits of the land...still, he had other resources. So rarely he'd used these, however, that he'd nearly forgotten how. The enchantments hung there at the back of his quivering mind; they were the merest suggestion, things practiced in childhood during walkabout.

"You die first," Eli repeated. "Slow and first, small man. Slow is best."

Slow, indeed. Barega drew upon those childhood memories, when he'd first learned he was *koradji*, and could dance with forces very few in the world knew existed.

Slow.

Slow...

S L O W.

The Aborigine fixated on the air surrounding Eli's skin and thickened it and gave it weight. So very long ago he'd done this, he wasn't sure at first that the enchantment had manifested properly.

But when Eli seemed sluggish raising his arm, as if a force pressed down, Barega knew he'd retained the skills. *Slow,* he thought, *S L O W,* making the air thicker and heavier still, rendering the Slayer lethargic.

"Slow," Barega whispered, finding some sensation with his own form returning. Perhaps his use of the old magic was forcing the stunning drug out of his system. If that was the case, he would use more.

"Kill...you...slow," Eli said, the words spilling out lazily. The monstrous-looking man seemed unaware a shamanic spell had wrapped around him.

Barega managed to turn his head, seeing Ninn stretched out, unmoving save for the slight and steady rise and fall of her chest. Not dead, just held in the stunning drug's clutches. If she was not so full of wires and metal and ceramic, the magic could flow to her more easily...so easily, as Barega had sensed her potential. But those manmade things had dampened her essence, crippling her to the world's possibilities. He would use the magic on her behalf, then. Mind stretching out, Barega felt the air above her skin and made it lighter, infusing it with some of his life energy, and then forcing that air deep into her lungs. He was doing the reverse of what he'd done to Eli...slow the monster, hasten the elf.

He nearly dropped the spells when he felt Eli grab his arm and squeeze, felt the bone break and the little splinters stab into his muscles. Adoni had felt this when the beast had grabbed his legs in the alley, squeezed so hard the bones shattered...Adoni's life shattered.

Barega focused and used the pain to fuel the next enchantment, one of the most potent the galah had taught him: air barrier. He pictured the air solidifying, becoming a shield that he directed to push the monster back. *Push! PUSH! Success!*

Eli grunted and let go of Barega's arm, stumbled back and into the side of the Plexiglas tunnel. A hammerhead shark swam close, curious.

The Aborigine pushed up on his good arm and tried unsuccessfully to tamp down the pain. "Dr. Tarr," he said, thinking a trip to the dwarf's medical parlor would be necessary...provided Ninn would get up and deal with the beast, who struggled against the invisible barrier. In the ocean beyond, a shark with dark tips on its tail passed by. There were other shapes in the water, more sharks, a few large and colorful blue striped goatfish, a yellow and black Crested Morwong that flitted out of the hammerhead's path. A rare Chinaman Leatherjacket swam at the edge of his vision, the light in the tunnel stirring the sleeping harbor fishes.

Eli was angry, spittle dripping from his mouth, eyes wide, chest heaving. Barega prayed his conjured wall would hold, because if it dropped the monster would make quick work of both of them.

"Nininiru! Wake up, Nininiru!" Barega formed a fist with his good hand, picturing his fingers as the air around Eli's neck, squeezing, seeing the beast's eyes bulge. For a moment Eli made headway and stepped away from the tunnel wall. *Push!* Eli stumbled back again, surprise and anger flitting across his wide face, mouth opened and metal teeth glimmering. If Adoni had been *koradji* too, he could have fought the Slayer in the alley, perhaps lived and sang on a bigger stage. And perhaps Barega would have traveled to hear the performance.

Unbidden, Adoni's incredible voice played in Barega's mind:

"Brother won't you find me, find me.
I'm lonely won't you keep me, keep me?

Keep me close to your heart, 'cause I'm dead and gone.
I caught someone's eye and he killed me, killed me."

Barega had a few more tricks, but he suspected that would spread his concentration too thin and weaken the weaves he'd already manifested. Better to work with what he'd already conjured, give them a boost.

"Nininiru!" He forced the air faster and deeper into her lungs and faintly energized the air against her skin. "Nininuru, wake, please!"

Barega saw the muscles in her legs bunch and her hands splay flat against the floor as if she'd been shocked. The elf gasped and pushed up into a sitting position, and the old shaman made the air dance faster.

"Move, Nininiru. Move fast! Hurry."

The elf made it to her feet just as Eli broke through the air barrier and furiously charged Barega.

"You die fast, old man!" the beast bellowed. "Fast and with pain!"

TWENTY-TWO
SLEEPING WITH THE FISHES

Ninn had been floating, satisfying the sweet spot in her soul with the delicious numbing buzz delivered by the neuro-stun. *Should try to fight it,* she thought, do something to nudge her trauma damper to jet out some enkephalins and—

In a rush, it felt like she'd stuck a wet finger in an outlet, a jarring sensation stabbing into her and making her teeth hurt. Couldn't have been the trauma damper; it didn't work that way. Ninn wondered if she'd had a defibrillator used on her, but that notion was discarded when she heard the Slayer growl.

She recalled where she was...in seriously deep trouble.

Her pulse quickened, her breath came fast, and she bolted up. In a heartbeat she was on her feet, drawing Mordred in the same motion, and firing. Despite the muzziness of the neuro-stun, she moved fast.

"Bam bam bam!" Mordred shouted in her head. *"'Bout time you got up, Keebs. Bam!"*

In reality, the gun made a harsh spitting noise.

The beast—even more vivid and ugly in person than in the vision she'd shared with Adoni's spirit—had been lumbering at Barega. Ninn only struck the monster once, the other two shots richoeting off the plexiglass and spooking a big seacarp in pursuit of a shiny longtom.

Just as the beast whirled to pursue her instead, Ninn got a good look at Barega. Cradling a broken, bloody arm, the old man stared at her with wild, wide eyes. He mouthed something, but she didn't catch it; the beast loomed in front of her on muscular legs as thick as beer kegs, blotting out everything else. She fired again and again, the slugs hitting the Slayer dead center, blood blossoming on a tattered khaki shirt.

Still he rushed at her, forming a fist and swinging. He struck her wrist so hard she heard the bone *snap*, the agony an icepick rammed in up to its hilt. Ninn howled, a mix of pain and fury. She took several long steps back while the Slayer loomed, gloating, pointed metal teeth glistening with saliva in the dim light. He could have finished her then, but he seemed to be relishing the moment.

"Kill the elf," the Slayer purred. "With pleasure, kill the elf. Sssssslow."

Ninn didn't understand what happened next, but she saw him stagger away from her, thick arms flailing. He opened his mouth wide and roared; the sound echoed off the Plexiglas and a school of blue devilfish scattered like a handful of tossed glitter. Some unseen force slammed him against the tunnel wall, and she took advantage of it. Her right hand useless, she scooped Mordred up with her left and aimed, looking over her shoulder at Barega.

"Did you do that? Did you shove him?"

"In a manner." The old Aborigine struggled to his feet, the tight expression on his wrinkled face showing his pain. He kept his eyes on the beast. "But it won't hold him long. It didn't before. Get us out of here, please."

Ninn wanted to kill the son of a bitch, but a glance at the Slayer showed the bullet holes already closing. He had a serious healing factor, augmented, certainly...definitely better than hers. She stopped herself from firing, fearing either the Plexiglas might break or a richochet could strike Barega or her.

"Fine. I'll get us out of here, old man." She rushed past him, holding her broken wrist against her, reaching the door and studying the panel. It should open from this side, a slide down bulkhead of a door that was probably used if the tunnel ruptured. But if there were controls on this side, she couldn't see them. Ninn dropped Mordred back in her pocket. Benzo clung to her ankles, twitching as if in fear.

"Bam bam bam! *Let me get him, Keebs! Let me shoot him while he's not moving!*"

With her good hand, she felt along the seams and pressed in the center of the door, thinking there some sort of contact release. *Wala-lang*. Not even a peephole she could look out of. Maybe the door at the other end could provide a way out. She swung around on the ball of her foot and dashed back, stopped when an inkblack fist shot out and connected with her rib cage. The Slayer had barreled through whatever Barega had thrown against him.

Ninn went flying against the opposite wall, the back of her head bouncing hard off the Plexiglas; the punch had been delivered with pile-driver strength. Not quite as big as a troll, the Slayer was definitely stronger than one; and more than muscle augmentation and bone lacing had to be involved. She'd boxed with augmented Lone Star officers in Chicago, and not even the biggest of them was capable of that.

Some ribs broke, she was sure of that. Wrist broke, Barega's arm busted, and the hulking inhuman Slayer was healing. She pulled Mordred out again, raised him and fired again and again and again.

The Slayer laughed like a villain in a bad B movie.

"I'm going low!" Mordred shouted. *"Careful, Keebs."*

"Great," Ninn muttered. "Why didn't you say something before now?"

"Because I thought you'd take him down before now."

"Crap." She wasn't the best aim with her left hand.

"Good for one more burst, Keebs. Bullet to the Head, 2012, Sylvester Stallone, Jason Momoa."

Ninn pushed to her feet just as Barega raised his good arm, palm out, and closed his eyes. Once more the Slayer was pushed back against the Plexiglas, and once more he roared.

Ninn wasn't going to waste the shot while the force she couldn't see kept him at bay. The bullet would bounce off like before. "Hold him as long as you can, Barega. I'll try to get us out of here."

The Slayer continued to rage.

"I will do my best, Nininuru. But this will not keep him—"

"—for long, I know." She was almost at the opposite door, still moving faster than normal, when she whirled at a thunderous THRUM THRUM THRUM. Mordred still clenched in her left hand, she saw the beast hammering with both fists against the Plexiglas.

"Oh, hell no!" Ninn yelled.

The clear tunnel withstood water pressure; and in the news vids she'd never heard of it failing. But the Cross Slayer was more than troll-strong and pissed off to boot.

"I'm good for one shot, Keebs. This ain't a good angle."

"Then I'll have to get close and make it count, eh?" Ninn took a deep breath and strode past Barega. "When I tell you, old man, get rid of your invisible wall."

Barega's voice was small behind her. "It is down, Ninn. That enchantment ran its course. He isn't held by me. Not anymore."

Gotta get him to face her, then. Gotta take the head shot. "One burst, eh, Mordred? Let's make sure one is good enough." The beast had an incredible healing factor, but she prayed a slug in his brain would stop that.

"Hey, ugly!" she hollered.

He continued hammering at the Plexiglas. Water bubbled in along a seam.

"Hey ugly, come and hit me instead!" She wanted him to face her, plug him in the center of his wide forehead. One shot, it had to be perfect. But when he wouldn't turn—maybe he was so intent on busting the tunnel he didn't hear her—she stepped to his side, held Mordred, and decided one to the temple would...

A fist slammed against the Plexiglas, the other drove at her so fast, an oil-black streak, knocking Mordred from her grip. The gun clattered away against the floor. The Slayer punched the tunnel wall again and the seam buckled, seawater sluiced in. At the same time Ninn planted her feet wide and hard, putting all her strength in her upper body. Only her left fist capable, she drove it forward, catching him under his arm. Again, she hit him, not lifting her legs because that would weaken her punches.

The Slayer made a keening sound, ignoring her and pulling his arms back, fingers interlaced into one big mallet of a fist that he brought down against the Plexiglas. The seam opened wide and the ocean poured in.

"Oh, hell no!" Ninn fought against the rush of water and followed with a jab, punch, uppercut, and hook, all with her left, and none doing anything. It was like punching a bag filled with wet duracrete. She turned and gave him a roundhouse kick to the back of his legs, which he answered with a swat that sent her reeling. A backhand sent her down to her knees and made her head spin.

Ninn bit her tongue hard in an effort to stay conscious, seeing Barega wobble, Benzo at his feet—

"Fetch!" she shouted to the dog spirit. "Fetch, Benzo! Fetch!"

Instantly the collection of furniture parts wiggled and yipped and scampered toward Mordred, the fabric tongue wrapping around the gun. "Fun fun fun. Fetch fetch fetch."

The spirit raced to her side, dropped the gun in her outstretched hand. She raised it just as the Slayer bent over her, his hideous, fang-filled mouth open in a roar loud enough to wake the dead.

"Bam!" Mordred said as the round hit the Slayer in an eye socket. *"And I'm out!"*

The Slayer's scream stopped short and he fell back, keg-sized legs twitching and fingers jumping like he was electrified.

"We should leave, Nininiru," Barega suggested, his voice a whisper in the *whoosh* of the rising water. He was at the opposite door. "Can you open this, please?"

"Fun fun fetch," Benzo said. "Good good dog."

"The best dog." Ninn was glad she'd never asked Barega how to dismiss a spirit. She gave the door a once-over. "No. I can't open this...not without tools, stuff I have—had—in my office. It's the same as the other door. Here's the emergency release, and it's fragged. They made sure we weren't getting out." She was equally sure someone was monitoring the tunnel. Draye and his dwarf crony had put the Slayer in here with them. They'd be able to open the doors from the other side...but they wouldn't.

An accidental tunnel breach would dispose of her and Barega, yielding the same results Siland had apparently wanted by siccing the monstrocity on them. She wanted desperately to get out of this and put all the puzzle pieces in the right places.

"Panicking yet, Barega?"

The Aborigine didn't say anything.

"I am," she told him. "Definitely panicking." Because a strong possibility existed they were going to drown.

The seam had opened wider wtill, water gushing in, up past their ankles now through the length of the very long tunnel. She slogged toward the Slayer, wanting to make sure he was really dead, stuffing Mordred in her pocket and crooking her neck to get Barega to follow her. He stumbled along, the broken arm no doubt painful, and maybe using his booga booga had taken a lot out of him, too. A glance at the seam, and she noted the tunnel walls on either side of it bulged ominously. The whole thing was going to give way, and soon.

"How the hell are we gonna get out here, Mordred?" She hadn't expected him to answer. But he did as she knelt next to the manlike Slayer and prodded him with her good hand.

"*Swim, Keebs. You go to the beach often enough, ya ken? Just swim.*"

Not that easy. Bottom of the harbor, water jetting in like a firehose had been turned on. What was she looking for? Why was she messing with the body? The lights in the tunnel flickered, adding to the image that she was living an awful horror movie... and wouldn't be living much longer. Why was she bothering with the corpse? She'd confirmed he was dead, and she had no desire to attempt to contact his spirit—that would be madness. Looked mostly human, in form anyway, the muscles hard and heavy, the skin black like oil but covered in fine black hair—all over, solid, like an animal. The ears small and flat against the sides of his head, a familiarity to them.

"What the hell were you?"

"Nininiru—" Barega had come up behind her.

She continued prodding. The water was over the body's chest and it took her considerable effort to lift the shoulders to look at the face, her keen cybereye vision noting a thin strip along the jawline where there was no hair. Something there. She zoomed in. *Renaixement C17* was tattooed in fine blue letters, like one might mark a cow.

"Moses on a moped." She'd seen the word in the computer. Renaixement therapy in connection with research animals sent from the zoo to the Moon Corp.

"Nininiru—"

Somewhere else, too, she'd read it. No, heard it. Accessing her coprocessor, she searched for the word. Asked Mordred to help.

"Keebs, we need to get out of here."

"Hey, buddy. Renaixement. Where did I hear that before?"

"Not a clue," Mordred answered. *"The Great Escape, 1963, Steve McQueen."*

"Nininiru—" This time Barega jiggled her shoulder. She glanced up. He was wide-eyed and focused on the bulge in the tunnel wall, had apparently called up his booga booga again, because where the seam had ruptured and widened, the water flow had stopped. "I can't...hold this...for long. The manifestation...was not meant...for such as this."

"Renaixement, Mordred."

"If you heard the word, it wasn't when I was along. My memory's perfect, Keebs," Mordred continued, as if oblivious to the danger. *"Perfect, 1985, Jamie Lee Curtis, John Travolta. But I think* The Great Escape *is a better notion. Chicago, ya ken?"*

So the RighteousRight bar, when she'd turned off Mordred's smartlink, or in the alley when she first answered Cadi's summons about his dead singer. She focused the coprocessor on that section of her memory, ignoring another shoulder poke by Barega.

A conversation replayed in her head: Gertie snorted. *"Hand to mouth she lived, spending it all on Renaixement and slips and slips and more slips. Bad habit she had. Her debts were square, I think."*

Adoni/Ella Gance was associated with Renaixement...which was linked to the Slayer and the slain biologist who'd apparently headed up the project...which was somehow all involved with Siland and this aquarium and the zoo.

"Nininuru, we—"

The rest of the Aborigine's words were drowned out by the rush of water as his enchantment and the Plexiglas tunnel gave in.

"Goodbye, Chicago," Mordred said.

The sound was as loud a thing as Ninn had ever heard, but it lessened as the sea pressed in and dashed her against the floor. The entire Shark Walk disintegrated under the pressure of Sydney's Darling Harbour. She barely had time to suck in a breath before the sea surged over her head and pushed her down.

The tunnel lights went out and the world went black. Then shadows intruded, her thermographic vision in her cybereye registering different heat signatures in the water. Large fish, nurse sharks from their shapes. Blood in the water from Barega's broken arm, from the head wound to the Slayer which, thankfully, did not heal.

"Sharknado XLIII," Mordred said. *"Starring—"* Then the smartlink cut out, shorted perhaps from the pounding saltwater.

A nurse shark nudged the Slayer.

She spotted Barega. The old man looked like a ragdoll held against the bottom of the broken tunnel. He wasn't moving. Ninn fought against the pressure and reached him, wrapped the fingers of her good hand around his unbroken arm and pulled him close. Then she kicked up. The gun was right; she could swim, and was good at it. But that was under normal circumstances...when the water wasn't beating at her and holding her down, where there weren't an abundance of sharks, and when she wasn't at the bottom of the harbor.

Sydney's Darling Harbour was complex, ranging from three to forty five meters deep in holes. Fortunately the shark walk split the difference. Ninn scissored her legs and aimed up, brushing by a black-tipped shark that twisted as if it was going to pursue her. She shot through a school of blue devils and broke the surface, continuing to kick even though she feared that was the worse approach. She would be attracting the attention of the many predators, certainly the sharks.

But there was a big, easy meal at the bottom, the Cross Slayer, and for once luck found Ninn, and she made it to shore without losing a limb. Tugging Barega up, she started breathing for him, tipping his head so he could cough up the water.

"You need a hospital, old man." She could use a good doc, too. Maybe Tarr, though she didn't have anything left to pay the dwarf. Mordred was the only thing that had managed to stay in the pocket of her coat. The opal was gone, so were the slips, which would have melted oh-so-nicely right now.

Barega shook his head. "No...hospital. We are too busy for that, Nininiru."

He didn't say anything else until he woke at dawn, sitting between Ninn and Stinky Stella under the bridge, watching the mana storm throw random pink bolts of lightning down on the surface of the water.

"Are we going to the zoo?" he asked.

TWENTY-THREE
A CHANGE OF CLOTHES AND SCENERY

Ninn had ripped her raincoat into strips to make a bandage for her broken wrist, had made a splint for Barega from a broken pallet, using more strips from the coat to serve as a sling. There wasn't anything worth saving left of the coat. The Aborigine had somehow slept through all of this, waking only a moment ago when a particularly loud boom of thunder shook the ground under the bridge and toppled a flowerpot off the roof of Stinky Stella's box house. Ninn hadn't been able to set his arm, which looked ugly, given the shattered ulna and radius, and which must have been quite painful. But she'd got the bleeding to stop, most of it anyway.

It looked like they'd been through a war.

Ninn thought it felt that way, though her trauma damper had started working again and kicked out enough endorphins and enkephalins to jazz her. Barega didn't have the benefit of the tech.

"Good good dog." Benzo sat on a pile of detritus that sloshed along the shore. The spirit looked well camouflaged amid the broken clutter.

"Yes," Ninn agreed. "A very good good dog." The outcome under the harbor might have turned out differently if the spirit dog hadn't retrieved Mordred for the final shot.

The gun lay in her lap; she'd have to find some ammo somewhere. Dried out, the smartlink was working again.

"I'm going back to Cadigal's," she said.

"Seriously? That's not a good move, Keebs. Siland might be there."

"Which is why I need to go."

"But I'm empty, remember?"

"I'll work on that, Mordred."

"Empty empty empty. Starving for some ammo here."

Shanties stretched across a section of Darling Harbour near the bridge, some under a section of the span, a mix of colorful and drab floating hovels where an assortment of raggedy people lived. They couldn't be called homeless exactly, as the hovels served as their homes. But they were a collective blight on an otherwise beautiful part of Sydney. A bolt of pink lightning came down and vaporized one.

"But I want to go back at night, Mordred, when the neighborhood's darker and the right crowd is out. Better chance of finding Siland then, I'm guessing. Easier to hide in all the shadows."

"*Shouldn't go back until I've got some ammo, Keebs. You can't shoot anyone by pointing your finger at 'em. You never bought that attachment.*"

"It's on my list. I have to get some nuyen first, Mordred. Nuyen, then ammo."

"I knew Cadigal's grandfather." It was the first Stinky Stella had spoken since she'd helped pull Barega out of the water. "He died up on that bridge in one of the bad storms, turned into one more rivet. But he was old and on his way out anyway." She blew out a deep breath that smelled awful, and then yawned, showing her rotted teeth. "His grandson was too young to be geeked, though. Pity."

"Cadi was a friend of mine," Ninn said absently.

"So I'll help. But you make it up to me sometime, understand? I like pressies." Stinky Stella retreated into her box and came out with four credsticks. "I find these things from time to time, an' I spend 'em when I go up the bank and want a night out, something new to wear." Ninn suspected the woman had not changed clothes in a few years. "But you use these to get you some bullets and better threads, understand? Cover up some of that skin. And you make it up to me sometime." She huffed and sat again. "Make it up real good, and she'll be apples."

Ninn focused to keep from retching at the woman's stench. "I'll make it up to you, Stella. Promise."

"Promises! Promises! *1963, Jayne Mansfield.*"

Ninn extended a hand and helped Barega up. "You need a hospital," she repeated as she tugged him up the bank. The pink lightning had stopped, and the rain had slowed to a steady drizzle. The cloud over the city had turned a shimmering pink in places, and the sky was full of birds.

"*I* need a hospital?" He stared at her bandaged wrist. "We need to go to the zoo."

The credsticks had a lot on them, more than enough to put her in a new, chic "urban mystic" outfit, nothing she'd normally wear, and that might help her continue to hide in plain sight. It was something made by Aztechnology and no doubt helpful to street mages, every shade of brown in the world cut through with a green pattern that looked like Egyptian hieroglyphs and seemed to complement her Aboriginal-design facial tattoos. It had a single deep pocket that Mordred and some spare clips fit into nicely, and an attached hood draped down her back. Ninn hoped she could keep the clothes intact; she liked them.

She put Barega in navy blue alley punk garb, one step above what a banger would wear, with a half cape that fell over his arm and a broad-brimmed slouch hat that shaded his face. There was enough nuyen left to get some ammunition for Mordred and to pay for their entrance into the zoo, some unhealthy food at one of the stands, and cover a couple of nights in a halfway decent hotel—though the mattress in the furniture store had been comfortable and free.

"You're going to the hospital after the zoo," she told him.

"And you are not my mother, Nininiru Tossinn."

"And what do you hope to find at the zoo?" Mordred asked.

"Some answers," Ninn replied. "Like what the hell Renaixement is. And is that one word at the heart of why Adoni and the others had been killed? Renaixement. What the bloody blue blazes is it?"

Barega gave her an odd look. She knew he still hadn't cobbled on to the fact that her one-sided conversations weren't really one-sided.

They took the ferry to the zoo. It was an antique operation, a big colorful wood boat that had to be at least a hundred years old—many of the harbor ferries were from before the Awakening—and it was a tourist attraction Ninn had often embraced. Sometimes she'd buy bags of soychips and hold them over the rail one at a time for the seagulls to come down and swipe. There were several tourists doing that now. The rain had stopped, the weather accommodating for a change, and she relished the feel of the sun sneaking down on her face.

Ninn didn't want to leave Sydney, despite the ever-present

massive cloud and oddball magical weather, and despite her often making homesick comments about Chicago. She'd come to love this city, the Cross especially. She fit in here, better than she had with Lone Star in the Windy City. Now if only she could get to the bottom of this Siland and Renaixement business, find a way to clear her name for the arson, and set up shop again...oh, and get clean. Maybe do something about Draye, too. Ninn was a little jittery; she'd been way the hell too many hours without a slip. The sweet spot in her soul was starting to beg. Maybe she could score some graypuppy if there were any go go gos at the zoo, or deepweed, which was more likely around this part of the city. She didn't like deepweed, the taste that glued itself to her tongue, but the effect...she'd settle for it if she had to.

"Nininiru, are you listening?" Barega nodded toward a couple sitting nearby. The man had a palm-sized comm, and was watching a news vid.

Ninn focused on her audial receptors to boost the sound and record it. She scowled. The news wasn't at all good.

"Sydney AISE Major Crime Division is searching for one of their own, an ex-cop-turned fugitive named Nininiru Tossinn." Ninn assumed they displayed a picture of her; she couldn't get a good enough angle to see the small screen. *"Tossinn, an American elf who once worked for Lone Star in the UCAS, has caused millions of nuyen in damage. From burning a historical building in the heart of Kings Cross, to setting explosive charges at the aquarium and destroying the famous under harbor Shark Walk, Tossinn is also sought for the deaths of four people in the building fire, a beloved Darlinghurst street doc Elizabeth Tarr, and attempted murder on AISE officers last night. A substantial reward is being offered by Hudson Siland, aquarium owner and Sydney philanthropist. Tossinn has been placed on the terrorist watch list and is considered extremely dangerous. She might be in the company of an unidentified elderly black man, whom AISE believes she has kidnapped. Anyone seeing her should contact the AISE hotline immediately. Do not approach, as she is armed and very dangerous."*

"Wonderful," Ninn said. AISE geeked Tarr. Why? Caught them on surveillance maybe at the morgue, matched Ninn's joygirl appearance there with security footage from the aquarium maybe. Questioned Tarr or killed her to eliminate a loose end. What the hell had Ninn stumbled into that was worth killing so many people over? At least the news report hadn't mentioned that Barega was an Aborigine; that designation would make the two of them easier to spot. And they hadn't mentioned the dog, which when it wasn't hiding, stuck out like a proverbial sore thumb.

She raised the hood so it cocooned her face and hid her elvish features. "We're more than at the top of most wanted list. We're the entire list."

Fortunately, no one on the ferry paid her any heed. Most of the tourists were interested in the view and the seagulls.

"So they know we did not die in the water tunnel." Barega's voice was so soft Ninn had to lean close to hear him. "Otherwise there would be no such news bulletin."

"Well, there'd be some mention of the aquarium tunnel. Gotta explain to the tourists why it's closed. But, yeah, the bakebrains knew we got out. I'm sure someone was watching the Shark Walk, monitors everywhere in the aquarium. I saw plenty, probably plenty I didn't notice. Someone was making sure Eli ripped us apart, wanted to watch the bloody spectacle. Someone had let him in there with us and sealed the doors."

"And that someone must be very unhappy. I am not bright in the ways of nuyen, Ninn, but I am certain Eli was expensive to engineer."

She nodded. "And I pray they only engineered one of them."

It was a twelve-minute ride, the ferry letting out on the wharf at Bradleys Head Road. Through overgrown brush, Ninn spotted an old wooden sign, the paint faded from age and weather. She could faintly read: TARONGA ZOO, its former name. And under it: CONCEALED CARRY ONLY.

"That is an Aboriginal word, Taronga," Barega said. "It means 'beautiful view.'"

Ninn hadn't known that, figured it was the last name of one of the zoo's original founders. It had been changed to Sydney Zoo before she'd moved to Australia. She thought Taronga sounded better, but maybe with the ruined bridge and the shanties stretched across the harbor the view wasn't so beautiful anymore.

"What does your name—"

"My name means 'the wind,' *Nininiru*. And yours?"

"Not even the slightest hairy idea."

The zoo stretched out over a high hill, and visitors were encouraged to start at the top and walk down. They could take either a tracked bus...the Mosman suburb's gridlink did not extend here...or an antique gondola lift, which she and Barega opted for, listening to the historical loop on the ride up.

"Opened in October 1916, during World War I, and originally operated under the auspices of the Taronga Conservation Society, the zoo covers more than two dozen hectares and is home to more than one thousand animals of four hundred and twenty species, some of them extinct in the wild." The voice was androgynous and even, and in the background birds twittered. *"Considered Australia's finest zoo, attracting visitors from throughout the world, it was Syndey's second. The first opened in 1884 in Billy Goat Swamp in Moore Park, which later became the site of the city's high schools. An exhibit in the information center has photographs from that first zoo and a VR immersion theater where you can relive the glorious black and white time. While you are here, visit the zoo shop for commemorative apparel, dine in our café where we feature a vegetarian buffet and Aboriginal cuisine, and walk across the restored Rustic Bridge. Enjoy your stay today at the Sydney Zoo."*

Ninn remembered looking at the photos of the first zoo. Lots of patrons in the shots, all of them human. But that was a long time before the Awakening. The RighteousRight would have been happy ducks.

"We could have walked up, Nininiru." Barega stared out the window, eyes fixed on a thin spot in the cloud. "It is my arm, not my legs that are broken."

"Would've drawn attention," Ninn whispered. "Summer like this, they don't want people walking up the mountain, heat strokes and heart attacks. We'll walk down." She noticed it wasn't the cloud after all that the Aborigine stared at. A pink and gray bird circled nearby, floating on a lazy updraft; Barega watched it. Before the ride to the top was finished, a second galah joined it. Ninn involuntarily shivered.

She'd been to the zoo a few times, when she'd first moved to Sydney and wanted to soak up the local attractions. Still, she consulted a map where the gondola let out. Ah…Administration… that's what she wanted. First they'd wander among the animal exhibits to not draw attention, and then she'd find her way into the small cluster of office buildings and go through some records, get to the bottom of Renaixement. If Talon were still alive, it would be so easy, wouldn't even need to be here. He could connect to the Matrix and dig, breaking through walls and slipping around passwords and retinal scans. She should've kept someone like him in her orbit, but in the past few years her PI jobs had been too simple, and she'd certainly never considered that Cadi's job would have turned into this.

The Platypus House and Nocturnal Exhibit were close to the administration building and veterinary quarantine center. They'd have to walk through the Rainforest Aviary on their way there. Bet there were galahs inside.

The weather as close to ideal as it got in Sydney, the crowd was considerable. Humans, metahumans, tourists, rakkies, all ages, all manner of dress, some poser-gang members, an obvious go go go. Only a few of them paid attention to Benzo. Ninn briefly thought about approaching the go go go, her skin itching for want of just one slip. But in the press of people she saw someone that changed her mind and made her go in the other direction—Draye.

What the hell was he doing here?

At his side was the dwarf from the aquarium. From the bulges in the dwarf's jacket, she guessed he was carrying at least three guns.

"Great Guns, *Laurel and Hardy, 1941,*" Mordred said, noting the bulges also. "*There's even some resemblance with that pair.*"

Ninn neither understood nor cared about the film reference. Draye had a handheld sniffer unit and was turning it one way and then the other. Clearly with the pair was a near-skeletal ork in a long tribal loincloth, feathers and beads hanging from his purposefully matted hair. He was heavily tatted, had a port in his chest with wires connected, hard to see just how many wires amid the tats. What was his game?

Bullet to the head, indeed. Should've shot Draye right between his beady eyes when I had the chance, Ninn thought. Grabbing Barega's good arm, she pulled him toward the Lemur Forest Adventure, Benzo following, but walking through the tall grass. They'd take a different route to the administration building.

"On the Run," Mordred said. "*1999, directed by Bruno de Almeida, a comedy—*"

"—of errors," Ninn finished.

TWENTY-FOUR
OF A FEATHER

Ninn noticed other lumpers along the path—zoo security mostly, another couple of AISE officers, one of them talking on a comm. Had there been this many on her previous forays and she just hadn't noticed? She'd been in tourist mode then, an employee of AISE, and more interested in the animals. Maybe she was just being paranoid. But now there were people actually out to get her—people with guns and badges, no less.

"How did he follow us, Ninn?" Barega tugged his arm free, and Ninn slowed her pace to accommodate him. "That officer? How could he know we are here?" The Aborigine tapped her arm and she looked over her shoulder, at Draye and his sniffer. The elf wasn't looking up, so engrossed in the screen in his hand, panning it right and left.

"Yeah, he is. But how? Just how the blue blazes is he following us?" The connection between the two was painfully obvious; Siland owned the aquarium...Draye had been at the aquarium. Siland was a shareholder in the zoo...Draye was now at the zoo. Siland apparently was the puppet master behind the Cross Slayer... Draye "investigated" the Cross slayings. Or perhaps Draye was orchestrating the investigation so the real killer wasn't found and no fingers were pointed in Siland's direction. He was likely just as much a puppet as the Slayer had been, just easier on the eyes.

As she thought it through, she realized there could be any number of reasons why the AISE officer was here—and the majority of them involved making sure Ninn and Barega's investigation didn't go any further.

Fortunately the zoo was crowded, with such nice weather and a discount admission day. Ninn stepped off the path, waited a beat, and then looked for Benzo, who edged out of the grass and stopped at her feet. Maybe thinking about him made him appear. Maybe she'd have to ask Barega to teach her more about this spirit booga booga. "Benzo," she whispered.

"Good dog, good good dog." Benzo wiggled his tail, a screw flying off into the foliage.

"See that thing in the big elf's hand?" Draye was closing the distance, glancing up now, between the screen and the people on the path. "The elf with the white hair. See it? In his hand?"

"Good good dog."

"Can you fetch that? The thing in his hand? Go get it, boy!"

"Fetch fetch fetch fetchfetchfetch." Benzo yipped and raced away, weaving through the legs of a group of schoolchildren. Approaching the cop, he vaulted, fabric tongue lolled out and wrapping around the sniffer, tugging it free and running back toward her.

Draye reacted immediately, drawing his Colt Agent Special. The people on the path scattered. Ninn suspected not many visitors to the zoo came armed, though she'd not seen a policy that prevented it.

Everything happened at once.

Benzo leaped into the bushes, dropping the sniffer into Ninn's left hand. She dropped it in her pocket and drew Mordred. She wanted a look at the sniffer, but being armed was a higher priority.

Amid the cacophony of people hollering, and the general animal sounds filling the air, she heard a shrill cry. A galah. Then a burst of static and pounding feet: zoo security on the way, likely. Someone blew a whistle.

"Urlu!" Draye shouted. "Bring Urlu!"

"Hope that's not a relative of Eli," Mordred quipped.

Sucks major swampwater to have a broken wrist, she thought. Ninn was working one-handed, and she was not left-handed. Probably shouldn't have had the spirit dog grab the sniffer and set all of this off. Sometimes she was her own worst enemy.

Barega chanted something in a language she couldn't understand, and with his good arm looked to be knitting a pattern in the space in front of him. She hoped it was that air barrier thing he'd used against the Slayer in the tunnel.

A pair of tourists returned on the trail, Turkish orks, taking photographs of Draye, who was still talking on his comm.

"Bam?" Mordred asked. *"C'mon, Keebs, let's get him. Not the orks, the elf."*

Ninn hesitated, finger trembling on the trigger, and drew farther back in the foliage, Barega keeping to her side. She noted he was still weaving, his eyes fixed on something farther away than the zoo and Sydney.

Draye fired, the shot spitting up mud near her. *Near*, but not close enough; he didn't see her, but he knew she was in the area. He fired again and again, and she drew back farther, keeping herself in front of Barega to be his meatshield.

The Turkish orks screamed.

The next shot was way the frag too close. Draye must have seen her, or at least noticed the bushes move. He charged straight at her and fired again. A siren went off.

"Bam, *Keebs? C'mon!*"

The elf reached the foliage and tripped.

"I did that," Barega said, sounding oddly pleased.

Ninn leaped forward and landed with a knee on Draye's back as he was starting to rise. He flattened to the ground with an *oof!* The Turkish orks took pictures of the two of them, chattering animatedly the whole while.

"Smile," the smaller one said. "*Tesekkür ederim. Tesekkür ederim.*"

"*Thank you. Thank you,*" Mordred translated.

Ninn stuffed Mordred under her armpit, then ripped Draye's comm loose and hurled it into the bushes. The smaller ork came closer, taking more pictures.

A voice came from speakers placed high on poles: "*Your attention, please. The Sydney Zoo is closing. The Sydney Zoo is closing. Please move to the nearest exit.*" The message repeated.

"Frag it," she growled, retrieving Mordred and waving the gun at the orks, who fled. "Swampwater, this broken wrist." She clocked Draye on the back of the head with Mordred, half-worried she might have hit him too hard. Didn't want to kill him...not yet, anyway. She wanted some answers. She mentally corrected herself. She was going to get some answers.

"We gotta move," she told Barega. "They're locking down the zoo. And company's coming." The pounding feet and whistle were coming closer. The siren persisted, it wasn't a regular police or fire sound; must be a zoo alarm. She struggled to hoist Draye over her shoulder so she could drag him deeper into the greenery just as more security arrived on the path behind them. "Barega—"

The Aborigine was knitting something in the air again; a cloud of sparkling mist, almost invisible, settled over them.

"Your attention, please. The Sydney Zoo is closing. The Sydney Zoo is closing. Please move to the nearest exit," the message repeated.

"So we move," he said. "Where?"

"This way." There were patches of foliage throughout the zoo, part of the atmosphere, and she was grateful for it. The underbrush was thick and choking here, but also concealing, and she picked her way through it more quickly than she'd expected. The *koradji* had done something to make her faster. Her skin felt tingly, and her muscles quivered, the sensation similar to that initial hit of graypuppy with an alcohol chaser before the mixture took hold and relaxed and swirled the world.

She felt hyper and took advantage of it, recalling the map she'd spotted near the entrance as she stepped over roots. The bird area was nearby, and beyond it the administration offices. She headed in that direction. Ninn tried to hear what was going on behind her, listening for more AISE or zoo security approaching, and picking up the cries of children dragged by parents, grumbling tourists being ushered out, the pounding of her heart, the chatter of birds and other animals, and the whistle.

"Your attention, please. The Sydney Zoo is closing," the announcement droned.

The cry of a galah intruded.

"Stop a minute," she said. "Can you do something to make us invisible?"

Barega shook his head.

"Harder to find?"

"Sorry, no. That is not how—"

She waved his words away and leaned Draye up against the trunk of a tall red jarrah, a tree Ninn suspected was a couple hundred years old. Marri and wandoo trees were also in this small grove, probably a representation of an Australian rainforest. The bottlebrush was thick, and there were plenty of golden wattles and round-leaved pig face. They scented the air and kept the odors of people and the city at bay, everything so lush because of the frequent rains.

"Don't have a lot of time here. His comm is on the other side of the path, so maybe they'll look there first. But they'll find him. AISE officers are chipped; they can home in on him. Can't you do...something magical?"

"I can stop the sound around us by putting us in a bubble of quiet."

"So no one can hear us?" Ninn was encouraged.

Barega nodded.

"Silence of the Lambs," Mordred said. *"1991, based on the novel by Thomas Harris."*

"Do it," she said. Adding a heartbeat later: "Please."

He was already knitting. Could he teach her these spells, enchantments...whatever the hell they were? She knew the Awakening had brought some kind of magic with it; the perpetual cloud over Sydney was evidence of that. Did she really have some kind of magic in her?

Ninn rubbed Draye's cheeks. "C'mon, c'mon, wake up. I didn't hit you that hard." To Benzo: "You keep watch. Can you do that? Let me know if anyone's coming back here?"

"Good good dog." The collection of furniture pieces sprinted away.

Ninn didn't know if the spirit understood, but it was worth a try. "C'mon, Draye. C'mon!"

He rolled his head and opened one eye. She noticed the other was swollen; he must have hit his handsome face against a rock when Barega tripped him. The AISE elf's lips curled and he tried to stand. Ninn straddled him and pressed a shoulder back against the tree, brought her head in close. Barega loomed in, too. The *koradji* had taken Mordred from under Ninn's arm and pointed the weapon at the AISE. The double threat seemed to amuse him.

"Should've stayed out of this, Toddlin' Town."

So he knew who she was, the disguise be fragged.

"Should've stayed drunk on Darlinghurst and left the Cross Slayer alone. Healthier for you."

"And how's your health, eh, *choob*? If you want to stay healthy, talk. Fast." Ninn was worried there'd be company soon, didn't matter that the other AISE couldn't hear them. They were tracking them somehow. She reached into her pocket and pulled out the sniffer. A soft red glow pulsed in the center of the screen. *Bullseye.* "How are you tracking me?" There were better questions, but this was the most immediate.

He laughed. "You're a homing beacon, Toddlin' Town. We're tracking your tech. Been tracking you since you hit the morgue. You're history, Chicago."

Not possible, she thought. All the stuff riding around in her innards, she'd bought trackless, paid the extra nuyen for stuff with no signatures, went with a smartlink with Mordred because wireless, while more convenient, could be hacked and traced.

"He can't be tracking you, Keebs. Can't be tracking me either. How 'bout you tell Barega to pull my trigger, put the elf out of his misery. He can't track nothing if he's dead."

But the dwarf might also have a sniffer, or that tribal-looking ork that was with them.

"So why do you need to geek me?" Again, there were better questions, but the selfish ones rose to the top.

He didn't seem to mind answering those. "You looked too close, asked too many questions."

"But I didn't learn anything."

"Couldn't be sure. And you certainly could have, nosy as you were. Learned something if you were at the aquarium, and now here."

"Just looking," she said. Ninn glanced up, seeing birds fly from the jarrah; maybe something spooked them. *Besides, I'm nothing,* she almost added, *a piss-poor private eye who follows ex-wives for enough nuyen to buy slips and booze and pay the rent.* "But that made me a loose end."

He grinned wide. "Snip snip, Toddlin' Town."

"Why'd Siland turn a monster loose in the Cross?" Finally, Ninn was getting to the heart of the matter. "A monster I geeked, by the way."

Draye shook his head, defiant rather than oblivious.

"What's his game?"

He made a *tsk-tsk*ing sound.

"Bam," Mordred coaxed.

"Since when did you get so bloodthirsty, Mordred?" Ninn noted that Draye's eyes went right and left, looking for whoever she was talking to.

"Since your keister's been close to taking a dirt nap, Keebs. How 'bout we go back to following ex-spouses so you can keep breathing? And how 'bout you take me from the Koori and shoot this sucker? I ain't any more bloodthirsty than you. La Cage aux Folles, *1978, Ugo Tognazzi."*

"What's Siland to you that you're so far in his pocket you'll never get out?" Ninn watched Draye's smug smile fade.

"Nuyen." She guessed he figured that question was all right to answer.

"That all?"

"A lot of nuyen, and I'm not the only one."

"The dwarf."

"His name is Damarcus, Sergeant Damarcus." A pause: "And he's not the only other one."

Lots—that's what it translated to in Ninn's mind. Siland had a lot of AISE on his payroll, probably Cross lumpers, too. "Put the right cops on the job and the job'll never get done, the murders never solved."

The shit-eating grin again.

"All right, the murders'll get solved all nice and tidy with a doer that didn't do it. The real murderer doesn't get caught. And the real motive never gets revealed."

"You're goin' down, Toddlin' Town, just 'cause you're nosy. Killing Elizabeth, the street doc, the explosion at the aquarium, millions of nuyen in damage. AISE has an order to shoot to kill you. Snip snip on the loose end. Too bad you didn't actually do that stuff. Wait, there was the arson."

"I didn't do that either, drekhead." Ninn pressed her thumb into his neck and twisted. She saw the pain flicker on his chiseled features. "So, what was the motive? Why did Siland need a biologist geeked? And folks in the Cross? What'd they do to get on the kill list? What's Renaixement, eh? What the hell is Renaixement therapy? Some program to churn out ugly oil-black monsters?"

His eyes were hard, glass beads that reflected her angry face. *Stalling*, she thought. *He's drawing this out so his buddies will find him.* "How the hell are you tracking me?" she repeated, each word spit out like it was a piece of rancid soybeef. "How the bloody blue blazes are you—"

Benzo bounded back, tail wagging, fabric tongue lolling out.

"Dr. Tarr!" Draye had called her Elizabeth. He knew her; maybe she was on Siland's payroll too, maybe a lot of people in the Cross were. "Something Tarr did to me. That's how you're doing it. Tarr put something in me or did something to me, and they got the signature from the fragging dwarf. And then they killed her. Snip, snip."

Ninn shoved Draye's head against the tree, knocking him unconscious again. She pushed off him and slammed her heel down on the sniffer, shattering it.

"We have to move," Ninn told Barega. "Benzo says someone's coming."

"Good good good dog." The collection of furniture parts raced after them.

Ninn glanced up as a shrill cry speared into her. Two galahs circled.

TWENTY-FIVE
COFFEE CLUTCH

Ninn would have enjoyed the rainforest aviary under most any other circumstance. She raced down the path, Mordred in her pocket, her pulling the Aborigine along and weaving between the tourists. Together, the two of them had one useable pair of arms, and she yelped when a boisterous teen bumped into her broken wrist.

"Sonofa—"

"Sorry, sorry lady!" he called.

She tried to tug Barega along faster.

Parents with children in tow gave her dirty looks as she jostled them on her mad dash, a go go go flipped a foul gesture at her, and one of the zoo employees got on her comm. Ninn caught something about reported felons in the area—so their current disguises weren't disguises anymore. Maybe Draye had come to and passed on their images; she could tell he had cybereyes; no doubt he'd recorded their current looks and broadcast it.

The birds of the aviary were splashes of amazing color amid the greens, and she jogged along she recognized stubble quail and painted snipe on the ground; lorikeets, cockatiels, and cockatoos of various sizes and colors perched above the heads of the visitors, squawking, singing, adding to the clamor. Glossy swiftlets swarmed overhead as thick as gnats; she'd read somewhere that the little birds spent most of their lives flying. Two galahs flew with them.

She followed the galahs and shoved a thickset man with a cyberarm out of the way, Barega apologizing in her wake.

"Good dog dog good dog." Benzo stayed on her heels.

"Where we going, Keebs? Chicago, I hope."

"This whole escapade has been nothing but bad ideas, Mordred," Ninn said. And it had...taking Cadi's case; thinking the RighteousRight was involved in the Cross slayings—which they weren't, though they most certainly were guilty of being narrow-minded rude bigots—letting Talon into her office; and not having a rigger or decker in her small circle of friends to pursue the leads through the Matrix—which would have beat the hell out of getting chased by AISE at the zoo. Shoot to kill order on her, how awesome was that? At least there were too many people around for the dwarf to pull his gun. He had to be getting close, though. "We're going there. Over there."

She tugged him harder, worrying that an old man like him might have a heart attack or stroke or just give out. Should've dropped him on a tram to the hospital, shouldn't've let him come here...but then she shouldn't have come here either.

Ninn angled down a narrowing path that cut between a line of red bopple nut and shaggybark trees. No ENTRANCE, the sign on the path said. A chain across it also made it forbidding, but was easy to slip past.

The path swept around behind a dunny and a storage building with a maglock on it. Couldn't waste a beat opening it. Another glance over her shoulder—no dwarf...yet. He'd find her; Draye had admitted they were tracking her. The next building was squat, green, and said CANTEEN on the side, likely the cafeteria for zoo employees. The door was propped open, and she darted in, dragging Barega. What would running in here do for her? Nothing. Maybe buy her a few minutes to think.

Three men—two of them human, one an elf with a tall camouflage mohawk, sat at a table drinking coffee or soykaf—zoo maintenance workers from their coveralls. Engrossed in their conversation, They'd probably come in here to get away from the press of tourists being ushered out. Ninn slipped right past them like she was supposed to be here and continued through a door at the back, which led to a kitchen. No cooks, no dishwashers, the place was empty. Staff would have probably been prepping for the lunch crowd if the zoo hadn't closed. She released Barega's arm, bent, and breathed deep. Benzo settled at her feet.

"Stay here," she said between gasps. "I'll lead them away. They're following me, tracking me, and until I can get rid of whatever is in me that they're homing in on, I can't shake them."

"I will stand by you, Nininiru."

"Stand by Me." Mordred's tone was sad. *"1986, based on a*

Stephen King novel about kids finding a body."

"They'll find two of them, Mordred." She locked eyes with the *koradji*. "Listen, old man, I've got Talon's death on my hands, as well as whoever else died in the fire because I made some Double-Rs as mad as a cut snake. I'm not getting you geeked, you understand? I can run faster without you. We'll stand a better chance. I don't have time to argue about it. Stay the hell right here, and after a while leave. Just go...somewhere." She glanced at the door next to a double-tub sink, *EXIT* stenciled on it. "Nice knowing you."

She had her good hand on the door when the dwarf and ork burst into the kitchen behind her.

"Moses on a moped," Mordred said.

The dwarf had a Fichetti machine pistol in his right hand—looked like a Military 100 model, and pulled a small Colt Agent Special out of his waistband with his left. He had a comm lead on the side of his head. "Got her, Draye. Taking her down now."

He fired both guns, but Ninn was moving, ducking and rolling behind an island counter, springing up and firing Mordred at the dwarf. Her aim wasn't as good left-handed, and the first three shots went wild, though one nearly hit the ork. She got a better look at him, the light streaming in from high windows around the kitchen making his body art practically glow. The tats weren't Aboriginal, but they were nothing she could describe, dizzying patterns that covered skin pulled so tight it looked like his rib bones were going to poke through. There was something arcane about him, she could sense it. He raised his hands and gestured at a row of pots hanging on the wall above the sink, they flew off and pelted her. The heaviest struck between her shoulders hard enough to almost make her drop Mordred.

The dwarf spun and then leaned out into the canteen. "Frag! The others're gone," he announced.

She took advantage of the dwarf's distraction and fired, clipping him in the shoulder, in the thin space between armor plates, hitting him in the back of the arm, the bullet lodging in padding. She fired on the ork, trying only to wound him, and catching him in the thigh. He dropped and grabbed his leg.

"Bloody bogger!" the dwarf shouted, whirling back and firing just as she ducked again, bullets hitting the stainless counter and ricocheting around the room.

"What the hell?" she hollered, skittering for a better position behind the counter, holding Mordred tighter, peeking up and firing again, this time hitting the dwarf square in the chest, which was so thickly armored he didn't even wince. "Why'd you have to shoot them? Those people out there! They did nothing!"

"Snip. Snip." The dwarf answered. Then he swung the gun on Barega. "Drop it, Tossinn. Drop your gun or I'll drop your mate here. I don't give a whit that he's not carrying. I'll splatter his brains. Drop it!"

Ninn paused, and more pots crashed into her, a fry basket hit her on the side of the head and she tasted blood. Her tongue ran over the remnant of a tooth.

"We're in the canteen, Draye," the dwarf said into his comm. "Tell Siland it's wrapped up. Right, she'll be." A pause: "Urlu, you ain't hit that bad. Finish her if she don't drop the gun."

A butcher knife hovered at the edge of Ninn's vision, held by invisible strings. The ork was on his feet, leaning against a counter. His eyes were ice blue, and she couldn't see any pupils in them. His face was heavily lined and dark, as if he'd spent a lifetime in the sun. One of the patterns on his skin moved. He wasn't without tech, though; wires led from a port high on his chest and wrapped around behind him. She should've shot to kill him when she had the chance.

"I'm gonna plug the old man, Tossinn. Last chance," the dwarf said. "If you don't drop it now. Now!"

"You win." Ninn set Mordred on the counter, held her arms out in a gesture of surrender and stepped back from the counter, which sat square in the center of the small room. She bumped into the double sink.

"Don't do this, Keebs," Mordred cautioned. *"Don't be letting me go. He's gonna kill the Koori anyway. You know that. And he's gonna kill you."* Softer: *"And then what's gonna happen to me?"*

"Snip, snip." The dwarf fired at Barega anyway, turning and firing next on Ninn, who presented a much better target standing away from the counter. At the same time, the ork gestured and the knife came at her, slicing through the air where her head had been. Ninn had dropped to her knees, saving her skin, somersaulting until she was up against the counter, too far away to grab Mordred. But...she spotted the spirit dog.

"Fetch, Benzo! My gun. Fetch it."

She heard a sound like an angry wind makes when it rushes in under a door, followed by more shots, and the clang of pans. A stack of heavy ceramic dishes cascaded on her, knocking her flat. Benzo appeared and dropped Mordred in front of her. Woozy from the onslaught of crockery, Ninn bit her lip to focus, pushed up with her good arm, grabbing Mordred's stock in the same notion.

The ork and Barega had squared off near a stove top, the ork with two hands raised and fingers wiggling, the *koradji* with one hand up, like they were in a magical showdown.

"You are a mere summoner, little dark man," the ork sneered. "I am your destruction. I can counterspell whatever hint of magic you toss at me. And I will utterly crush you and feed on your astral essence."

Barega bled from two sizeable holes in what had been his good arm, made by rounds from the dwarf's machine pistol. Ninn couldn't tell if the *koradji* was hit anywhere else. But it was a testament to the old man that he could still stand after the impact from those heavy bullets.

So where was the dwarf? In the other room? Ninn didn't hear him, didn't see him at first, the counter blocking her view of the floor. She stepped around it, feet crunching on shattered plates, edged closer to Barega. A clear shot now, she fired repeatedly on the ork, not caring he wasn't armed. The bullets hit some invisible barrier and dropped like wads of spit-out gum.

"Getaway, *2013*," Mordred said. "*Keebs...get away.*"

There was the dwarf...flat on his stomach in the kitchen doorway, the butcher knife that had been poised near Ninn protruded instead from the back of his thick neck, in a gap between pieces of his armored clothing. Blood pooled around the body.

"I did that," Barega said. "Stay out of this, Ninn."

The air felt electric and the hairs stood up on her arms. At first she thought it was her body crying for a slip, as she'd been way the hell too long without one. But the sensation changed, becoming hot and cold waves that chased each other from her heels to the top of her head. Her throat tightened, and she nearly pulled the trigger again, but stopped when a ring of flames sprung up around the ork.

Who'd done that? Did he? Some kind of defense?

There were faces in the fire, and it made a laughing, cackling sound. The ork cried out in agony. Barega had brought the fire. Then the flame wall suddenly dropped and a dozen kitchen knives flew past her at Barega, striking an invisible barrier—perhaps the same enchantment he'd used in the tunnel. The blades clattered to the floor.

"Nice," the ork said. "But it will only delay your death."

The comm on the dwarf's corpse squawked. *"On my way,"* Draye said. *"I called Siland."*

"Get out of here, Nininiru."

She'd never heard that tone from Barega before. It sent a chill down her spine.

"The back door, go through it. I'll join you in a few minutes, or I will not."

Ninn hesitated, and in that instant *really* took a look at the Aborigine. Since the day he'd appeared in her office, she'd considered him a frail old man, one step removed from a nursing home. The "old" part was still accurate, but there was nothing frail about him now. His eyes burned like coals, and thick ropy veins stood out on his neck, the envy of a bodybuilder. His jaw set, his thin lips worked, a faint singsong chant drifting out. She felt something emanating from him in pulses, power of some sort. The energy skittered through her, and she could feel her teeth. Old? Yeah. Slow? Yeah, he was that, too. Weak? Frail? No way in hell. He looked scary.

"Keebs—"

"Yeah, Mordred, we're leaving."

That sound she'd heard moments ago...of an angry wind slipping under a door...it returned and intensified as she slipped out the back door. The squawks and tweets from the nearby aviary, the shushing sound of the leaves in the breeze, the chatter from the crowd on the other side of the tree line...it drowned out all of that. The crescendo blotted out all the sound in the world, and then it abruptly stopped. Tentatively, the other noises returned.

Barega met her outside the kitchen a minute later.

She stopped herself from asking what happened to the ork, and whether Barega could teach her whatever he'd done in there. Instead, she pointed to another building, one that poked around the side of the Administration Centre that she'd originally sought. "We're going there. Maybe we can get rid of the homing beacon riding around in my innards before Draye finds us again."

"I hope there is something inside to sit upon," Barega returned. "Old men lie if they tell you their feet do not hurt. And... what is the expression? Yes. My arms hurt like hell."

TWENTY-SIX
THE DOCTOR IS INTERESTED

The veterinarian—Dr. Aiden Kappa, by the embroidery on his shirt—was tall and had the silhouette of a dagger, with the broad shoulders of a swimmer that tapered down to his slim hips and faux-suede Wellies. Ninn waved Mordred at him and looked around the office. Besides him, it was empty; her audio receptors didn't pick up anyone hiding behind the shelves and antique file drawers.

"Close the door," she told Barega. "Lock it if there is one."

She heard the latch flip.

The large room was the shape of a shoebox, twice as wide as Ninn was tall, and twice that in length, there were two other doors on the far wall, likely leading to examination rooms. Three desks were in a row along the near wall, each with a vet's nameplate. The largest desk matched Kappa's tag; he must be in charge.

"Where are the others?"

"We have five full-time veterinarians on staff. The others are on rounds because of the lockdown, making sure the animals are all right." He looked down his long nose at her. Despite being human, he had a handful of inches on her. "But they'll be back." She noticed his eyes were a startling, almost unnatural green; probably dyed irises or top-of-the-line cybereyes that looked real. "If you're looking for drugs, we don't keep any here."

"My friend there has two bullets in his arm." Ninn had noted there were no exit wounds, so the rounds had stuck. Barega didn't appear to have any other holes in him. "And his other arm is badly broken."

"And for both of those counts he needs a hospital." He pointed to her poorly bandaged wrist. "It looks like you could benefit from one as well."

Ninn waved Mordred again for effect. "Yeah. Well, I don't have time to go into it, but a hospital isn't an option right now." Those startling green eyes widened. "You're the two they're looking for."

She noted the scanner on the center desk, and quickly glanced around for surveillance. There had to be some, right? If there was, she didn't see it with a cursory look. "Mordred," she whispered. "Any video feeds in here?"

While she waited, she gestured with the gun, nodding Barega's way. "My companion needs help, and you're going to help him."

"Or you'll shoot me? And then who'll help him?" His smug reply was a poor attempt to mask his worry; Ninn saw his bottom lip quiver, and his fingers tapped together nervously. A close look at him: didn't see any obvious tech.

"But before you help him, you need to—"

"No video feeds in here, Keebs."

"What? I need to what? Call for help? We both know no one's going to hear me unless they're passing by."

"You need to remove my tattoos." Ninn had figured out that was the only thing that might have a signature. Tarr had repaired her, not added anything—except the nanite tattoos. The dwarf wouldn't have done anything else because she hadn't been paid for anything else. "The nanites under my skin."

"Your tattoos," Dr. Kappa said. "Really?" The disbelief was thick in his voice. He glanced at Barega, then back at Ninn. "Your friend is bleeding like a stuck warthog and you want me to excise your tats."

"Yeah," Ninn said. Sounds filtered in through the windows, nothing alarming yet...birds, leaves rustling, no pounding footfalls or shouts. "I really need them out. And if you value your skin, you'll do it."

He let out a breath that whistled between his teeth. "I suppose I can do that here. The middle desk, it's pretty empty. I suppose you'll want me to get some pain killer for both of you."

That sounded absolutely delicious, a little bit of numb would mollify that sweet spot in her soul.

"No," she said. "No pain killer, nothing to knock me out." She stepped over to Barega. "That arm working?" She indicated the one with the bullets. He didn't answer, but he flexed his fingers, and she stuck Mordred in them. "My friend here will shoot you if you do anything funny."

Ninn hopped up on a desk and lay down, staring at the ceiling, the faux wood uncomfortable and sticky from the summer heat against the back of her arms.

"Why do you want them removed? It's nice work." As the vet leaned over her, she noticed he had a small tat on the side of his neck, an all-too-familiar one.

She groaned. "RighteousRight."

"You want the tats removed because of the Right?" Dr. Kappa made a *hnnnnnnning* sound. "Or because it's easier to identify you? You're pretty distinctive looking regardless."

"Someone is tracking her," Barega said. "Probably by the tattoos."

Ninn grimaced. The vet didn't need to know that.

"Possible," Dr. Kappa returned. He reached into a desk drawer and pulled out a small kit, opened it and came up with a needle pack. "Difficult, quite. But possible. Nanotattoos are hard machines, and embed themselves as a lattice. They're basically liquid crystal microdisplays that hang just under your skin. PAN commands make the tattoo do something. Some provide camouflage, like military fatigues, some change colors, in your case the nanotattoos move—and quite beautifully so, I would say. Preprogrammed animation, decorative."

"How do you know so much about them? Ouch."

"Sorry. No pain killer, as you said, so this is going to hurt." He probed her cheek with a needle attached to a small coprocessor. "Well, some of our animals are tattooed, especially the ones we loan to other systems, and I usually do it, the tattooing. Sometimes I remove the tats if we sell the animals. We have five full-time veterinarians here, but I handle the tattooing. I worked in a tat parlor when I was going to uni."

"I bet the Double-Rs don't approve of tattoos. Except for those little neck things."

"Tattoos? Sure. They've no problem with tattoos and body art." Dr. Kappa rolled up his sleeve and held his arm above Ninn's face. An artistic ЯR with red and blue scrollwork wrapped around his forearm. "Regular ink, sure. Nanotattoos, no way. I had a couple when I first went to meetings. I liked what I heard there, liked the people, and so I had the nanotattoos removed. Got this ink instead." The vet turned and washed his hands in a small sink, put something on them and rubbed his palms furiously back and forth. "The Right believes putting anything foreign like that *in* your body is sacrilege."

"They don't like elves, either."

The vet shrugged. "Some in the Right. The real radicals. Shades of the Klan, huh? But really it's all about the additions. Like I said, I had a couple of nanotats when I worked at the parlor. I was particularly fond of a kangaroo that hopped up one arm and down the other."

"But the Right—"

"Wouldn't've liked it. Didn't like it, actually. I joined them about a year after I finished vet school. A lot of what they say makes sense. Not everything, but a lot."

"Tattoo, 1981," Mordred cut in. "*No more tats, Keebs.*"

"So, a tattoo...just how the hell can they trace me with a drekkin' tat?" Ninn knew Talon would have had the answer, and also probably a friend who could have removed all the nanites for her. How long was she going to beat herself up about him dying in the building fire? Until uber-resistent Alzheimer's kicked in?

"They'd have to get the signature of the nanites from whoever put them in."

That would be Dr. Tarr, and they could have got it out of her by roughing her up, maybe even torturing her. Or more likely she happily gave it to them, either she was an ally or easy to buy off. And they still killed her in the end to cut a loose end. Snip snip, as Draye and the dwarf were fond of saying.

"The more advanced tats can be changed—colors and patterns with a wireless device controlled by a commlink. Yours are preprogrammed, still having a signal. Someone searching the Matrix can find your signature. They'd have to be good, but it definitely could be done, even if the nanotattoo is in hidden mode."

The vet poked Ninn harder, and she tried not to wince. She suspected he was trying to cause her pain. "Be a lot of trouble, I'm thinking, to find someone through a tat. Someone wants you awfully bad. But then that's pretty evident by the bulletin circulated through the zoo, and the lockdown." He shoved the needles in faster. "Stay still, and I'll get rid of it for you. I'm basically vacuuming the nanites out. If I miss a few, it won't matter; there won't be enough of them left to give off a signature. In fact, the signature was disrupted the moment I sucked out the first one. I have a four-year-old daughter at home."

By that comment, Ninn guessed the vet figured she was going to kill him.

"I should use a trauma patch, but I don't have any in the office.

They're in the clinic two buildings over. Would mask the pain."

"It's fine," Ninn said. "I probably won't notice." She really wanted to shout "ouch!"

"So, what did you do?" Dr. Kappa asked. "To get a group of Aces on your elf ass?"

Apparently the zoo bulletin hadn't gone into detail. Ninn pulled her lips into a straight line, deciding whether to answer that.

"You and the Aborigine, what did you do?"

Barega started talking. In the span of the few minutes it took the vet to work on Ninn's tattoos, he supplied a short version of everything. His description of Eli in the tunnel was graphic.

The vet seemed to take their entire story in stride. "I have serious issues with the Renaixement program," Dr. Kappa said as he unwrapped the raincoat bandage from Ninn's wrist. "I'll need the clinic for this." He nodded at Barega. "And definitely for your friend. You shouldn't have been so pushy, elf. Should've gone there right away."

"Pushy is her nature," Mordred said.

"Couldn't waste the footsteps," Ninn said. "I needed the tats gone." A pause: "You know about Renaixement?" She pushed off the desk with her good hand and started recording everything.

"A little." The startling green eyes filled with ire.

"What do you know?"

"Spill," Mordred said. *"Make him spill, Keebs."*

"Only a little, I said. But enough for me to know Renaixement is nothing good."

TWENTY-SEVEN
SUBTERFUGE REBORN

Dr. Kappa used trauma patches on Barega, working on the surgical table in the large-animal clinic room. The place was immaculate, state-of-the-art, and at the back of the building, the only room with a maglock on the inside. Ninn thought that odd, but perhaps it was important that people couldn't just walk in during surgery on a lion or something. What was even odder was the lack of video surveillance. She'd noticed feeds throughout the rest of the clinic, and kept her hood up as they walked past. But there were no feeds in here, and Mordred confirmed it.

The gun was in her pocket now, unfolded; she'd decided the vet wasn't a threat...at least not at the moment.

The *koradji* closed his eyes and his lips worked, and Ninn wondered if perhaps he was "dreaming."

"About Renaixement," Ninn prompted.

The doctor grimaced. "You are pushy."

Desperate, Ninn thought.

"I had to look it up, the word," Dr. Kappa began. "It's Catalonian. An area in the north of Spain, southwest of France, on a good day about a hundred thousand or so people still speak it. The word translates as 'rebirth' or 'reanimation,' 'revitalization,' 'revivification,' all those sorts of things."

"It explains your brother," she told Barega. "Older than you, right? Looked young enough to be your granddaughter. Pretty revitalized. It might...maybe...explain some of the other entertainers. Maybe. But why have them killed?"

"Isn't that what I hired you for, Nininiru?" The Aborigine gave her a stern look. "To discover?"

"And you think it's 'nothing good,' eh?" Ninn turned back to Dr. Kappa and used his own words for it. "Nothing good?"

"Not when it involves the animals in this zoo." He continued working on Barega while Ninn stared at the chrono on the wall. Her hand drifted down to touch Mordred, finding a little measure of comfort in the gun's presence. She worried someone would come in here and she'd have to start shooting again—lefthanded. If Draye came with significant backup, it would be snip, snip. There was no other exit out of this room.

Dr. Kappa cleared his throat. "I don't think anyone's going to walk in on us. No surgeries scheduled today. My comm would buzz if there was an emergency. And Renaixement doesn't use these rooms during zoo hours."

Ninn still didn't relax; she'd had enough people after her the past couple of days to make that impossible. A slip might help. Just one, if she could manage to find it. There had to be slips around here, all these meds.

"The Right burned my office, the whole building in the Cross. You hear about that fire the other night? AISE says I did it. The Double-Rs did it, magnesium. I've got a few ideas how to prove it, too."

"Some elements of the Right are...militant. *Some.* There's a rough pocket in the Cross, a couple of troublesome ratbags I have nothing good to say about. But more good folk than bad. It's like any organization." The vet spoke to Barega now, softly and Ninn decided not to overhear. She was recording everything anyway, and could play it back later if she felt the need. Better that she just sit and fume for a while. More good folk than bad...like any organization...like AISE? Really?

Several minutes later, Dr. Kappa helped the *koradji* off the table and onto a bench against the wall. "Not very comfortable, sorry," he said. "No plush surfaces—germs, you understand."

Barega nodded.

"Next?" The vet beckoned Ninn over. "Let's see the wrist."

She thought about telling him it was fine, not to worry about it. She wanted to get out of here. And go where? But it was easier to shoot with her right hand.

"About Renaixement," she prodded again. "You said you know a little. Beyond what the word means."

"*Spill,*" Mordred said. "*And get him to do it while you and the* Koori *are still breathing.*"

"Renaixement..." The vet used a stim patch and injected her with something that stung like the blazes. Then he motioned, and a medical drone came out of a cabinet and started working on her wrist.

"You didn't use that on my friend's arm," she said.

"Didn't need to. Your friend has some magic in him. A little juice here, and I just helped augment what he was already working on. He'll be apples soon enough. The bullets, though. I had to dig them out."

"Renaixement," she repeated.

"Yeah, Renaixement." He continued working, offering her nothing for the pain. Payback, she figured, for waving a gun at him. "I began noticing things a while back," he continued. "So I started recording things, copying a few files on micro drives. I've no tech inside me, you understand."

"How righteous of you."

"There were some healthy young animals marked for study, 'Renaixement Therapy,' the records listed. Healthy. Perfect. They were lumped in with old, diseased animals, and a few that had been born missing a limb or two. Usually an insalubrious animal... if we can't correct it with a minimally invasive measure, behavior adjuster or the like...we set them aside for research. But the young, healthy animals. No. I looked into that."

"And—"

"Why are you so interested?"

Barega chimed in again. "The Cross Slayer was both a man and an animal, or perhaps a man with animal parts grafted to him, and he had a Renaixement identifying number tattooed on his face. He looked like a mix of human and sea lion."

The ears! Ninn had thought something familiar about the ears. They'd looked like a seal's ears. She'd thought him perhaps part killer whale, but Barega was right. And the Slayer's skin. It was covered with fine, black hair. Like a seal.

"What the hell," she mused. "A seal. Listen, Doc, I need to access your system, look up Renaixement, the Moon Corporation. See what they're doing to people, what they did to Ella."

"Adoni," Barega said. "My brother."

"You won't find anything. It was there, pieces of it, like a puzzle missing parts. Maybe I didn't know how to look and put it all together. Doesn't matter. Now it's all gone. Maybe too many people looking where some higher-ups didn't want anyone looking."

"And you looked. A lot?"

A shrug. "In the past three months, a scattering of healthy animals have disappeared, most of them from new litters. I saw a couple of crates—the kind you put live animals in—being loaded on a Moon Corporation helivan in the staff lot. I almost hitched a ride. But I have a daughter. I looked into it—the Moon Corporation is a bio-firm about fifty klicks south of Whoop Whoop." He finished with her wrist, dismissed the drone, and helped her sit. "A good long way from here if you're on foot. The research center's located in the low part of the Blue Mountains, around the ruins of Windsor."

A long way. A Milton quote flashed in her head: "Long is the way and hard that out of hell leads up to light." Prophetic? Ninn flexed her wrist and moved her fingers. Sore, but it worked. Really sore. God, she could use something for the pain and to take the edge off. She slid from the table, seeing deep scratches on the surface that had been made by some large animal.

"I asked around, looked maybe once too often. I'm into causes, you understand. Animal rights. Human rights."

Ninn frowned. "Righteous rights."

"No one had answers...where the animals had disappeared to. I thought perhaps more were being marked for this Renaixement Therapy, and that they'd stopped recording that. The other vets had been asking questions, too. We were all talking a little. Maybe talking too much. Now all the Renaixement citings in our system are gone. All of them. Not a mention left." He took off his gloves and stuffed them in a biohazard disposal unit. "The biologist on the project ended up dead. And he was the one we posed our questions to."

"The Slayer's first victim," Barega supplied. "The biologist died by the monster."

"Then one of our staff vets...moved...though no one seems to know where. Supposedly moved. Canberra, somebody said. I stopped asking questions. I have a four-year-old daughter. This posting pays well. I think I make a difference here."

"I get you," Ninn said. "But what else?" There was something in his face. He was holding something back.

"Wave me at him, Keebs. I'll make him talk," Mordred said.

"I came in after midnight a month back, to check on a sick lion. She was resistant to the antibiotic nanites. I wanted to look in personally."

Hypocrite, Ninn thought, *eschew tech for you, jump in bed with the Double-Rs, but use it on the animals.* He'd probably used some healing nanites on her, delivered through the drone.

"I checked on her, no change. There were lights on in here, so I thought I'd see if someone had an emergency, maybe help out if they needed it. In this room, through the monitor, I saw a bear on this table." He drummed his fingers on its surface. "Records said the bear had fallen into a moat, injured too severely to save it. But it wasn't a regular necropsy they were doing, and the vets weren't the zoo's regular staff. I'd never seen them before. Two of them, cutting slabs of tissue, had organ transport boxes and were stuffing them full. I came back the next morning, and there was no record of any necropsy, just a note that the bear's body had been disposed of. We give the carcasses to a fertilizer company. The video feed of what I'd saw had been wiped, and a maglock had been installed *inside* the room." He pointed to the door, which he had locked when they came in. "There are no video feeds in this room any more. That's against protocol. And it used to be against regulations...back when the city owned the zoo."

"You think it's related to Renaixement? The bear?"

He shrugged. "One of the people working on the bear...I saw her mug in one of the files that mentioned Renaixement Therapy, saw her with Henry, too. I don't suppose she really was a vet."

"Henry?"

"The lead biologist who got—"

"—geeked by the Slayer. Snip. Snip." Ninn blew out a deep breath. "So what the bloody blue blazes is so...I dunno, secretive, dangerous...that people are dying over this? Being killed? Cadi? Ella Gance? There's companies out there working to extend lives, make people more beautiful. I don't think they're using a monstrous serial killer to take out their clients."

"It's dangerous to dig into this," Dr. Kappa ran his fingers through his sandy blond hair. The startling green eyes looked troubled. "I think about Henry. Then I think about my kid."

"Dangerous or not, we have to know," Barega said. "The galah led us here." He'd come off the bench and stood behind Dr. Kappa.

"I told you I stopped asking questions. I have a daughter."

"I don't have anyone left," Ninn said. "I have nothing and no one to lose."

"They're still searching for you." Dr. Kappa glanced at the chrono now. "Even though the zoo is closed, if you go out there while they're looking—"

"You will hide us until it is dark, all right?" Barega's eyes were wide, and Ninn saw the hint of bulging veins in his neck. Was the *koradji* doing magic, or merely asking politely?

"I can try, but I don't want trouble."

"But it bothered you enough to poke," Ninn said quietly. "Bothered you enough to risk a little trouble."

"Easier to get you out at night, I'd think. Won't have to wait long for that." The vet wiped off the table, made sure the room looked undisturbed. "Easier to hide in the shadows."

"The shadows are my friend," Ninn muttered.

"In the Shadows, *2001, James Caan.*"

TWENTY-EIGHT
MOON OVER NEW SOUTH WALES

They didn't have to wait long at all, however. Sydney's mana cloud intervened and both ruined and improved the day.

The wind came first, strong enough to rattle the siding on the clinic building. Power flickered, everything went dark, and then the lights came back on.

"The Weatherman *said it should be fine all day,*" Mordred said. A pause: "*2005, Nicolas Cage.*"

"Generator," Dr. Kappa said. "Feeds the clinic and main offices, and the security grid." Ninn hadn't asked. "Some people head for the trams when the big ones come. The regulars ride it out in the nocturnal exhibits, reptile house, all the places with walls and roofs."

"A good time for us to flee for a tram," Ninn said.

"We're going back to my office first."

From there he called his mother. "I might be late. Pick Ann up from Kiddie Care. If something happens...if I don't come home—take care of her for me." He ended the call and rummaged in his desk drawer.

"Do you have any slips?" Ninn kept her voice low. "Pain slips? Slips...something." Her fingers itched. She'd been way too long without. "I need something..."

"Sorry, everything's monitored. As it is, I'll have to come up with a reason why I used stim patches, trauma patches, nanites from the drone. Emergency surgery on something, a boomer."

Large male kangaroo, she mentally translated.

He retrieved a Walther Secura, an old gun that European security favored ages back. Ninn cocked her head in question.

"Bought it when I first noticed the odd things going on around here." He jammed the magazine in, put an extra one in his pocket, then went to the middle desk and looked through its bottom drawer. "We can't stay here. Jake'll be back any minute. He hates these bad storms." Dr. Kappa pulled out a slightly larger gun, a Taurus Multi-6; Ninn had owned one in the States. It was a reliable revolver.

He handed the Secura and spare mag to Barega, who took it without argument. "Just in case," Dr. Kappa told him. "My brolly's on the hook. One of you can use it. I'll borrow Jake's. I'll try to help you get out, or close to it. *Try*, understand. I've my own skin to think about."

"And your daughter. I get it." Ninn grabbed the umbrella and passed it to Barega, who put the Secura in his pocket so he could hold it. "For all the good this will do against that," he said, gesturing out the door to the sheets of rain pounding down.

No sign of pink lightning. *Nothing wrong with a good summer drenching,* Ninn thought...*if no funky colored lightning bolts accompanied it.*

The trio cut through the thicket beyond the canteen, avoiding an AISE recovery crew there for the bodies of the dwarf and the ork and the coffee drinkers—no doubt all those deaths would be blamed on her, too. They hurried down one twisting path after the next, avoiding the larger exhibits where Dr. Kappa said video feeds were more numerous. Down and around they jogged, everything looking like smeared watercolors because of the rain, puddles up to the tops of their shoes because the ground and the drainage system couldn't absorb it fast enough.

"I think you can make it from here," Dr. Kappa said. They were on Taronga Road, near the cassowary enclosure, backs against a thick boab tree. "Straight through—"

"I know where we are. I think you should come with us." Ninn had been thinking about the vet on the scamper down the hillside. "I think you'll be safer."

He laughed and nervously stared through the curtain of water. Small clumps of zoo workers stood under an overhang by the cassowaries, a few more under the canopy of another thick boab. "I took bullets out of him." He pointed to the *koradji*.

"Barega."

"I fixed your wrist—"

"Ninn," she said. "Nininiru Tossinn. But you probably know my name from the alerts."

"Yeah, they mentioned it."

"AISE killed people drinking coffee in the canteen, Doc. Those folks saw me, and saw the AISE goons coming after me. They died because of that. No witnesses. If you're on any video feeds with us, they'll kill you, too. Your vet buddy who moved. We both know he didn't leave Sydney. He went belly up with Henry. These are bad people, Doc, snipping off any loose ends to protect whatever it is they're doing. No witnesses, get it? And my aim is to the cut the numbers of these very bad people so I can keep on breathing. If you're not coming with, you should leave here right now, get your daughter, leave the city, and never come back."

With nothing left to say, she darted forward, Barega following, her audial receptors faintly picking up the *slap-slap-slap* of the old man's shoes. He was keeping up, but she wasn't running full out.

She'd thought the vet might come along, but was glad he didn't. She didn't need to be looking out for one more soul; it was hard enough to keep Barega and her alive. Anyone else was potential collateral—like Talon. She doubted Dr. Kappa would ever see his four-year-old daughter again.

They cut through the brush by the petting zoo, slipped across Marine Parade, where an AISE quartet armed with assault rifles stood, drenched and huddled over a shared handheld monitor. Maybe they were still trying to track her, and maybe that monitor would lead them to the clinic where the vet removed the nanites. Kappa would have been safer with them, or at the very least he should have beat feet out of the zoo and found safety fifty klicks away.

The path here was slick with mud where earth had washed away from the patches of foliage, and it clung to her feet. They hugged the building by the Macquarie Island exhibit; looking through the window, she saw it was packed with visitors avoiding the storm. Two more AISE officers were outside on the opposite corner—these with Ares Sigma-3 submachine guns.

What were the odds she and Barega would live to see the end of the day?

There were more AISE officers and zoo security at the lower turnstile, but Barega managed a way around them. At the edge of a service path, he created another one of his air barriers, canting it so that he and Ninn could climb it—up and over a fence that had a bevy of sensors. No doubt someone would see them leaving when they reviewed the feeds.

Minutes later, they were on Bradley's Head Road, that

wrapped around the zoo and led to a parking lot usually full of tour buses. No video feeds that she could see, or that Mordred could detect—except for the big, obvious one at the lot entrance. The lot was mostly empty now.

"That's big." Barega tipped the umbrella toward the far end of the lot, the widest point, where a streamlined helicopter parked, rotors slowly turning.

"I need to get closer to that." Ninn crept around the edge of the duracrete lot, using the few remaining vehicles and the overhang of trees for concealment. Benzo followed her. She didn't see any video feeds, but there might be some in the vehicles that AISE would access.

"Aerospace Emblem," she said, pulling up the information through her coprocessor. "It's a shuttle helicopter, can pack in quite a few passengers. See the logo?"

The copter was sleek and black, looking malevolent in the downpour. On its side was a blue-white pockmarked circle with a stylized *CORP* in the center.

"I'd say that's the logo for the Moon Corporation, dontcha think?" She let out a low whistle. "Bet that's expensive as the Blue Mountains. Rode in something similar once, AISE officers taking advanced training in Queensland. Smart materials, ducted props to cut the noise. Listen, you can't even hear those blades turning, can't hear the engine, and it's on. The one I rode in was from Aztechnology. But the small print on the lead door says—" She enlarged the image with her cybereye and recorded it. "Prometheus. The upshot, that's my ticket to the Moon Corporation. Vet said the place is fifty klicks south of Whoop Whoop."

"I don't know where Whoop Whoop is."

"Just a phrase, Barega. Pure Aussie. It means in the middle of nowhere." She studied his face. He looked so very old, shadowed by the big umbrella and the overhanging tree limbs. "So your brother...Ella...was into Renaixement somehow. This entertainer I talked to, Hurdy Gertie...she said Ella gave a lot of nuyen to Renaixement. I figure somehow it held back time for her."

"Turned back time," Barega corrected. He pulled deeper into the brush, and Ninn followed, still keeping her eyes on the 'copter.

"Good dog," Benzo said.

One man inside that she could see—the pilot. There might be more, the windows darkened against prying eyes. Another man standing outside talking on a comm, seemingly oblivious to the rain. The man outside was in deep blue coveralls with the same circular logo on the breast.

"There are things in this world—magic maybe, technology, medicine—that can stave off the years, or let you hold onto your youth longer," Barega continued. "I know about this world, Ninn. I've been to this city, other cities before. I lived with my brother in a flat in Canberra forty years ago, even took some courses at the uni. I tried civilization on and off, and found the blues to my liking...and some of the food. But I prefer the Outback and my solitude. My brother wanted nothing to do with the quiet places."

He paused, eyes seemingly locked on a caterpillar clinging to the underside of a leaf. But Ninn thought he was looking at something far away and long ago.

She glanced at the helicopter; no one had moved.

"Adoni aged, Ninn, like any man should, and he tried things... medical things...to hold off the years. And surgery, a procedure to make his face more feminine. He did not want surgery to change his sex, however. Adoni said he was not transsexual or dualsexual or asexual, that he considered all such labels useless and judgmental and unnecessary. He said he was simply a female impersonator. A very good one." He closed his eyes. "Very, very good, Ninn. When I visted him in Sydney to hear him sing, only nine years ago, he was younger, and I hardly recognized him. The years had turned back and back and back, and he would not discuss it. Ninn, it was not cosmetic. Not *merely* cosmetic."

"Renaixement, I get that. Whatever it all entails. Your brother was part of that."

"And when I saw his body in the morgue...he looked younger still."

"Time is not a subtle thief of youth," Ninn said, paraphrasing Milton. "I'm going on the 'copter, see if I can stow away. Stay here, old...friend." She scurried around to the far side of the helicopter.

The man outside continued talking on his comm, but looked up suddenly. Ninn worried he might have spotted her and Benzo. He said something to the pilot, and then started toward a brace of elf-high flowering acacias at the edge of the lot. They gyrated madly, despite the lack of wind, as if someone was snared inside. Ninn was curious, too, but rather than investigate used the distraction to slip onto the copter. Benzo leaped in on her heels. Heartbeats later Barega followed, and they found cover at the back behind empty crates marked "live animals."

"I did that," he whispered. "Moved the bushes."

Ninn glared. If someone removed the crates to fill them, she
and Barega would be caught and geeked. Bad enough she felt responsible for Talon's demise. "Let's hope, old man, that the Moon
Goons are not taking animals today. Because if—"

He knitted with his fingers, a pattern she called up through
her coprocessor. It matched his gestures when he'd created the
silent bubble. Good timing, as a half-dozen men in deep blue coveralls came on board. Ninn had watched them approach through
the tinted windows. Each had a holdout pistol in a holster at their
waist, and a serious threat hanging on their shoulder—looked like
a Colt Cobra by their shapes.

Minutes later the helicopter lifted off; Ninn hoped the pilot
was good, given the heavy rain.

Ninn pulled Mordred out of her pocket and placed his clear
barrel just past the edge of the crate. "You be my eyes here; let me
know if anyone's coming back this way."

"*Right as rain,*" the gun said.

"And Mordred," she subvocalized, not wholly trusting Barega's spell to stop the sound. "What do you know about Windsor,
in the Blue Mountains? Got anything in your programming?"

She'd never heard of the place, though she'd been to the
mountains and visited a koala sanctuary. That's where the vet had
said the Moon Corporation was...if he was correct. She wondered
if Dr. Kappa was still sucking in oxygen.

"*North of Sydney, settled in the late 1700s,*" Mordred said, his
voice monotone like a recorder playing a school lesson. "*Third
oldest British community on the continent. Windsor was a breadbasket
in those early days. A rumor crossed the governor's desk in 1813 that
the French were going to sail up the Hawkesbury River and cut off the
Windsor granary, playing foul with Sydney. The invasion never happened, the community grew to about eighteen hundred, and then the
first big storm came and took them all, leveled most of the buildings.
Not a survivor, and no one moved in and rebuilt—maybe because the
river often floods...all the rain, ya ken? Or maybe out of fear, maybe out
of respect for the dead.*"

Except the Moon Corporation, Ninn thought. *Moon doesn't seem
to respect anyone.*

In the back of her mind, she heard the dwarf in the canteen
gun down the coffee drinkers.

Snip snip...

TWENTY-NINE
THE CORPSE SOLUTION

Medical science advanced every day. Ninn had brought her sister to Sydney because the city was known for its "miracles," though no miracle had happened. The treatments had merely prolonged the end.

She still kept up on stuff, mostly because she liked upgrading her bioware and cyberware and put new options on her shopping list. She knew about chemicals and bio-attachments that slowed aging, and figured that at some point she'd embrace some of that—if she had the nuyen. Adding years was expensive. Hadn't thought a whole lot about it, though. Elves had long lifespans. But humans...like Ella-Adoni, they burned out fast. Trolls and orks burned out faster.

"Wonder what this place looks like from the outside, you know...above." The helicopter had landed several minutes ago, the engine shut down, passengers filed out. No one disturbed the crates. Someone moved around the outside; she heard panels open and close, probably the pilot inspecting the engine.

"Does it matter?" Barega looked exhausted.

"I suppose not." Ninn glanced out the tinted window. It wasn't raining here, but by her estimation, they'd traveled far enough that they were out from under Sydney's cloud. It looked sunny. "Unless someone comes out to take this bird for another ride, I want to wait until it's dark."

Barega curled up behind a crate. Benzo lay at his feet.

"Then I'll find a way in...provided we really are at the Moon Corp, get on a computer—"

"You will not need a computer, Nininiru."

She huffed. "Siland...whoever's here...they're not going to volunteer anything, Barega. I need computer records to find out—"

"A *koradji* such as yourself does not need a computer...or Siland or anyone else *living* inside to confess their sins." Barega closed his eyes. "But a gun would be useful. I am sure you will have to shoot somebody. You always have to shoot somebody." In a heartbeat, he was sleeping.

"Shooter, *2007, Mark Wahlberg*. The Shooter, *1997, Randy Travis.*"

Getting inside hadn't been as difficult as Ninn had expected; there were badges in the helicopter, and she found spare deep blue coveralls in the copter bay...which was on the roof of a large, round building on stilts perched over the river.

The badges got them through security doors, and they took the stairwell, where, if there was surveillance, she couldn't see it. A barracks, chapel, social room, mess—the top level looked military...and fortunately had a video room, where two security guards watched feeds from throughout the complex and the surrounding sodden grounds and who—thankfully—tried pulling matching Thunderbolt pistols when she stepped inside. It took two seconds to draw Mordred from her pocket. The men were dead in two more, the door closed and maglocked, and she and Barega seated at the console, looking from one screen to the next.

"I was correct," the Aborigine said. "You had to shoot someone."

"Sometimes they need to be shot."

Barega nodded and smiled faintly.

"You understand there's a strong possibility we won't be getting out of this." Ninn studied a screen slightly larger than the others. It showed a lab. Most of the screens showed labs.

"I am not afraid of death, Nininiru. I am only a visitor to this time and place."

"I know about some of this," Ninn spoke aloud, but it was only for her benefit. "When I brought my sister to this stinking big island, I learned about skin grafting and regrowing flesh...that's what they're doing in this little lab here. See these tanks and monitors? I recognize this stuff. They're doing some other things too, with this tank and this one, but these tanks up front, that's flesh regrowth. See? This tank even has a woman in it, on oxygen feed. Back in the city, they had my sister in one of those tanks. Not as fancy as that one, though."

She looked at the next monitor and moved the stick to pan the room. "This place is pretty big. I count nine labs, and this one here...this is like an organlegging operation."

"And this—" Barega pointed to the view of a room bathed in blue light.

"Dunno. It's got...seals. We need to go there."

"And this—" Barega pointed again.

"That looks like a morgue. Yeah, that's a morgue."

"We need to go *there*," Barega said.

"Yeah." Ninn scrutinized the old man. "You really didn't need me for any of this, did you? Investigating your brother's death? You could have done this all on your own."

"The galah sent me to you, Nininiru."

"You didn't need me. Did you?"

"I suppose not." Barega tipped his head in acknowledgement, his eyes mirthful. "But you needed me."

The Moon Corporation's morgue made Sydney's counterpart look like a relic. Corpses were stored in tanks filled with a gelatinous material that Ninn guessed kept the flesh from decaying. The tanks were stacked three-high, *again the military similarity*, she thought. The dead looked like they were sleeping in watery army bunks. Four banks of tanks, for a total of one dozen corpse nests. Half were occupied, and one held an all-too-familiar body.

The Slayer.

"They brought him back here." She touched the glass. It felt cold, but not like in Sydney's morgue, more the pleasant chill of a summer drink type of cold. "Why?" *So his body wouldn't be discovered floating belly up in the harbor? So they could study him? Make another one, if they hadn't already?* His corpse was so big, the legs and arms were pressed against the side of the tank. "I'd thought the sharks would have eaten him."

It should smell in here, she thought, *chemicals or death or floor cleaner...something.* But all she could detect was her own pong from going too long without a bath.

"He is held here, Ninn, the Slayer's spirit. I feel it. Held by something, like my brother is held to his perfect body."

She felt it, too. His was the middle tank, eye level to her. She pressed the side of her face against the glass. It felt good, the coolness, her skin still aching from the nanites being culled. The vet could have given her something for the pain. Dear God, she needed a slip. She felt her insides quivering for a hit of graypuppy. If she got out of here, somehow, made it back to the Cross, she knew a man who would cut her credit on some graypuppy. High interest, a veritable loan shark, but it would be worth it. She needed it bad.

"Clear your mind, like you did before."

"When I danced with your brother," Ninn whispered. "Like I did then? You could do this, Barega. Easier for you."

"I could watch the door." The Aborigine had the borrowed gun in his hand, and put his back to hers. "Benzo and I will keep watch." The dog trotted after him.

In *Paradise Lost*, Milton wrote: *Millions of spiritual creatures walk the earth unseen, both when we wake, and when we sleep.*

Did she really want to connect with the spirit of this monster? There were five other bodies in this place...two men, one an elf; three women, one an ork that had similar tribal markings to the fellow in the canteen. Perhaps one of their spirits still clung to this place.

Just do this. Clear your mind. Do this, do what it takes to get your answers or some measure of justice. For Cadi. Do this and escape, drown in graypuppy and mollify the sweet spot. Her fingers trembled for need of the drug.

Ninn stared at the body in the viscous liquid. The smooth, shiny black skin was marred from the struggle in the tunnel; chunks were missing where a shark or sharks had eaten part of him. That the entirety of the monster had not been devoured was a puzzle. Maybe the beast tasted awful. Again she was struck by his darkness. Black like pitch, like oil that had been spilled and somehow hardened. His ears were holes—those of a seal, truly. His mouth looked like a seal's. The teeth...those were man-made and seriously nasty.

"Concentrate. Focus."

Was that Barega talking? Whoever it was, the voice came from far away.

"Release the physical world." It sounded like Barega, but the voice was a whisper. "Release the—"

Like in the morgue in downtown Sydney, a mist formed around her, the foggy wisps forming arms and legs, the mist cocooning her. But it had a different feel. This was cloying and damp, and the fog grew thicker and more opaque, and she swore her feet left the floor and that she floated in the same viscous liquid as the Slayer's corpse.

A face emerged, black and wide, beadlike eyes—seal eyes or human eyes? She felt herself floating *inside* him, looking out through those beady eyes and suddenly seeing...an office? The abrupt transition nearly threw her out of the connection.

She'd been here before, in this office, when she'd gone upstairs at Cadigal's and met...

Siland was in front of her, talking to her...to the Slayer, except it wasn't the Slayer...it was a man. Looking out through his eyes, she saw human hands, old and wrinkled and blue veins standing out, liver spotted, and realized they were his.

"Lover, won't you find me, find me?
I'm lonely, won't you keep me, keep me?"

It was Ella's voice, coming in through a speaker on the desk. Applause followed. Siland must be listening...must *have been* listening...to the performance downstairs on Cadigal's stage. She tripped through the memories of the person Siland spoke to—Elijah Moon, the head of Moon Corporation, major shareholder in the Sydney Zoo, and owner of who-knew-what-else. Elijah Moon, who later became the monster Eli.

The men discussed their fortunes and properties and immortality.

Hudson Siland.

The realization hit her like a bolt of pink lightning.

In her first meeting with Siland, he'd said: "My great great grandfather Hudson owned this entire block, passed it along, eventually to my father who kept most of it and passed it on to me when he died." The antique picture on the wall of Siland's great-great-grandfather...it was *his* picture. He was the *original* Hudson Siland. There'd been no passing it down. He'd retained it, probably making it look like he'd died and given it to a child. Records were easy to forge. *But it was the original man.* Hudson Siland had cheated death with science, continued to postpone it through whatever was cooked in the labs here. And Moon?

She looked through the spirit's eyes, taking in the office. That picture of the original Hudson...the man with him in one of the photographs was Moon. Younger, most certainly, than the relic with the liver spots. Same man. Same men.

Why had Siland been able retain his youth, and Moon had aged?

Ninn tripped through Moon's muddled mind, and the spirit obliged her. In fact, Elijah Moon seemed desperate to tell his sordid tale.

They were biologists, come to Australia many decades ago, bent on studying the indigenous animals and plants, and discovering a proprietary formula that allowed them to live well past their years. The mana storm affected their crops and studies, and they were forced to expand their quest for immortality in other directions. They owned so much, and Australia's sea and wildlife were theirs to toy with. So wealthy, they improved their laboratories and acquired the best scientists—who gladly worked with them for a taste of immortality. They discarded the ones deemed a risk.

They experimented with the locals.

And then with people in the Cross.

Adoni. Ella Gance.

Moon had first heard her sing in Katoomba, a middle-aged drag queen that the years had not been especially kind to. But that voice. That amazing voice.

"Lover, won't you find me, find me?
I'm lonely, won't you keep me, keep me?"

Adoni was quick to embrace the possibility of renewed youth, and promised to sing for Moon forever. Siland and Moon required Adoni to pay them for the bioware that continued pumping the precious elixir into her system. It kept her on a leash, never able to gain enough nuyen to go elsewhere, always under Moon's thumb...and then Siland's thumb. Had they loved her? Or was she just a pretty, singing toy to them?

But Adoni grew tired of the influence and so threatened to spill their secret, let everyone know that two well-known businessmen were the ultimate geezers who should be ashes, and that they were sitting on a true fountain of youth. Moon was certain Adoni's threats had no substance, that the singer would do nothing that might jeopardize her own health. But they considered their toy broken. She had to die...along with a scattering of other entertainers who were nothing more than a ruse to draw the public away from the one necessary death. The public loves a good serial killer story, Moon's muddled mind thought.

And the necessary death before Adoni's, a cocky biologist who talked too much and headed up the animal culling operation.

"Snip snip," she heard Siland say to Moon through her spirit dream. "All the loose ends gone, we'll be safe to live forever."

Cadigal? He was a loose end too, wasn't he? Ninn thought. Hiring Ninn, demanding to discover who killed his favorite impersonator...snip. One more victim of the Cross Slayer.

Eli...Elijah Moon.

She realized the two men couldn't let their secret get out. Governments would step in to regulate it, other corporations would take any measures to steal it, even militaries might intervene. To keep it their own, to keep their immortality, it had to remain secret.

"What happened?" Ninn breathed. "What happened to you?"

The Slayer was eager to share. The days and months melted in a dizzying blur of images that Ninn tried to digest as she floated in the corpse sludge that cocooned the creature that used to be Elijah Moon.

His body had begun rejecting the bioware that pulsed with the serum that gave him years, reversed decades...and had reversed the years for Ella Gance and a handful of chosen others. Other means to dispense the serum were tried on Moon, then variations on the serum, then experimenting with animals that they'd already been testing for other research...cures for diseases. Splicing animal DNA into metahumans had met with some success, and that's what Moon opted to do, though he was human—and that type of splicing had not been tried in their labs. Change his DNA just enough so he'd no longer reject the bioware, and so that the precious serum would again work and return him to a robust man seemingly in his prime. But even that yielded minimal results. So they tried again because he was aging, the years catching up and the grave calling.

Seals. That showed the most promise. With a touch of killer whale, platypus, and shark DNA.

Tried everything.

A DNA soup.

And, in so doing, made Moon into a monster.

His spirit let Ninn know he was not displeased. Strong, vibrant, vision incredible, the years held at bay again. Indestructible. He could heal at a marvelous rate. He'd lost some of his magnificent scientific mind along the way. Was to be expected, he understood, like in the old days when a man underwent hardcore chemotherapy and "chemo brain" resulted. Moon called his condition "seal brain." An acceptable loss for the gain of immortality.

He grew to like the killing.

So proud of this house of horrors, the Slayer's spirit treated her to a tour of the facilities, reveling in the twisted painful science inflicted on humans, metahumans, and creatures from the Sydney Zoo. Ninn felt twisted inside, but she paid attention and committed the place to memory...room-by-room, level-by-level, storage containers especially.

When at last she distanced herself from the spirit, she came to on the floor, Barega hovering over her. Was that worry on his face? She was wet with a slime that covered only her skin. Oddly, it had not touched her borrowed coveralls. The liquid the Slayer floated in? Or something else?

"No one deserves to live forever, Nininiru."

"We are all visitors to this time, this place," she replied. "We are just passing through. Our purpose here is to observe, to learn, to grow, to love...and then we return home."

"And in a few years, I will return home. But I will use that time to teach you."

"I want to learn it all." Ninn took a last look around the morgue. "Gotta go," she told Barega and Benzo. "There's a routine the guards walk. I've got it." She disabled the monitors as she talked. "It's rather predictable, and they're well-armed, but not overly jumpy. Who would come all the way out here, after all? Got a couple of labs to visit, a handful of things to disconnect. We time this right, we don't get caught. We time this very carefully, and I'll be an apt student."

They gathered oxidizers, reducing agents, magnesium, broke open solvents, mixed them well and set them ablaze in key places.

"Now we run like the wind, Barega."

This time he had little trouble keeping up with her.

They watched the inferno consume the building from the safety of the swollen riverbank, just at the edge of the Great Ghost Dance. It was barely dawn and the single, nacreous cloud at the top of the sky was all milky blue and opalescent gray, shimmering, beautiful, shiny, a hint of rosy pink. It invited Ninn to stand beneath its pulsing strands in wonder and appreciation while she watched the Moon Corporation come down. Just beyond the edge of the cloud, the rain couldn't reach the big round building to help put out the fire.

Sirens, lights, men scurrying...nothing could save the place. Ninn had made sure to disable the elaborate and state-of-the-art sprinkler system first.

The stench was incredible, but it dissipated, a wind whipping up and blowing the worst of it away.

"I want to learn more, Barega. All of it."

"I have a great deal to teach you, Nininiru." He pointed to the northwest. "I live there, a hundred or so klicks from Whoop Whoop. You'll be able to find me when you are ready. The galah will show you."

"I've a few things I need to do first."

"I understand." Barega nodded. "Bring some coffee when you come, the real stuff."

THIRTY
SNIP SNIP

It took her two weeks to make it back to the Cross. On the way, she stopped at the outskirts of Sydney at a sheep farm owned by a RighteousRight family who was not militant about her tech. There was a *Help wanted* sign posted outside.

The Sydney Zoo vet was correct, she decided, *not all the Double-Rs were bad.* She traded some manual labor for a place to sleep, a pocketful of nuyen, and a change of clothes...coveralls that somehow fit her fine, topped with a floppy hat, both an effective disguise. The spirit dog nearly stayed behind, apparently relishing nipping the heels of his temporary charges. But in the end, he followed her.

Now they strolled along Darlinghurst late at night, the sidewalk slick from a recent rain, puddles reflecting the swirling colors of the signs of restaurants, pubs, and sex parlors. The cloud looked heavy, promising another downpour to make the puddles bigger.

"Going Home," Mordred pronounced. *"1971. Jan-Michael Vincent was nominated for a Golden Globe for Best Supporting Actor for his portrayal of Jimmy. He lost to Ben Johnson."*

"Not my home anymore," she said. "Not for long anyway."

Cadigal's Corner had a CLOSED banner spread across the entrance, and the colorful advertisements that had been on the building exterior—including the poster of the beautiful Ella Gance—had been removed. Ninn wondered if Hurdy Gertie and the others had found work elsewhere. She hoped so. Maybe in the next few evenings, she'd poke her nose into some of the tawdry houses along the strip to see if they had. Wouldn't be a bad way to spend a little of the nuyen from her sheep-herding.

The back door to Cadigal's was shuttered, wood planks nailed across it, along with a simple maglock she had no trouble defeating. She slipped inside, picking up the scents of perfume and floor cleaner and memories, and wondering if Cadi's spirit was tied to this place. Ninn stopped herself from trying to find out.

She popped the next lock and took the stairs up. If Siland wasn't home, she'd wait for him; he'd show eventually. Deciding to make an entrance either way, Ninn kicked the door at the top open.

"You again!" It was the familiar thug, recognizing her in spite of the coveralls. She figured he must have tech or had memorized her face. He reached for his gun, but she and Mordred were faster.

He fell, a hole dead center in his forehead.

She moved quickly now, like the lightning that had flickered beyond the windows lining the long hall. In a heartbeat she was at the office door, which was opening for her.

Siland.

"Convenient," she said, smiling, glad she didn't have to wait for him. She waved Mordred at him.

Siland didn't budge for a moment, seemingly nonplussed at the threat of the weapon. "My guard—"

"Don't worry about him," Ninn said. "Just worry—"

"—about myself?" His voice was smooth, like perfectly aged whiskey. "No worries," Siland said, adding a feigned Aussie accent to it. "No worries, mate. Come in, please, Miss Tossinn. I wondered whatever had been keeping you."

"Sheep," Mordred said. *"And sheep poop had been keeping her."*

He turned his back to her, and Ninn watched his hands; they hung loose at his sides, not reaching for a weapon. Siland settled into his high-backed chair, rested his elbows on the desk, and appeared to study her.

She didn't detect a trace of concern on his ageless face, not a single drop of sweat on his forehead. How could a man be so smug? Could enough nuyen make him that way? Power? The drugs coursing through his system, eradicating old age, eliminating the specter of death?

"Impressive what you managed at my facility," he said. "I could use someone like you in my employ." He nodded to the chair opposite. "Sit, please. Would you like some brandy?"

Yes. "I'm not thirsty."

"Let me shoot him." From Mordred. *"Several times."*

"I've read up on you, Miss Tossinn. About your sister, your AISE record. The force shouldn't have dropped you, a fine officer, really. And a good private investigator. Too good."

Ninn sat. She'd been on her feet a lot today; it felt good to be off them. She listened closely; the floorboards in the hallway outside had creaked when she'd come in, and she wanted to make sure no backup was coming.

"Does death frighten you that much?" Ninn began after a few moments of silence. "That you had to create Renaixement? Experiment on people, animals. Does death—"

Siland laughed. The first time she'd heard the laugh, she thought it rich and pleasant-sounding. Now it sent a shiver down her spine. "It's what leads up to death, Miss Tossinn. Age. Infirmity. Unable to control your bowels. Your mind slipping away. Your joints aching because all the treatments and nanotech in this advanced world can only postpone the misery. But Renaixement? It gets rid of what leads up to death. It gives you forever."

"He's mad," Mordred judged. "It's a Mad, Mad, Mad, Mad World. *1963, Spencer Tracy."*

"Everything dies," Ninn said softly. "Everyone."

"Maybe not." Siland fixed her with an unblinking stare. "I can offer you immortality, Miss Tossinn. I'll rebuild the laboratory. Maybe in the Cross this time. I've refined things, don't need as much space, as many tanks. You could have it too, if you wanted. All you've got to do is say yes. I've even got the serum here. You could start your first treatment right—"

She pulled Mordred's trigger several times, although the first shot had been sufficient.

"That felt good, Keebs," Mordred said. "But it was a nice offer he'd made."

"I don't want to live forever," she returned.

Mordred made a sound that passed for a sigh. "Forever Young, *1992, Mel Gibson. He was an Aussie, ya ken."*

Ninn ignored him as she searched the office, quickly finding what had to be the cache of serum in his desk. She trashed the rest of office to make it look like a burglary, then left.

Outside, she smashed the vials on the ground, grinding them into the dirt until the last of the immortality serum was nothing but a dark stain on the ground.

Sirens coming from the opposite direction made her look up, then start walking away. As she did, the sky opened up, and the rain fell again, cleansing everything, washing the Cross clean, at least for a little while.

Ninn lifted her head and let the rain fall on her face for a few moments, then quickened her pace as she rounded the corner and vanished out of sight.

It turned out Ninn didn't have to worry about the arson charge. Someone in the RighteousRight ratted out a few of the brothers who had set the blaze. Dr. Aidan Kappa had survived after all.

She kept her cybereye and Mordred's smartlink. The rest of her tech...she went under the knife at a reputable street doc and had it ripped out, selling it all as payment for the operation.

The spirit voices came easier to her now. She could see creatures in a swirl of dust stirred up by a breeze and in the puff of moisture preceding a storm. The spirits were everywhere...now that she knew how to look for them. She kept Benzo, too; Ninn *had* always wanted a dog.

A few more months, that's what she intended to give the Cross. It would be hard to leave the earthy neighborhood; she loved its rhythm and colors and humans and metahumans and everyone and everything in between. Just a few more months. Something she had to do during that time. Then she'd be worthy of Barega.

Across the park from the restored El Alamein Fountain and above a chemist's was a small meeting room. She went there every third night. A few more months of it, and she'd be good to go...to go a hundred klicks from Whoop Whoop.

Follow the galah.

"My name is Nininiru Tossinn," she said as she stood. "Ninn for short. I am an addict."

"G'day, Ninn," the rest of the room returned.

"G'day, Keebs," Mordred echoed.

IDENTITY: CRISIS
BY PHAEDRA WELDON • COMING SOON!

SHADOWS OF MYSTERY...

One morning, Oliver Martin wakes up to find he no longer exists, with no job, SIN, nuyen, or even a place to live. He's been completely wiped from the Matrix, with a new identity replacing his. Only this one's on Lone Star's Most Wanted List, and Oliver's usual morning turns into the first run of his life.

Boston's mean streets hold the keys to Oliver's fight to reclaim himself and discover who's behind his redacted identity. Falling in with a shadowrun team, he uncovers a conspiracy within MIT&T that could bring down the corporate walls of the city before it's through—and take him right along with it.

PROLOGUE
SOUTH BOSTON
THURSDAY, AUGUST 1, 2075
NEAR MIDNIGHT

In front of me, I saw a deserted alley.

Behind me was darkness.

My memories lived in that darkness, like a spirit not yet wishing to be seen as it hovered on the edge of manifesting in this world, or remaining safe in its own. It whispered to me as I looked up through the broken rooftops, above the glittering lights of Boston in the distance, north of where I found myself. Rain tapped my cheeks, my forehead, my bare shoulders as my cold feet scraped across the oily, pitted asphalt beneath them. The smell of the alley ahead was rich with decay, the foul odor of death and desperation.

Or was that *my* desperation I smelled? My sweat beneath the rain, beneath the night sky, beneath the ravaged ruins of the dark world I found myself in. I also smelled something I couldn't forget. The coppery scent of blood.

My blood.

I pressed my filthy hands against my ripped and shredded shirt on my chest to stanch the bleeding. It didn't hurt, but it should. My heart thundered against my palms as my head told me to keep moving, reasoned with my intellect, telling it that my chance of survival would be higher if I disappeared into the alley instead of remaining here in the open, along a deserted road between empty stores, their signs hanging by wires corroded by time and the elements.

Neon was the light to see by, its pink, green, and blue hum filling the dark spaces in the night as I caught my breath. I held something in my right hand. I could make out its silver surface, soft blue and white glow of a screen and blood, sticky and full of hair on one of its corners. I'd taken this from someone, hadn't I? I had a half-formed memory of striking someone, but I couldn't see their face.

It was a commlink. Unlocked and untraceable.

I heard their boots beating the asphalt, the whisper of their communications in my ears, but I couldn't make out what they were saying. I shivered as I looked to my left, my right, and then dove headlong into the darkened alley in front of me.

I wasn't prepared for just how dark it was. The neon from the street didn't reach far enough inside, and I hissed as my battered feet caught on rocks and sharp objects. But I kept running because I knew on an instinctual level my life depended on it.

I wanted to puke. I wanted to rest. I wanted to find someplace warm.

But above all, I wanted to live.

Suddenly I could see down the narrow alley as everything turned an eerie shade of green. I stopped and blinked several times, putting a bloody hand to my face, to my cheeks below my eyes as a faint memory came to me. *Cybereyes...* At least that memory returned when I wanted it.

I held up the commlink. My eyes had paired with it. I engaged the local grid to access RFID tags—that is, if anything in this foul place still had them.

A few things popped up on the augmented reality provided by the commlink, projected as an overlay on the scene in front of me. Manufacturers' tags, mostly. But I could see now, and I easily picked my way through even as I caught the shadow of something flying overhead. It cast enough shade through the green light for me to know someone or something had just jumped from one building to the other, across the alley.

Could they see me? I didn't know, so I stopped, looked around, and spotted a dark indentation in one of the walls low to the ground. I slid inside and curled up before quietly pulling a piece of trash closer to cover me.

Their footfalls slowed, but I could see them coming. Three shapes. I knew there had been four before. I spotted the human girl and man, and the bulk of the troll with them. Most of them had cyber implants, upgrades that gleamed in my green vision.

The girl was looking around as if scanning. Probably had the same night vision as me, so I pushed myself as far into the hole as I could and held my breath. If she had infrared to see my body heat, I was dead.

Abruptly, something landed inches away from me, but in front of them. Here was the fourth pursuer. I kept my breathing shallow as I watched the boots join the other three. I couldn't see his face. He stood with his back to my hiding place, but I did see a long, blond braid swing down to his lower back. The end was decorated with a large bead of some kind. "He came in here."

"Yeah, I know," the girl said, and I could see she had goggles on top of her head. Small sparkles followed her nose and jawline and a tag popped up that read *Josef's Tattoo and Piercings*, and gave me the address. I dismissed it.

"We saw him run in here, too." She lowered the weapon she kept balanced on her hip. "How is he still moving? I nailed him in the fraggin' chest."

"Then obviously you missed," said the mystery man. His speech pattern, pronunciation was very different than the other three.

"We ain't got time for fight'n," the troll said, his deep voice low enough to feel it rumble against the asphalt beneath me. "If we don't find him and make sure he's dead, we don't get paid."

"Sloppy," said the male human. He raised his arm, and I could see a slim Fairlight Excalibur deck hanging over his shoulder. Pretty pricey piece of equipment. I knew this because my love of decking units resurfaced. The girl had a commlink on her wrist. None of their weapons or equipment had tags. Smart.

I assumed they were all SINless, just like me.

But I'd had a SIN, hadn't I? I knew I needed one to interact with this world, but I...

I couldn't *remember*.

I noticed a bow attached to the human's back. I knew about bows and arrows. I didn't know how I knew, but I flexed my left hand and *remembered* having gripped a bow before. *Come on brain, if you can remember that, why can't you remember my name?*

"Yeah well, you do the killing next time, Mort," Goggle Girl said.

The human had a name: Mort.

"You're the one keeping a score card," Mort turned, scanning the narrow corridor, and I held my breath again. "This alley runs for a quarter-mile with two breaks. If he's bleeding like you say he is, he should be easy to track."

The troll pointed at the sky. "Not with this rain. It's already washing the blood away with the rest of the garbage."

"He's dead," Goggle Girl piped up. "Or he'll be dead soon. Ain't nobody in this part of town gonna help him. They'll kill 'im and rob 'im first. I say we done the job, and we go get paid."

Mort shook his head. "I'm not going back to Mr. Johnson without the trophy."

Goggle Girl made an unpleasant noise. "That's disgusting, you know that? Why take the guy's head?"

"Because he's got information in it. I don't know what or how, I just know what was requested. So no head, no nuyen for any of us." Mort sounded confident.

The mystery man with the braid moved back. "You three can do what you want—as long as you find him." He disappeared, leaving the three of them standing in the cramped alley.

I exhaled slowly, tried to quiet my anxiety. I was getting light-headed due to loss of blood. Adrenaline and pure fear had kept me going so far, and now that I was still, I was dying faster.

I needed to move. But I couldn't if these three were still following me.

The logical thing to do would be to eliminate them. But I didn't have a weapon.

Something sung in my arms and legs, a power that surged straight into my toes. My muscles vibrated, subtly at first, as the memory in my body came alive and I realized I'd just loaded an activesoft into my skillwires.

I had skillwires—why would I have those?

I glanced around the area where I hid. I spotted several objects that could be used for combat, a few as shields and a few as projectiles. Something in my head calculated the odds, coming up with the predictive analysis of certain movements and outcomes. The only variables were the opponents, since I hadn't seen them fight.

"Don't know about you two," the girl said. "But I'm bettin' he's in there, hidin' somewhere. Ain't your cybereyes showin' you anything, Peter?"

The troll answered. "I ain't got infrared, just tactical. And I ain't got a map downloaded for this side of town."

"There's the real threat," Mort said. "We're in Ancients territory. I'm surprised they haven't showed up yet."

"You want 'em to?" the girl said. "Stupid piece of drek. We don't need no ganger troubles. I say we go down the alley, and if we don't see him on the other end, we get the hell outta here. There's no way that soft piece of corp drek survived my bullets."

Peter the troll moved out ahead of them, stomping past my position. As I saw it, I had very few options, and I ran through both of them in an instant. I could wait where I was until they passed and hit the end of the alley just like Goggle Girl said and they would leave. But that scenario brought up worries about the mystery man, the one that disappeared. Was he waiting back at the entrance? Was he still around, maybe waiting for them to flush me out so he could make the kill shot...and take my head?

I still hadn't quite gotten over that piece of information.

That possibility brought me to option two. I take out these three and grab their weapons. I'd at least be armed and had a fighting chance if mystery man came back. Or one of these "Ancients" showed up.

A quick, petulant war went on in the back of my brain as I thought. A strong voice agreed with option two, assuring me I could do what I saw as the impossible, against a smaller, softer voice that insisted hiding was the proper thing to do, insisting I wasn't trained or in any condition for this kind of heroic stuff.

The stronger voice reminded me about the wires, the singing I could feel in my spine, radiating through my limbs, the power I sensed, ready and waiting for me to tap it.

I put my hand on my chest where a hole still leaked blood. The deciding thought I felt was my own. I was dead either way. I could go out by bleeding to death as I hid from my enemies, or I could take a few of them with me.

After that, there wasn't much of an argument anymore.

I slowed my movements—which wasn't difficult, given the loss of blood—and waited for the male and then the female to move past before creeping out of my hiding place. The troll was far enough down the alley so if I took out these two first, I could be armed by the time he came at me.

In theory.

I wanted to be stealthy about it, but I was too wobbly on my feet. The girl bringing up the rear sensed someone behind them first.

She whirled and started firing her Ares Light Fire 70. I dropped straight down, but felt air split as the bullets flew over me. When she paused I listened to the wires, gave them control, and launched back up, grabbing the muzzle of the gun and shoving it up into her face. Her yell, as well as the spray of blood from her nose over my forearm and face, was my reward.

I didn't wait for her to fall or drop or die. I yanked the gun from her hands and turned it, aiming it at the troll's head. I didn't see Mort the human, and the troll was already closer than I anticipated.

The wires hummed as I aimed and fired through the green light of my cybereyes. His head exploded like an overripe cantaloupe as it sprayed bone and brain matter all over the place.

A shot zinged past my right shoulder from behind, grazing the skin. I pivoted around and crouched lower, knowing he'd have to reset his next shot, and aimed the gun on Mort as he stupidly stood exposed in the middle of the alley. I didn't know how he'd doubled back, and it didn't matter as the bullets struck his neck.

I'd aimed at his head. But my aim was off thanks to the stinging wound on my shoulder. He gurgled and choked and grabbed his throat to stop the blood, but I could see it cascade through his fingers like a waterfall.

Within two minutes they were all lying at my feet, and I was on my hands and knees, puking my guts out.

Killing...was bad. I knew this. I didn't know my name, but I knew from somewhere in my head that this wasn't me. It *couldn't* be me. But I'd done it. I'd taken three lives in less time than it took me to make the decision to act.

The control from the wires eased back, and I started shaking. Bad shaking. This wasn't just the cold anymore. This was worse. I knew it was shock setting in. I was gonna die out here in this alley if I didn't get someplace warm, with medical supplies and a place to rest.

The rain thickened and washed away whatever had been left in my stomach. I was driven to take what I needed and fast, because I didn't know where braid man was, and I was pretty sure he or someone else had heard those shots.

I went to the human male first. Mort was about my size and height. I wasn't exactly a small man, and at forty five—I knew my age?—I was in decent shape. I stripped him of his weapons, deck, commlink, and his coat and boots. The boots were a little big, but nothing I couldn't handle. The coat was long and had a hood, so I used that to hide my face. The bow and the pack of arrows I kept on the synthleather strap at my hip. I tucked the tech into a coat pocket and then stripped the other two bodies of everything I could find and carry, including weapons.

Once I had what I needed, I took off down the alley and turned onto the first street it intersected. There weren't any people around, not in this weather. I slipped into the doorway of what might have been an old electronics store, but had long since been raided, the windows broken and then boarded up, and then broken into again. The grungy, black-and-white tile floor clicked under my new boots as I stumbled toward the back of the place, where I assumed the office was.

There I stripped everything off, dumping it unceremoniously on a couch I was sure had been home to more than just vermin and other squatters. I used what was left of my mangled shirt, now covered in dirt, grime, oil and all manner of garbage and pressed it against the wound in my chest.

Nausea almost brought me to my knees again, so I stumbled into the remains of a bathroom. The water had been shut off long ago, and the toilet stunk of piss and shit. The mirror had been smashed, but I could just make out my face in the remaining shards. It somehow felt fitting that I saw my self, my eyes, my hair, all in the fragmented pieces of a mirror, just like the missing pieces of my memory.

I finally looked down at the bleeding hole in my chest. I was too squeamish to reach in and find these bullets Goggle Girl said she'd pumped into me. Why wasn't I dead? How was I still moving around?

After I asked myself that question, dizziness nearly dropped me to the floor. I felt another wave of it as I staggered back into the office.

I collapsed behind the desk and couldn't get back up. The water-stained ceiling, the smell of stale cigarettes, all of it twisted my stomach again as I turned on my side and curled up.

I was gonna die here, in some stranger's past. A man who couldn't remember his own past, but had fought hard for his future.

At least, that's what I was thinking when closed my eyes for what I thought would be the very last time...

IDENTITY CRISIS

BY PHAEDRA WELDON

COMING SOON!

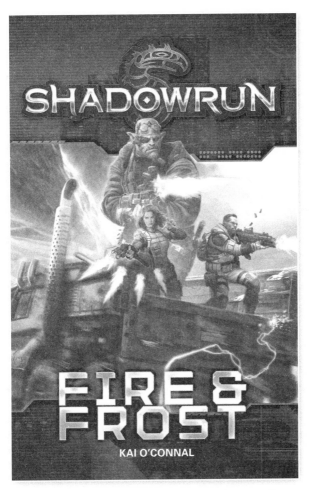

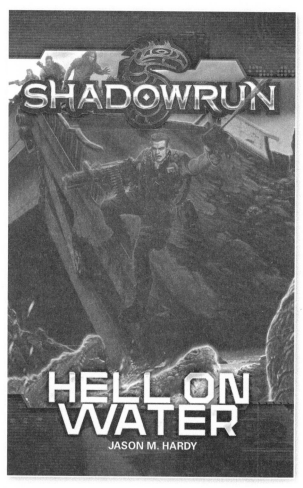

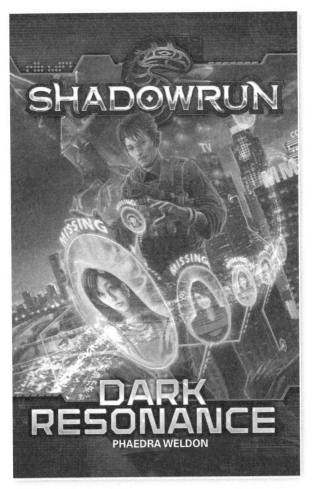